Looking North

Looking North

Writings from Spanish America on the US, 1800 to the Present

Edited by
JOHN J. HASSETT AND BRAULIO MUÑOZ

THE UNIVERSITY OF
ARIZONA PRESS
TUCSON

THE UNIVERSITY OF ARIZONA PRESS

© 2012 The Arizona Board of Regents
All rights reserved

www.uapress.arizona.edu

Library of Congress Cataloging-in-Publication Data
Looking North : writings from Spanish America on the US, 1800 to the present / edited by John J. Hassett and Braulio Muñoz.
   p. cm.
   ISBN 978-0-8165-2998-8 (pbk. : alk. paper) 1. United States—Foreign public opinion, Latin American. 2. Public opinion—Latin America. 3. United States—Relations—Latin America. 4. Latin America—Relations—United States. 5. Spanish American literature—Translations into English. 6. United States—In literature. 7. Americans in literature. 8. United States—Civilization—Foreign public opinion, Latin American. 9. United States—Literary collections. I. Hassett, John J., 1943– II. Muñoz, Braulio, 1946– III. Title: Writings from Spanish America on the US, 1800 to the present.
   F1418.L66 2012
   327.7308—dc23   2012003244

Publication of this book is made possible in part by the proceeds of a permanent endowment created with the assistance of a Challenge Grant from the National Endowment for the Humanities, a federal agency.

Manufactured in the United States of America on acid-free, archival-quality paper containing a minimum of 30% post-consumer waste and processed chlorine free.

17 16 15 14 13 12   6 5 4 3 2 1

For Elizabeth, Nancy, and Joan

Contents

Introduction   1

Part I: The Two Americas

Simón Bolívar, "The Angostura Discourse" (Selection, 1819)   11

José Martí, "Our America" (1891)   21

José Enrique Rodó, *Ariel* (Selection, 1900)   30

Manuel Baldomero Ugarte, "An Open Letter to the President of
the United States" (1913)   45

Gabriela Mistral, "The Infantilism of the North American" (1944)   52

Leopoldo Zea, "The Culture of the Two Americas" (1971)   56

Salvador Allende, "Chile: Address to the United Nations General
Assembly" (1972)   68

Irene Zea, "U.S. Hegemony on the American Continent" (1975)   90

Octavio Paz, "Mexico and the United States: Positions and
Counterpositions" (1978)   109

Sergio Marras, "The First New Days: A Conversation with Roberto
Fernández Retamar" (Selection, 1991)   127

Armando Roa, "The Historic Significance of the
United States" (1997)   143

Mario Vargas Llosa, "A Wall of Lies" (2006)   153

Part II: Travelers from the South

Domingo Faustino Sarmiento, "Moral Geography" (1847)   161

Ciro Alegría, "The Race Problem" (1941)   174

Germán Arciniegas, "English Lessons" (1945)   178

Luis Alberto Sánchez, "The First Surprise" (1945)   181

Ernesto Cardenal, "A Trip to New York" (1973)   186

Víctor M. Espinosa, "We Didn't Go North to Pick Flowers" (1992)   204

Eduardo Galeano, "Mea Culpa" (1992)   216

Mario Vargas Llosa, "New York, New York" (2008)   220

Part III: The United States as Literary Theme

Rubén Darío, "To Roosevelt" (1905)   227

Nicolás Guillén, Selected Poems (1967)   230

Gabriel García Márquez, *One Hundred Years of Solitude* (Selection, 1967)   237

Pablo Neruda, Selected Poems (1970, 1973)   242

Mario Benedetti, "The Weeping of Jimmy Swaggart" (1988)   247

Esmeralda Santiago, "The American Invasion of Macún" (Selection, 1993)   250

Christine Granados, "Inner View" (2006)   254

Looking North

Introduction

This book is intended to bring together a variety of texts that deal with how Spanish Americans from different nations, periods, and backgrounds have viewed the United States over the past two centuries. Our aim has been to provide a significant glimpse into a complex and ever-changing landscape of facts and opinions that have been instrumental in shaping the South's perceptions of its neighbor. Our endeavor is by no means unique in its theme. Others have gone before us who have attempted to understand this often-perplexing relationship between the two Americas and we are indebted to their work.

One of these initial efforts was José de Onis's *Los Estados Unidos vistos por escritores hispanoamericanos* (Madrid: Ediciones de Cultura Hispánica), published in 1956. Despite its groundbreaking importance, today this book has several limitations. On the one hand, it was published more than a half century ago, with selections by literary authors who today would not be considered as important as many of the writers we have chosen to include in our study. In addition, the book focuses exclusively on the perceptions of creative writers. Unfortunately, it is also out of print and was never available to an English-speaking audience. A second book, John T. Reid's *Spanish American Images of the United States 1790–1960* (Gainesville: University of Florida, 1977), is a highly intelligent, readable contribution to the ongoing discussion of the topic. However, whereas this author's approach is a personal analysis of a number of Spanish American texts, our intent has been to go a step further. We offer a broad selection of materials to be judged on their own, asking our readers to be sensitive to the evolution of the historical relationship between the United States and Spanish America as they listen to the voices of the authors included. The Reid book is currently out of print and was first published more than thirty years ago. Carlos Rama's *La imagen de los Estados Unidos en la América Latina* (Mexico: SepSetentas/Diana, 1975) is closest to ours in approach since it represents a selection of materials from the world of history and politics. Unlike ours, it contains neither the voices of travelers to the United States nor those of the region's creative writers. This book is also no longer available and its most recent entry dates from 1972. A fourth book, Carlos Rangel's *The Latin Americans: Their Love-Hate Relationship with the United States* (New Brunswick, N.J.: Transaction Books, 1987) is essentially one man's insightful and at times controversial reading of a long history shared by the Americas. While his understanding of this history is often fascinating, it is, nonetheless, one individual's reading of the period. Again, as with the other works already mentioned, this text is also out of print. Finally, David Viñas's *Viajeros, turistas y testigos argentinos* (Buenos Aires: Instituto Movilizador de Fondos Cooperativos, 1997) contains a number of travel essays written by Argentineans concerning their experience of life in the United States. This small collection addresses the responses of tourists and travelers from only one country in Spanish America. Additionally, this book has not been made available in English.

Any attempt to capture Hispanic America's perceptions of the United States must begin with a recognition that Spanish Americans do not speak with one voice when it comes to such a profound influence in their lives. In other words, we certainly do not wish to posit some kind of regional mind-set in this regard. And yet, taking into account the obvious variety of perspectives that have evolved, the writings included here also show that Spanish Americans share some clear and fundamental cultural positions, which makes it possible to at least speak of a Hispanic American point of view. We will discuss below in some detail the grounds Spanish American cultural leaders present in support of the claim that the majority of people in Hispanic America share a set of fundamental cultural values. Before we do so, however, we want to articulate the criteria used for choosing the specific texts included in this volume.

First, we have limited our selection to texts originally authored by Spanish Americans. We have not included important extant works in either Portuguese or French. To be sure, these languages and their cultures contribute significantly to Latin America's worldview, but their inclusion would have made our task even broader than it already is. This would have been particularly the case had we considered Brazil as part of this study. Rather, we believe, given the limitations of space, that Brazil and Haiti deserve separate attention. Similarly, we are all well aware that over the centuries there have been important texts written in the native languages of the continent, particularly in Central America and the Andean region. Samples of these texts have not been included here because they do not engage the issues that primarily concern us. All selections included in this volume have been written, in some cases spoken, by individuals whose principal language is Spanish.

At first glance, it might appear that to speak of a Spanish American perspective is highly questionable. After all, even when we refer only to the Spanish-speaking areas of Latin America, the territory included is extremely vast. There are more than twenty independent nations in this region, each with its own complex historical experience regarding the colossus to the north. Mexico, which shares a vast border with the United States, sees its neighbor in markedly different ways than, for example, Peru. And there is little doubt that Cuba, only ninety miles from the US mainland, may view the North very differently than a country like Paraguay. The texts included here, however, show convincingly that during the past two hundred years Spanish Americans as a whole have come to view the recurrent political, economic, military, and cultural incursions by the United States with a wary eye. It would appear that despite the political boundaries or economic interests at play throughout these different countries, when it comes to incursions of any kind from the North, Spanish Americans tend to join hands as citizens of a Latin American nation first dreamed of by Bolívar. This attitude is particularly manifest in the political discourse included in this volume.

The notion of a unified nation of Spanish America, long proposed by the area's cultural leaders, has, to a certain extent, been made a reality through at least the following factors: (1) an ever-increasing linguistic integration; (2) an enduring religious tradition; and (3) a *mestizo* cultural tradition.

Even though there are still in Hispanic America large populations of people who speak a language other than Spanish, the fact is that over the last two centuries Spanish has become hegemonic. The self-understanding of Spanish Americans and their essential differences with their neighbor to the north and their view of the world in general are things that have been articulated and grounded in Spanish. Spanish Americans have brought significant changes to the language of Cervantes and it is no accident that there are now ten academies of the language in Hispanic America. In other words, the linguistic integration of Spanish America is an undeniable social fact. It is in this sense that the assertion by cultural leaders, that in fundamental questions of self-understanding Spanish Americans speak with one voice, seems justified.

This linguistic homogeneity across Spanish America has contributed to the notion of an identity that is contrastable with that of their northern neighbor. In this sense, the United States becomes the linguistic "Other." Spanish Americans view their English-speaking neighbors as having a different sensibility concerning matters of life and the cosmos. Within the context of historical coincidence the consolidation of English as the language of the United States, following the neutralization of indigenous languages as well as French and Spanish, has its counterpart in a similar process in Hispanic America where Spanish prevailed. These similar processes of consolidation contributed greatly to the differences between the Hispanic and Anglo-Saxon worldview.

In the area of religion, despite continuing resistance by native populations, the recurrent attempts at secularization, and the inroads made by Protestant dominations over the last few decades, there is little doubt that for the most part Spanish Americans continue to consider themselves Catholic. A practicing Catholic from Lima can worship in absolute comfort in, for example, Bogotá, Colombia. Of course, given the profound influence of religion on all aspects of culture, this particular Catholic worldview provides Spanish Americans with a strong and almost homogeneous view of life and the cosmos. This worldview is largely based on a Humanist tradition that celebrates the life of contemplation. By contrast, Protestantism has been a determining factor in the affairs of the United States from the time of its founding until roughly the middle of the twentieth century. Even today, despite the growth of other religions—particularly Catholicism—there is a Protestant feel to religion in the United States. Its spirituality privileges not contemplation but action upon the world. Spanish Americans, particularly the cultural leaders who wrote in the nineteenth century, have tended to portray these religious differences in stark terms. Consequently, the people of Hispanic America have come to see themselves as occupying a clear and distinct position from the United States, which they view as a Protestant nation.

Finally, ever since Bolívar, Spanish Americans for the most part have viewed themselves as *mestizos*. This is so in spite of the continuous attempts by some cultural leaders to characterize the Latin American nation as either indigenous or European. The term *mestizo* is not only a biological concept—the miscegenation between whites, native peoples, Asians, and Africans—but it is also a cultural concept. The notion of hybridism in Spanish America is at least five hundred years old. Its cultural leaders have viewed this phenomenon as an essential contrasting element in relationships between the two Americas.

Most of the commentators whose works we have included in this study perceive the English-speaking Protestant United States as averse to viewing mestizo culture as a value. Spanish American cultural leaders judge experiences such as Jim Crow as a palpable sign that the United States is profoundly opposed to any notion of hybridism. This is not to say that these same cultural commentators were blind to discrimination and racism in their own back yard. On the contrary, they are quite vocal in their rejection of racial prejudice and view it as something intrinsically indefensible and harmful to a society as a whole.

These different attitudes toward *mestizaje* have had direct and personal consequences in the process of self-understanding for Spanish Americans. Several of the texts included here present the United States' history of racial intolerance as a judgment of its citizens as human beings and neighbors. Their authors detect an air of racial intolerance in the political, economic, military, and cultural posture of the United States and its representatives in Spanish America. The long history of indigenous reservations, Jim Crow, and the internment of Japanese-Americans during World War II are never far from their minds when thinking about their northern neighbor. The inflammatory discourse against immigrants from Latin America to the United States in the past few decades and the recent immigration law passed by the Arizona legislature only exacerbate such perceptions of the United States.

From the foregoing it would appear that Spanish Americans might have only negative views of the United States, but such is not the case. In reading the selections that compose this volume it is obvious that there is a profound ambivalence experienced by Spanish Americans when commenting on their northern neighbor. Perhaps this attitude is best captured by Octavio Paz, who suggests in "Mexico and the United States: Positions and Counterpositions" that two very different moralities prevail in the United States: one for domestic consumption and the other for export. For Paz it becomes a question of profound contradiction between what the United States is domestically—a democracy—and what its actions abroad constitute—an imperialistic power.

As a democratic nation the United States is seen by Spanish Americans as having made important contributions to the modern world, not only in the fields of science and technology but also in the area of civil rights and freedom of expression, and this serves as a beacon of hope to many citizens of Hispanic America. Hispanic Americans also recognize that US culture has produced, throughout the ages, a memorable literature with soulful reflections on life and the cosmos. Intellectuals such as Jefferson, Lincoln, Whitman, Emerson, Poe, Faulkner, and Merton are greatly admired. The United States is viewed as a place where individual achievement is celebrated, where hard work and fair play are rewarded, and where social mobility is more than just a remote possibility. And for many Spanish Americans, their neighbor embodies a nation that is striving to achieve increasing social equality and tolerance. When confronted, however, with its international behavior the image of a true democracy quickly evaporates in the eyes of most of the citizens of the South.

Spanish Americans do not view the United States as an empire in the sense of an England or Spain during the height of their international power. American expansionism takes place in such fields as economics, politics, technology, and culture rather than in the conquest of new territory. Nonetheless, there is a fundamental similarity in the behavior of all empires: the United States does not extend the same treatment and rights to others that it offers its own citizens. Spanish Americans are all too aware that their neighbor does not hesitate to prop up dictators, to bribe and co-opt potential revolutionaries, and to threaten the use of its mighty war machine in order to protect its political and economic interests. As far as most Spanish Americans are concerned, the United States is more than willing to undermine entire countries for the sake of preserving the "American way of life."

This highly ambivalent attitude toward the United States is unlikely to go away anytime soon. Nonetheless, the selections we offer chronologically here are meant to shed some light on its trajectory across time and instill in the reader a more profound understanding of what unites as well as separates the two Americas.

Our book is divided into three parts. The first underscores the similarities and differences between the two Americas. It opens with Bolívar's proud declaration in 1819 of Hispanic America as a mestizo land and it closes with Mario Vargas Llosa's comments, written in 2006, on the controversial wall being constructed between North and South and the dreams that bring mestizos to the United States. The second part is composed of travel essays and begins with Domingo Sarmiento's fascination with the United States during his travels in 1847. It ends with an essay written in 2008 by Mario Vargas Llosa, who sees the city of New York as the new, exciting Babylon but who experiences, at the same time, "a certain anxiety and a feeling of solitude" as he wanders its streets. Finally, in the third part we have included works that treat the United States as a literary theme. It starts with Rubén Darío's restatement in 1905 of the essential differences between Hispanic America and the United States and ends with Christine Granados's witty short story on Hispanic perceptions of Anglo culture.

Given recent changes in political and demographic landscapes, we expect that Spanish America and the United States will become increasingly important to one another in the years ahead. A greater sensitivity toward one another's differences and similarities will ensure that the relationship between these two neighbors can be a more fruitful one, based on mutual respect and understanding.

Unless otherwise noted, all translations are by John J. Hassett.

PART ONE

The Two Americas

The Angostura Discourse (Selection)

Simón Bolívar

Simón Bolívar (1783–1830) was, together with José de San Martín, one of Spanish America's most important leaders in the struggle for independence from Spain and, to this day, he is remembered as the Great Liberator. After the triumph over the Spanish monarchy he was instrumental in founding Gran Colombia, and served as president of this newly created nation from 1821 to 1830. In addition, he was president of Perú (1824–1826) and Bolivia (1825–1826). His name is forever linked to the independence of present-day Venezuela, Colombia, Ecuador, Perú, Panamá, and Bolivia. This selection is from *Selected Writings of Bolívar*, vol. 1: *1810–1822*, edited by Harold A. Bierck, compiled by Vicente Lecuna, translated by Lewis Bertrand, published by the Bank of Venezuela (New York: Colonial Press, 1951), 173–197.

Angostura, February 15, 1819

Gentlemen:
Since, therefore, by this profession of mine in support of Venezuela's freedom, I may aspire to the glory of being reckoned among her most faithful sons, allow me, Gentlemen, to expound, with the frankness of a true republican, my respectful opinion on a *Plan of Constitution*, which I take the liberty of submitting to you as a testimony of the candor and sincerity of my sentiments. As this plan concerns the welfare of all, I venture to assume that I have the right to be heard by the representatives of the people. I well know that your wisdom needs no counsel, and I know also that my plan

may perhaps appear to be mistaken and impracticable. But I implore you, Gentlemen, receive this work with benevolence, for it is more a tribute of my sincere deference to the Congress than an act of presumption. Moreover, as your function is to create a body politic, or, it might be said, to create an entire society while surrounded by every obstacle that most peculiar and difficult situation can present, perhaps the voice of one citizen may reveal the presence of a hidden or unknown danger.

Let us review the past to discover the base upon which the Republic of Venezuela is founded.

America, in separating from the Spanish monarchy, found herself in a situation similar to that of the Roman Empire when its enormous framework fell to pieces in the midst of the ancient world. Each Roman division then formed an independent nation in keeping with its location or interests; but this situation differed from America's in that those members proceeded to reestablish their former associations. We, on the contrary, do not even retain the vestiges of our original being. We are not Europeans; we are not Indians; we are but a mixed species of aborigines and Spaniards. Americans by birth and Europeans by law, we find ourselves engaged in a dual conflict: we are disputing with the natives for titles of ownership, and at the same time we are struggling to maintain ourselves in the country that gave us birth against the opposition of the invaders. Thus our position is most extraordinary and complicated. But there is more. As our role has always been strictly passive and our political existence nil, we find that our quest for liberty is now even more difficult of accomplishment; for we, having been placed in a state lower than slavery, had been robbed not only of our freedom but also of the right to exercise an active domestic tyranny. Permit me to explain this paradox.

In absolute systems, the central power is unlimited. The will of the despot is the supreme law, arbitrarily enforced by subordinates who take part in the organized oppression in proportion to the authority that they wield. They are charged with civil, political, military, and religious functions; but, in the final analysis, the satraps of Persia are Persian, the pashas of the Grand Turk are Turks, and the sultans of the Tartary are the Tartars. China does not seek her mandarins in the homeland of Genghis Khan, her conqueror. America, on the contrary, received everything from Spain, who, in effect, deprived her of the experience that she would have gained from the exercise of an active tyranny by not allowing her to take part in her own domestic affairs and administration. This exclusion made it impossible for us to acquaint ourselves with the management of public affairs; nor did we enjoy that personal consideration, of such great value in major revolutions, that the brilliance of power inspires in the eyes of the multitude. In brief, Gentlemen, we were deliberately kept in ignorance and cut off from the world in all matters relating to the science of government.

Subject to the threefold yoke of ignorance, tyranny, and vice, the American people have been unable to acquire knowledge, power, or (civic) virtue. The lessons we received and the models we studied, as pupils of such pernicious teachers, were most destructive. We have been ruled more by deceit than by force, and we have been degraded more by vice than by superstition. Slavery is the daughter of Darkness; an ignorant people is a blind instrument of its own destruction. Ambition and intrigue abuse the credulity and experience of men lacking all political, economic, and civic knowledge; they adopt pure illusion as reality; they take license for liberty, treachery for patriotism, and vengeance for justice. This situation is similar to that of the robust blind man who, beguiled by his strength, strides forward with all the assurance of one who can see, but, upon hitting every variety of obstacles, finds himself unable to retrace his steps.

If a people, perverted by their training, succeed in achieving their liberty, they will soon lose it, for it would be of no avail to endeavor to explain to them that happiness consists in the practice of virtue; that the rule of law is more powerful than the rule of tyrants, because, as the laws are more inflexible, everyone should submit to their beneficent austerity; that proper morals, and not force, are the bases of law; and that to practice justice is to practice liberty. Therefore, Legislators, your work is so much the more arduous, inasmuch as you have to reeducate men who have been corrupted by erroneous illusions and false incentives. Liberty, says Rousseau, is a succulent morsel, but one difficult to digest. Our weak fellow citizens will have to strengthen their spirit greatly before they can digest the wholesome nutriment of freedom. Their limbs benumbed by chains, their sight dimmed by the darkness of dungeons, and their strength sapped by the pestilence of servitude, are they capable of marching toward the august temple of Liberty without faltering? Can they come near enough to bask in its brilliant rays and to breathe freely the pure air which reigns therein?

Legislators, meditate well before you choose. Forget not that you are to lay the political foundation for a newly born nation which can rise to the heights of greatness that Nature has marked out for it if you but proportion this foundation in keeping with the high plane that it aspires to attain. Unless your choice is based upon the peculiar tutelary experience of the Venezuelan people—a factor that should guide you in determining the nature and form of government you are about to adopt for the well-being of the people—and, I repeat, unless you happen upon the right type of government, the result of our reforms will again be slavery.

The history of bygone ages affords you examples of thousands of governments. Visualize the nations that have shone in brightest splendor and you will be grieved to see that virtually all the world has been, and still is, the victim of its governments. You will note numerous systems of governing men, but always their purpose has been to oppress them. If our habit of looking upon the human species as being led by its own shepherds did not diminish the horror of so distressing a spectacle, we should be stunned to see our docile species grazing upon the surface of the earth, like meek flocks destined to feed their cruel keepers. Nature, in truth, endows us at birth with the instinctive desire for freedom; but, be it laziness or some tendency inherent in humanity, it is obvious that mankind rests unconcerned and accepts things as they are, even though it is bound forcibly in fetters. As we contemplate humanity in this state of prostitution, it would appear that we have every right to persuade ourselves that most men hold this humiliating maxim to be the truth: It is harder to maintain the balance of liberty than to endure the weight of tyranny. Would that this maxim, which goes counter to the morality of Nature, were false. Would that this axiom were not sanctioned by man's lack of concern respecting his most sacred rights!

Many ancient and modern nations have shaken off oppression; yet those who have enjoyed even a few precious moments of liberty are rare, as they have speedily returned to their old political vices; because peoples rather than governments repeatedly drag tyranny in their train. The habit of being ruled makes them insensible to the attractions of honor and national prosperity, and they regard with indifference the glory of living in the free sway of liberty, under the protection of laws dictated by their own free will. The records of the universe proclaim this awful truth.

Only democracy, in my opinion, is amenable to absolute liberty. But what democratic government has simultaneously enjoyed power, prosperity, and permanence? On the other hand, have not aristocracy and monarchy held great and powerful empires together century after century? Is there any government older than that of China? What republic has lasted longer than Sparta or Venice? Did not the Roman Empire conquer the earth? Has not France had fourteen centuries of monarchy? Is there any nation greater than England? Yet these nations have been or still are aristocracies and monarchies.

Despite these bitter reflections, I experience a surge of joy when I witness the great advances that our Republic has made since it began its noble career. Loving what is most useful, animated by what is most just, and aspiring to what is most perfect, Venezuela, on breaking away from Spain, has recovered her independence, her freedom, her equality, and her national sovereignty. By establishing a democratic republic, she has proscribed monarchy, distinctions, nobility, prerogatives, and privileges. She has declared for the rights of man and freedom of action, thought, speech, and press. These eminently liberal acts, because of the sincerity that has inspired them, will never cease to be admired. The first Congress of Venezuela has indelibly stamped upon the annals of our laws the majesty of the people, and, in placing its seal upon the social document best calculated to develop the well-being of the nation, that Congress has fittingly given expression to this thought.

I am forced to gather all my strength and to exert every effort of which I am capable in order to perceive the supreme good embodied in this immortal Code of our rights and laws. But how can I venture to say it! Shall I dare, by my criticism, to profane the sacred tablets of our laws ... [sic]? There are some feelings that a true patriot cannot retain in his heart. They overflow, forced by their own violence, and in spite of one's efforts to restrain them an inner force will make them known. I am thoroughly imbued with the idea that the government of Venezuela should be reformed; and, although many prominent citizens think as I do, not all of them possess the courage necessary to recommend publicly the adoption of new principles. This consideration obliges me to take the initiative in a matter of the greatest importance—a matter in which the utmost audacity is required—the offering of advice to the counselors of the people.

The more I admire the excellence of the federal Constitution of Venezuela, the more I am convinced of the impossibility of its application to our state. And, to my way of thinking, it is a marvel that its prototype in North America endures so successfully and has not been overthrown at the first sign of adversity or danger. Although the people of North America are a singular model of political virtue and moral rectitude; although that nation was cradled in liberty, reared on freedom, and maintained by liberty alone; and—I must reveal everything—although those people, so lacking in many respects, are unique in the history of mankind, it is a marvel, I repeat, that so weak and complicated a government as the federal system has managed to govern them in the difficult and trying circumstances of their past. But, regardless of the effectiveness of this form of government with respect to North America, I must say that it has never for a moment entered my mind to compare the position and character of two states as dissimilar as the English-American and the Spanish-American. Would it not be most difficult to apply to Spain the English system of political, civil, and religious liberty? Hence, it would be even more difficult to adapt to Venezuela the laws of North America. Does not *L'Espirit des lois* state that laws should be suited to the people for whom they are made; that it would be a major coincidence if those of one nation could be adapted to another; that laws must take into account the physical conditions of the country, climate, character of the land, location, size, and mode of living of the people; that they should be in keeping with the degree of liberty that the Constitution can sanction respecting the religion of the inhabitants, their inclinations, resources, number, commerce, habits, and customs? This is the code we must consult, not the code of Washington!

The Venezuelan Constitution, although based upon the most perfect of constitutions from the standpoint of the correctness of its principles and the beneficent effects of its administration, differed fundamentally from the North American Constitution on one cardinal point, and, without doubt, the most important point. The Congress of Venezuela, like the North American legislative body, participates in some of the duties vested in the executive power. We, however, have subdivided the executive power by vesting it in a collective body. Consequently, this executive body has been subject to the disadvantages resulting from the periodic existence of a government which is suspended and dissolved whenever its members adjourn. Our executive triumvirate lacks, so to speak, unity, continuity, and individual responsibility. It is deprived of prompt action, continuous existence, true uniformity, and direct responsibility. The government that does not possess these things, which give it a morality of its own, must be deemed a nonentity.

Although the powers of the president of the United States are limited by numerous restrictions, he alone exercises all the governmental functions which the Constitution has delegated to him; thus there is no doubt but that his administration must be more uniform, constant, and more truly his own than an administration wherein the power is divided among a number of persons, a grouping that is nothing less than a monstrosity. The judicial power in Venezuela is similar to that of North America: its duration is not defined; it is temporary and not for life; and it enjoys all the independence proper to the judiciary.

The first Congress, in its federal Constitution, responded more to the spirit of the provinces than to the sound idea of creating an indivisible and centralized republic. In this instance, our legislators yielded to the ill-considered pleadings of those men from the provinces who were captivated by the apparent brilliance of the happiness of the North American people, believing that the blessings they enjoy result exclusively from their form of government rather than from the character and customs of the citizens. In effect, the United States' example, because of their remarkable prosperity, was one too tempting not to be followed. Who could resist the powerful attraction of full and absolute enjoyment of sovereignty, independence, and freedom? Who could resist the devotion inspired by an intelligent government that has not only blended public and private rights but has also based its supreme law respecting the desires of the individual upon common consent? Who could resist the rule of a beneficent government, which with a skilled, dexterous, and powerful hand, always and in all regions, directs its resources toward social perfection, the sole aim of human institutions?

But no matter how tempting this magnificent federative system might have appeared, and regardless of its possible effect, the Venezuelans were not prepared to enjoy it immediately upon casting off their chains. We were not prepared for such good, for good, like evil, results in death when it is sudden and excessive. Our moral fiber did not then possess the stability necessary to derive benefits from a wholly representative government; a government so sublime, in fact, that it might more nearly befit a republic of saints.

Representatives of the People! You are called upon to confirm or to suppress whatever may appear to you worthy of preservation, modification, or rejection in our social compact. The task of correcting the work of our first legislators is yours. I should like to say that it is your duty to cloak some of the charms that are displayed in our political code; for not every heart is capable of admiring all beauty, nor all eyes able to gaze upon the heavenly light of perfection. The Book of the Apostles, the teachings of Jesus contained in that divine work, so sublime and so sacred, that Providence has sent us for the betterment of mankind, is now a rain of fire in Constantinople; indeed, Asia would burst into fiery flames if this Book of Peace were suddenly imposed upon her as a code of religion, law, and customs.

Permit me to call the attention of the Congress to a matter that may be of vital importance. We must keep in mind that our people are neither European nor North American; rather, they are a mixture of African and the Americans who originated in Europe. Even Spain herself has ceased to be European because of her African blood, her institutions, and her character. It is impossible to determine with any degree of accuracy where we belong in the human family. The greater portion of the native Indians have been annihilated; Spaniards have mixed with Americans and Africans, and Africans with Indians and Spaniards. While we have all been born of the same mother, our fathers, different in origin and in blood, are foreigners, and all differ visibly as to the color of their skin: a dissimilarity which places upon us an obligation of the greatest importance.

Under the Constitution, which interprets the laws of Nature, all citizens of Venezuela enjoy complete political equality. Although equality may not have been the political dogma of Athens, France, or North America, we must consecrate it here in order to correct the disparity that apparently exists. My opinion, Legislators, is that the fundamental basis of our political system hinges directly and exclusively upon the establishment and practice of equality in Venezuela. Most wise men concede that men are born with equal rights to share the benefits of society, but it does not follow that all men are born equally gifted to attain every rank. All men should practice virtue, but not all do; all ought to be courageous, but not all are; all should possess talents, but not everyone does. Herein are the real distinctions, which can be observed among individuals even in the most liberally constituted society. If the principle of political equality is generally recognized, so also must be the principle of physical and moral inequality. Nature makes men unequal in intelligence, temperament, strength, and character. Laws correct this disparity by so placing the individual within society that education, industry, arts, services, and virtues give him a fictitious equality that is properly termed political and social. The idea of a classless state, wherein diversity increases in proportion to the rise in population, was an eminently beneficial inspiration. By this step alone, cruel discord has been completely eliminated. How much jealousy, rivalry, and hate have thus been averted!

The people of Venezuela already enjoy the rights that they may legitimately and easily exercise. Let us now, therefore, restrain the growth of immoderate pretensions, which, perhaps, a form of government unsuited to our people might excite. Let us abandon the federal forms of government unsuited to us; let us put aside the triumvirate which hold the executive power and center it in a president. We must grant him sufficient authority to enable him to continue the struggle against the obstacles inherent in our recent situation, our present state of war, and every variety of foe, foreign and domestic, whom we must battle for some time to come. Let the legislature relinquish the powers that rightly belong to the executive; let it acquire, however, a new consistency, a new influence in the balance of authority. Let the courts be strengthened by increasing the stability and independence of the judges and by the establishment of juries and civil and criminal codes dictated, not by antiquity nor by conquering kings, but by the voice of Nature, the cry of Justice, and the genius of Wisdom.

My desire is for every branch of government and administration to attain that degree of vigor which alone can ensure equilibrium, not only among the members of the government, but also among the different factions of which our society is composed. It would matter little if the springs of a political system were to relax because of its weakness, so long as this relaxation itself did not contribute to the dissolution of the body social and the ruination of its membership. The shouts of humanity, on the battlefields or in tumultuous crowds, denounce to the world the blind, unthinking legislators who imagined that experiments with chimerical institutions could be made with impunity. All the peoples of the world have sought freedom, some by force of arms, others by force of law, passing alternately from anarchy to despotism, or from despotism to anarchy. Few peoples have been content with moderate aims, establishing their institutions according to their means, their character, and their circumstances. We must not aspire to the impossible, lest, in trying to rise above the realm of liberty, we again descend into the realm of tyranny. Absolute liberty invariably lapses into absolute power, and the mean between these two extremes is supreme social liberty. Abstract theories create the pernicious idea of unlimited freedom. Let us see to it that the strength of the public is kept within the limits prescribed by reason and interest; that the national will is confined within the bonds set by a just power; that the judiciary is rigorously controlled by civil and criminal laws, analogous to those in our present Constitution—that an equilibrium between the powers of government will exist, the conflicts that hamper the progress of the state will disappear, and those complications which tend to hinder rather than unite society will be eliminated.

The formation of a stable government requires as a foundation a national spirit, having as its objective a uniform concentration on two cardinal factors, namely, moderation of the popular will and limitation of public authority. The extremes, which these two factors theoretically establish, are difficult to define in practice; but it can well be conceived that the maxim that must guide them is mutual limitation and concentration of power, in order that there may be the least possible friction between the popular will and the constituted public authority. The science of achieving the balance is acquired almost imperceptibly, through practice and study. Progress in the practice of this science is hastened by progress in the enlightenment of the people, and integrity of mind and spirit speeds the progress of enlightenment.

Love of country, love of law, and respect for magistrates are the exalted emotions that must permeate the soul of a republic. The Venezuelans love their country, but they cannot love her laws, because these, being sources of evil, have been harmful; neither can they respect their magistrates, as they have been unjust, while the new administrators are scarcely known in the calling that they have entered. Unless there is a sacred reverence for country, laws, and authority, society becomes confused, an abyss—an endless conflict of man versus man, group versus group.

All our moral powers will not suffice to save our infant republic from this chaos unless we fuse the mass of the people, the government, the legislation, and the national spirit into a single united body. Unity, unity, unity, must be our motto in all things. The blood of our citizens is varied: let it be mixed for the sake of unity. Our Constitution has divided the powers of government: let them be bound together to secure unity. Our laws are but a sad relic of ancient and modern despotism. Let this monstrous edifice crumble and fall; and, having removed even its ruins, let us erect a temple to Justice; and, guided by its sacred inspiration, let us write a code of Venezuelan laws. Should we wish to consult monuments of legislation, those of Great Britain, France, and the United States of North America afford us admirable models.

Our America

José Martí

José Martí (1853–1895) is considered Cuba's greatest national hero. He was a poet, essayist, translator, journalist, and political revolutionary. Through his writings and political activism he became one of the most important voices for Cuban independence from Spain during the nineteenth century. He was also one of the principal commentators on the threat of U.S. expansionism in Latin America and his essays on this subject are still widely read today by new generations of Latin Americans. Throughout his life he epitomized the engaged intellectual for social and political change. He died in Cuba's war for independence in 1895. Some of his most important works include: *El presidio politico en Cuba* (1871, The Political Presidio in Cuba), *El amor con amor se paga* (1876, Love Is Repaid by Love) Essays: *Nuestra América* (1881, Our America), *Emerson* (1882), *Whitman* (1887), *Bolívar* (1893), *Ismaelillo* (1882), *Norteamericanos* (1884, North Americans), *Versos sencillos* (1891, Simple Verses), and *Versos libres* (1913, Free Verses). The selection included here appeared originally in Spanish in *El Partido Liberal*, in Mexico, on January 30, 1891.

January 1891

The parochial villager believes that the entire world is contained within his village and as long as he can become mayor or humiliate the rival who stole his sweetheart, or provided his savings increase in his bank, he considers everything is fine in the world, without recognizing that giants wearing seven-league boots exist who can crush him underfoot and that comets traveling through space while he is asleep clash in the sky, devouring whole worlds. What is left of this village mentality in America must wake up. These are not times to be sleeping in a nightcap but rather with weapons as a pillow, just like the men of Juan de Castellanos: weapons of the mind that defeat all others. Bunkers of ideas are worth far more than those of cement.

There is no prow that can cut through a cloud of ideas. An energetic idea, unfurled at the right time before the world, repels, like the mythical flag of the Last Judgment, a squadron of heavily armed men. People who do not know one another must, like brothers in arms, hasten to get to know each other. Those who shake their fists at each other, like jealous brothers desiring the same land, or those who live in small houses and covet the house of their neighbor, must all shake hands as if they were one. Those who beneath the umbrella of a criminal tradition and with their sabers dripping in blood appropriate the lands of their defeated brother, a brother punished much beyond his culpability, if they do not want to be called thieves, they should return the lands to their rightful owner. The honorable man does not collect debts of honor in cash, at so much a slap. We can no longer be a people like foliage that lives in the air, loaded with flowers, bursting or fluttering at light's whimsical caress, or being buffeted and tossed by the storm: our trees must form ranks so that the seven-league giant will not pass! Now is the time for reappraisal and for the united march. We have to march together, side by side, like the silver lodes in the depths of the Andes.

Only weaklings will lack the necessary courage. Those who have no faith in their land are weak men. And because they themselves lack courage, they deny it to others. They cannot reach the high branch with their puny arms, with hands sporting painted fingernails and bracelets, arms of Madrid or Paris, and who say that the tree cannot be climbed. The ship must be loaded with these harmful insects who eat away the marrow of the country that nourishes them. If indeed they are Parisians or Madrilenians, let them stroll beneath the streetlamps to the Prado or go to Tortoni's for a sherbet. These sons of carpenters who are ashamed that their fathers are carpenters! These men born in America who feel shame because they wear the apron of their Indian mother, and renounce their sick mother, the scoundrels, and abandon her on her sickbed! Who is the real man? The one who stays with his mother, to help cure her illness, or the one who puts her to work where no one can see her and lives off her in these rotten lands, wearing fancy cravats, cursing the womb that bore him, displaying the sign of the traitor on the back of his paper cassock? These sons of our America, which will have to be saved by its Indians, only increase in number; these traitors who request a rifle in the armies of North America, which drowns its Indians in their own blood, who only continue to decrease in number! These delicate sons who are men but refuse to do the work of men! Washington, who forged this land, did he go to live with the English, to dwell with them during the years in which he saw them marching against his own country? These "incroyables" of honor drag honor over foreign soil, just like their counterparts in the French Revolution, dancing and bragging and rolling their r's!

In what country can a man be more proud than in the sorrowful republics of our America, built from among the mute masses of Indians by the bleeding arms of a hundred apostles, and at the sound of battle between the book and the church candlestick? Never in history have such advanced and compact nations been created so quickly, and out of such disparate elements. The proud man believes that the earth was created to serve him as a pedestal, simply because he has a glib pen or his speech is colorful, and he views as worthless and incapable of change his native republic because its virgin jungles do not provide him with a way to continually travel throughout the world, like a famous tycoon, riding Persian ponies and carelessly spilling champagne. The question of incompetence does not lie with the emerging nation in its demand for forms that represent a certain suitableness and functionality, but rather with those who seek to dominate unique nations, of a special and violent composition, with laws derived from four centuries of free practice in the United States and nineteen centuries of monarchy in France. A decree from Hamilton does not stop the advance of the plainsman's colt. And a statement by Sieyés does not unblock the congealed blood of the indigenous peoples. Where governance takes place, one must pay attention, in order to govern well; and the good governor in America is not the one who knows how to govern the Germans or the French, but who knows what the elements are that make up his own country and how he can successfully manage them as a whole through methods and institutions that are native to the country itself, so that the desirable state in which every man can realize his potential may be attained, and so that everyone may enjoy the abundance that Nature has bestowed on all members of the nation, which they enrich with their work and defend with their lives. A government has to emerge from the nature of the country itself. The form it takes must agree with the way it is constituted. Government is nothing more than a balance between all the distinct natural elements that make up a nation.

For this reason the imported book has been conquered in America by the natural man. Natural men have defeated the artificial men of letters. The native born mestizo has conquered the exotic Creole. The struggle is not between civilization and barbarism, but between false erudition and nature. The natural man is good and he respects and rewards superior intelligence, provided that it does not take advantage of his submission to do him harm, or it does not offend him by disregarding him, which is something that the natural man will not tolerate, prepared as he is to recover by force the respect of the one who hurt his pride or endangered his interests. It is because of this conformity with scorned natural elements that tyrants in America have arisen and they have fallen as soon as they have betrayed these same elements. Republics have paid with tyrannies for their inability to recognize the true elements of their respective countries and to derive from them the proper form of government to govern accordingly. To govern in a new country means "to be a creator."

In nations composed of cultured and uncultured elements, the uncultured will govern, because of their tendency to be aggressive and to resolve all doubts by force, whenever the cultured fail at governing in office. The uncultured masses are lazy and timid when it comes to matters of the mind, and they want to be governed well, but if the government harms them in any way they rebel and govern themselves. How are those that govern supposed to be trained in the universities if there is not one university in America that teaches the rudiments of the art of government, which have to do with the analysis of the elements peculiar to America? Our young people go out into the world wearing Yankee or French spectacles and aspire to govern, by guesswork, a nation they simply do not know. We should deny entry into a political career to anyone who does not understand the rudiments of politics. The prize given in competitions should not be for the best ode, but for the best analysis of a country's principal elements. Newspapers, universities, and schools should emphasize the study of these elements. They need only be stated plainly and without distortion because whoever disregards, either willingly or through forgetfulness, any portion of the truth is ultimately doomed to fail, because the truth he lacked will grow due to such negligence and undermine whatever is constructed without it. It is easier to resolve the problem after recognizing its elements than to try to resolve it without such recognition. The natural man arrives on the scene indignant and strong, and topples the accumulated system based on books because justice was not administered in accord with the needs of the country. Knowledge is the solution. Knowing the country and governing it according to that knowledge is the only way to free it from tyranny. The European university must cede its place to the American university. The history of America from the Incas to the present should be taught thoroughly, even if it means that the history of Athenian magistrates is not. Our Greece is more important than the Greece that is not ours. That is to say, it is more important to us. Our national politics must replace exotic ones. Let the world be grafted to our republics, but its trunk has to be our republics. And let the vanquished pedant be quiet, because there is no country in which a man can have greater pride than in our long-suffering republics.

With the rosary in our hands, our head white and our body mottled, both Indian and Creole, we came boldly into the world of nations. We set out to conquer liberty under the Virgin's banners. A priest, a few lieutenants, and a woman erect a republic in Mexico on the shoulders of Indians. A Spanish cleric, under the protection of his cape, instructs a few magnificent students on questions of French liberty and they in turn choose a Spanish general as the leader of Central America against Spain. In the red silk banners of monarchy Venezuelans in the North and Argentines in the South set out to build nations. When the two heroes clashed and the continent was about to erupt, one of them, who was not the lesser of the two, decided to turn back. But heroism is scarcer during peacetime, because it is less glorious than during war; it is easier for a man to die with honor than to think in an orderly fashion. Governing when the emotions are exalted and unified is more feasible than leading, after the fight is over, when diverse, arrogant, exotic, or ambitious thoughts take control. The forces defeated in the epic conflict sought to undermine, with the feline caution of the species and the weight of reality, the edifice that had emerged, which embraced the coarse and unique territories of our half-breed America, and the cities of the naked leg and the Parisian frock, under the flag of nations nourished by a governing vitality and skilled in the practice of reason and liberty. The hierarchical constitution of the colonies resisted the democratic organization of the republic, and the capitals where the cravat prevailed left the countryside of riding boots waiting in the vestibule. Educated leaders did not understand that the revolution, whose triumph had aroused and set free the soul of the nation, had to govern within that soul and not against or without it. America thus began to suffer and still suffers from the fatigue produced by trying to find an accommodation between the discordant and hostile elements it inherited from a despotic and malicious colonizer, and from the imported forms and ideas that have retarded the adoption of a logical form of government because they do not reflect local reality. The continent, disjointed by three centuries of rule that has denied men the right to use their own reason, has embarked on a form of government based on reason, but disregarding or not listening to the uncultured masses who have helped in its redemption; it was supposed to be the reason of all in matters that concerned everyone, and not the intellectual reason of some over the provincial reason of others. The problem of independence was not due to an alteration of forms, but to a change in spirit.

With the oppressed it is necessary to make common cause, in order to guarantee a system that is contrary to the interests and ruling tendencies of the oppressors. The tiger, scared off by a flash of gunfire, returns in the darkness to the haunts of his prey. He dies with his eyes flashing and his claws exposed. He cannot be heard approaching; he walks on paws of velvet. When the prey awakes, the tiger is already upon him. The colony continued to exist within the republic, and our America is saving itself from its gravest error—the arrogance of the capital cities, the blind sense of triumph of those living in the countryside, the excessive importation of foreign ideas and formulas, the perverse and rude disdain for the aboriginal race—through a superior virtue, supported by the necessary blood, of the republic that struggles against the colony. The tiger waits curled up behind each tree. He will die with his claws exposed and his eyes flashing. But "these countries will be saved," as the Argentine Rivadavia proclaimed, whose sin was to be too refined a person during very crude times. A scabbard made of silk does not go with a machete nor should the lance be discarded in a country won over by the lance, because it becomes angry and presents itself at the door of Iturbide's Congress demanding that "the blond man be made emperor." These countries will be saved because of a genius for moderation found in Nature's serene harmony in this continent of light, where a new real man is now emerging for these real times, who is steeped in the critical reading that has occurred in Europe and which has replaced the literature of trial and error and utopianism that was instilled in the previous generation.

There was a period when we were a strange sight, with the chest of an athlete and the brain of a child. We were a masquerade wearing English trousers, a Parisian vest, a North American jacket, and a Spanish cap. The Indian, silent, circled us in wonder, and then went into the mountains to baptize his children. The scrutinized black, alone and unknown, sang his music from the heart among the rivers and wild beasts. The *campesino*, the creator, rose up in blind indignation against the city that scorned him, against his own child. We were all epaulets and tunics in countries that came into the world with sandals on their feet and headbands instead of hats. The intelligent thing would have been to join the headband and the tunic with the charity of the heart and the daring of the founding fathers, to empower the Indian, to make an appropriate place for the black man, to fit liberty to the body of those who rose up and triumphed in its name. We were left with the judge, the general, the intellectual, and the prebendary. Angelic youth as if caught in the tentacles of an octopus cast themselves toward heaven, only to fall back in futile glory, their heads crowned with clouds. The natural people, driven by instinct, and blinded by a sense of triumph, swept away the golden staffs of authority. Neither the European nor the Yankee book could provide the answer to the Spanish American enigma. Hate was attempted and each year countries deteriorated more and more. Tired of a useless hatred, of the struggle between the book and the lance, of reason against dogma, of the city against the countryside, of the impossible empire of urban castes divided over the question of a natural nation, whether tempestuous or inert, we begin, almost without knowing it, to try love. Nations stand up and greet each other. "What are we like," they ask, and they begin to tell each other what they are like. When a problem arises in Cojimar, they are not going to look to Danzig for a solution. The frock worn is still French but thought begins to emanate from America. The young in America roll up their sleeves, sink their hands in the dough and make it rise with the leaven of their sweat. They understand that too much has been imitated, and that salvation is to be found in their creativity. Creativity is this generation's password. Our wine is from plantains and if it happens to be sour, at least it's our wine! It is understood that the forms of government in a country have to be linked to its natural elements; that absolute ideas, in order to avoid committing an error of form, have to be expressed in relative forms; that liberty, in order to be viable, has to be sincere and complete; that if the republic does not extend its embrace to everyone and move forward with them, it will perish. The tiger within enters through the opening and the tiger from without as well. The general accommodates the march of his cavalry to the pace of the infantry, because if he leaves the infantry behind, the enemy will surround his cavalry. All politics is strategy. Nations must possess the ability for self-criticism, because criticism is healthy: but it must always be carried out with one heart and one mind. Reach down to the worst of the wretched and raise them up in your arms. With the fire of the heart, dissolve America's clotted blood. Make its natural blood flow and throb through its veins. Standing proudly, with happiness in the eyes of workers, the new Americans salute each other from one country to another. The natural statesman emerges out of his direct study of Nature. He reads to apply what he has learned, not to copy it. Economists study the origins of a problem. Orators begin to sound uplifting. Playwrights create natural characters for their stage. Academics discuss viable themes. Poetry cuts its romantic locks and hangs its colored vest on the glorious tree. Prose, sparkling and in bloom, is filled with ideas. Governors in indigenous republics learn Indian.

America is beginning to be saved from all of its dangers. The octopus is still sleeping on top of some of the republics. Others, because of the law of equilibrium, rush into the sea in frenetic and sublime haste to make up for the centuries lost. Others, forgetting that Juárez rode in a mule-driven wagon, hitch their wagon to the wind and then hand over the reins to a soap bubble. Poisonous luxury, the enemy of liberty, rots the corrupt man and opens the door to the foreigner. Others, where independence may be threatened, strive to purify the virile character of man. And still others, in their rapacious war with their neighbors, breed an undisciplined military that may at some point devour them. But perhaps there is another danger for our America that does not come from within, but from the differences in origin, methods, and interests between the two entities that make up the continent. The time is fast approaching when our America must confront an enterprising and vigorous nation that will seek close ties with us without knowing who we are and perhaps even scorning us. And since aggressive countries, the product of the rifle and law, love and only love other aggressive countries, and since the hour is still not so near at hand, even to the most timorous eye, when North America frees herself from her recklessness and ambition, if the purest aspects of her blood are to predominate; and since she could be driven by her vengeful and sordid masses, her tradition of expansionism or by the ambition of a powerful leader, there is not enough time to display the continual, discrete pride with which to confront and dissuade her; and since her self-respect as a republic creates for North America, in the eyes of the world, a kind of brake that neither her puerile grievance nor her pompous arrogance nor the parricidal grievances among the nations of our America can easily remove, the urgent need of our America is to show herself as she is, united in mind and purpose, the swift conqueror of a suffocating past, stained only by the fertile blood emanating from hands in struggle to put an end to the damage and scars left by our masters. The disdain of our formidable neighbor, who does not know our America, is the greatest danger facing all of us; and it is urgent, since the North's visit is coming soon, that our neighbor understand us, know who we are so that she will not scorn us. Through ignorance, perhaps, she might go so far as to covet us. Out of respect, once she knows who we are, she will remove her hands and refrain from such behavior. One must have faith in the best in man and distrust the worst. We must give every opportunity to this potential for good so that it prevails over the bad. If not, man's worst behavior will certainly dominate. Nations should have a pillory for those who fan the flames of unnecessary hatred and another for those who do not speak the truth in time.

There is no such thing as racial hatred, because there are no races. Weak thinkers and pseudoscholars string together and reheat old bookshelf notions of race, which the fair-minded traveler and the cordial observer seek in vain in Nature's justice, where the universal identity of man stands out in a victorious love and a turbulent lust for life. The soul emanates, equal and eternal, from bodies that are different in shape and color. The one who foments and propagates opposition and hatred among the races sins against humanity. But in the potpourri of nations are compressed, in the proximity of other diverse nations, unique and vital characteristics, of thoughts and customs, of expansion and acquisition, of vanity and greed, which from the latent state of national concerns could, during a period of internal chaos or the precipitation of the accumulated national character, become a serious threat for neighboring countries, isolated and weak, which the strong country may declare perishable and inferior. To think is to serve. It should not be supposed, out of provincial antipathy, that the blond continent to the north suffers from an innate and fatal evil simply because it does not speak our language, nor see the world as we do, nor resemble us in its political flaws, which are different from ours, nor regard favorably the ill-tempered and dark-skinned peoples, nor view charitably, from the heights of its questionable eminence, those who are less favored by History, who attain through heroic deeds the road to republicanism. Nor should the obvious facts of the problem be hidden, because it can be resolved, for the benefit of centuries of peace yet to come, through the timely study and the tacit and necessary union of the continental soul. Because our unified hymn is already being sung, the current generation carries on its shoulders a hard-working America along the road paved by their sublime fathers. From the Río Grande to the Straits of Magellan, the Great Semí, seated on the back of the condor, has sowed the seed of the new America throughout the romantic nations of the continent and the sorrowful islands of the sea!

Ariel *(Selection)*

José Enrique Rodó

José Enrique Rodó (Uruguay, 1872–1917) was a foremost Latin American essayist. He is best known for his book *Ariel* (1900), in which he attempted to capture the essence of Latin American identity and how it differs from that of its neighbor to the north. During a period dominated by utilitarianism and materialism, Rodó sought to offer Latin America's youth an alternative lifestyle based on the values of idealism, spirituality, and humanism. This selection is from *Ariel*, foreword by James W. Symington, translation, reader's reference, and annotated bibliography by Margaret Sayers Peden (Austin: University of Texas Press, 1988), 70–90. By permission of the University of Texas Press.

1900

The inextricably linked concepts of utilitarianism as a concept of human destiny and egalitarian mediocrity as a norm for social relationships compose the formula for what Europe has tended to call the spirit of *Americanism*. It is impossible to ponder either inspiration for social conduct, or to compare them with their opposites, without their inevitable association with that formidable and productive democracy to our north. Its display of prosperity and power is dazzling testimony to the efficacy of its institutions and to the guidance of its concepts. If it has been said that "utilitarianism" is the word for the spirit of the English, then the United States can be considered the embodiment of the word. And the gospel of that word is spread everywhere through the good graces of its material miracles. Spanish America is not, in this regard, entirely a land of heathens. That powerful federation is effecting a kind of moral conquest among us. Admiration for its greatness and power is making impressive inroads, in the minds of our leaders and, perhaps even more, in the impressionable minds of the masses, who are awed by its incontrovertible victories. And from admiring to imitating is an easy step. A psychologist will say that admiration and conviction are passive modes of imitation. "The main seat of the imitative part of our nature is our belief," said Bagehot. Common sense and experience should in themselves be enough to establish this simple relationship. We imitate what we believe to be superior or prestigious. And this is why the vision of an America de-Latinized of its own will, without threat of conquest, and reconstituted in the image and likeness of the North, now looms in the nightmares of many who are genuinely concerned about our future. This vision is the impetus behind an abundance of similar carefully thought-out designs and explains the continuous flow of proposals for innovation and reform. We have our *USA-mania*. It must be limited by the boundaries our reason and sentiment jointly dictate. When I speak of boundaries, I do not suggest absolute negation. I am well aware that we find our inspirations, our enlightenment, our teachings, in the example of the strong; nor am I unaware that intelligent attention to external events is singularly fruitful in the case of a people still in the process of forming its national entity. I am similarly aware that by persevering in the educational process we hope to modulate the elements of society that must be adapted to new exigencies of civilization and new opportunities in life, thus balancing the forces of heritage and custom with that innovation. I do not, however, see what is to be gained from denaturalizing the character—the *personality*—of a nation, from imposing an identification with a foreign model, while sacrificing irreplaceable uniqueness. Nor do I see anything to be gained from the ingenuous belief that identity can somehow be achieved through artificial and improvised imitation. Michelet believed that the mindless transferal of what is natural and spontaneous in one society to another where it has neither natural nor historical roots was like attempting to introduce a dead organism into a living one by simple implantation. In a social structure, as in literature and art, forced imitation will merely distort the configuration of the model. The misapprehension of those who believe they have reproduced the character of a human collectivity in its essence, the living strength of its spirit, as well as the secret of its triumphs and prosperity, and have exactly reproduced the mechanism of its institutions and the external form of its customs is reminiscent of the delusion of naïve students who believe they have achieved the genius of their master when they have merely copied his style and characteristics.

In such a futile effort there is, furthermore, an inexpressible ignobility. Eager mimicry of the prominent and the powerful, the successful and the fortunate, must be seen as a kind of political *snobbery*; and a servile abdication—like that of some snobs condemned by Thackeray in *The Book of Snobs* to be satirized for all eternity—lamentably consumes the energies of those who are not blessed by nature or fortune but who impotently ape the caprices and foibles of those at the peak of society. Protecting our *internal* independence—independence of personality and independence of judgment—is a basic form of self-respect. Treatises on ethics often comment on one of Cicero's moral precepts, according to which one of our responsibilities as human beings is zealously to protect the uniqueness of our personal character—whatever in it that is different and formative—while always respecting Nature's primary impulse: that the order and harmony of the world are based on the broad distribution of her gifts. The truth of this precept would seem even greater when applied to the character of human societies. Perhaps you will hear it said that there is no distinctive mark or characteristic of the present ordering of our peoples that is worth struggling to maintain. What may perhaps be lacking in our collective character is a sharply defined "personality." But in lieu of an absolutely distinct and autonomous particularity, we Latin Americans have a heritage of race, a great ethnic tradition, to maintain, a sacred place in the pages of history that depends upon us for its continuation. Cosmopolitanism, which we must respect as a compelling requisite in our formation, includes fidelity both to the past and to the formative role that the genius of our race must play in recasting the American of tomorrow.

More than once it has been observed that the great epochs of history, the most luminous and fertile periods in the evolution of humankind, are almost always the result of contemporaneous but conflicting forces that through the stimulus of concerted opposition preserve our interest in life, a fascination that would pale in the placidity of absolute conformity. So it was that the most genial and civilizing of cultures turned upon an axis supported by the poles of Athens and Sparta. America must continue to maintain the dualism of its original composition, which re-creates in history the classic myth of the two eagles released simultaneously from the two poles in order that each should reach the limits of its domain at the same moment. Genial and competitive diversity does not exclude but, rather, tolerates, and even in many aspects favors, solidarity. And if we could look into the future and see the formula for an eventual harmony, it would not be based upon the *unilateral imitation*—as Gabriel Tarde would say—of one people by another, but upon a mutual exchange of influences, and the fortuitous fusion of the attributes that gave each its special glory. In addition, a dispassionate examination of the civilization that some consider to be the only perfect model will reveal no less powerful reasons to temper the enthusiasms of those who demand idolatrous devotion, reasons other than those based on the thesis that to reject everything original is both unworthy and unjustifiable. And now I come to the direct relation between the theme of my talk and the spirit of imitation.

Any criticism of the Americans to our north should always be accompanied, as in the case of any worthy opponent, with the chivalrous salute that precedes civilized combat. And I make that bow sincerely. But to ignore a North American's defects would seem to me as senseless as to deny his good qualities. Born—calling upon the paradox that Baudelaire employed in a different context—with the *innate experience* of freedom, they have remained faithful to the laws of their origins and with the precision and sureness of a mathematical progression have developed the basic principles of their formation. Subsequently, their history is characterized by a uniformity that, although it may lack diversity in skills and values, does possess the intellectual beauty of logic. The traces of their presence will never be erased from the annals of human rights. From tentative essays and utopian visions, they were the first to evoke our modern ideal of liberty, forging imperishable bronze and living reality from concepts. With their example they have demonstrated the possibility of imposing the unyielding authority of a republic upon an enormous national organism. With their federation they have demonstrated—recalling de Tocqueville's felicitous expression—how the brilliance and power of large states can be reconciled with the happiness and peace of the small. Some of the boldest strokes in the panorama of this century, deeds that will be recorded through all time, are theirs. Theirs, too, the glory of having fully established—by amplifying the strongest note of moral beauty in our civilization—the grandeur and power of work, that sacred power that antiquity degraded to the abjectness of slave labor, and that today we identify with the highest expression of human dignity, founded on the awareness of its intrinsic worth. Strong, tenacious, believing that inactivity is ignominious, they have placed in the hands of the mechanic in his shop and the farmer in his field the mythic club of Hercules and have given human nature a new and unexpected beauty by girding onto it the blacksmith's leather apron. Each of them marches forward to conquer life in the same way the first Puritans set out to tame the wilderness. Persevering devotees of that cult of individual energy that makes each man the author of his own destiny, they have modeled their society on an imaginary assemblage of Crusoes who, after gaining their crude strength by looking out for their self-interests, set to weaving the stout cloth of their society. Without sacrificing the sovereign concept of individualism, they have at the same time created from the spirit of association the most admirable instrument of their grandeur and empire. Similarly, from the sum of individual strengths subordinated to a plan of research, philanthropy, and industry, they have achieved marvelous results that are all the more remarkable, considering that they were obtained while maintaining the absolute integrity of personal autonomy. There is in these North Americans a lively and insatiable curiosity and an avid thirst for enlightenment. Professing their reverence for public education with an obsessiveness that resembles monomania—glorious and productive as it may be—they have made the school the hub of their prosperity, and a child's soul the most valued of all precious commodities. Although their culture is far from being refined or spiritual, it is admirably efficient as long as it is directed to the practical goal of realizing an immediate end. They have not added a single general law, a single principle, to the storehouse of scientific knowledge. They have, however, worked magic through the marvels of their application of general knowledge. They have grown tall as giants in the domains of utility; and in the steam engine and electric generator they have given the world billions of invisible slaves to serve the human Aladdin, increasing a hundredfold the power of the magic lamp. The extent of their greatness and strength will amaze generations to come. With their prodigious skill for improvisation, they have invented a way to speed up time; and by the power of will in one day they have conjured up from the bosom of absolute solitude a culture equal to the work of centuries. The liberty of Puritanism, still shedding its light from the past, joined to that light the heat of a piety that lives today. Along with factories and schools, their strong hands have also raised the churches from which rise the prayers of many millions of free consciences. They have been able to save from the shipwreck of all idealisms the highest idealism, keeping alive the tradition of a religion that although it may not fly on wings of a delicate and profound spiritualism does, at least, amid the harshness of the utilitarian tumult, keep a firm grip on the reins of morality. Surrounded by the refinements of civilized life, they have also been able to maintain a certain robust primitivism. They have a pagan cult of health, of skill, of strength; they temper and refine the precious instrument of will in muscle; and obliged, by their insatiable appetite for dominance, to cultivate all human activities with obsessive energy, they build an athlete's torso in which to shelter the heart of free man. And from the concord of their civilization, from the harmonious mobility of their culture, sounds a dominant note of optimism and confidence and faith that expands their hearts; they advance toward the future under the power of a stubborn and arrogant expectation. This is the note of Longfellow's "Excelsior" and "A Psalm of Life," which their poets, in the philosophy of strength and action, have advocated as an infallible balm against all bitterness.

Thus their titanic greatness impresses even those who have been forewarned by the enormous excesses of their character or the recent violence of their history. As for me, you have already seen that, although I do not love them, I admire them. I admire them, first of all, for their formidable strength of *volition* and, as Philarète Chasles said of their English forebears, I bow before the "school of will and work" they have instituted.

In the beginning was Action. A future historian of that powerful republic could begin the still-to-be-concluded Genesis of their national existence with these famous words from *Faust*. Their genius, like the universe of the Dynamists, could be defined as *force in motion*. Above all else, they have the capacity, the enthusiasm, and the blessed vocation for action. Will is the chisel that has sculptured these peoples in hard stone. Their outstanding characteristics are the two manifestations of the power of will: originality and boldness. Their history, in its entirety, has been marked by paroxysms of vigorous activity. Their typical figure, like Nietzsche's *superman*, is named *I Will It*. If something saves him, collectively, from vulgarity, it is that extraordinary show of energy that leads to achievement and that allows him to invest even the struggles of self-interest and materialism with a certain aura of epic grandeur. Thus Paul Bourget could say that the speculators of Chicago and Minneapolis are like heroic warriors whose skills of attack and defense are comparable to those of Napoleon's veteran *grognards*. And this supreme energy that seems to permit North American genius—audacious and hypnotic as it is—to cast spells and the power of suggestion over the Fates is to be found even in those peculiarities of their civilization that we consider exceptional or divergent. For example, no one will deny that Edgar Allan Poe is one such anomalous and rebellious individual. He is of the elect who resist assimilation into the national soul, a person who successfully, if in infinite solitude, struggled among his fellows for self-expression. And yet—as Baudelaire has so tellingly pointed out—the basic characteristic of Poe's heroes is still the superhuman persistence, the indomitable stamina, of their will. When Poe conceived Ligeia, the most mysterious and adorable of his creatures, he symbolized in the inextinguishable light of her eyes the hymn of the triumph of Will over Death.

With my sincere recognition of all that is luminous and great in its genius, I have won the right to complete a fair appraisal of this powerful nation; one vital question, however, remains to be answered. Is that society achieving, or at least partially achieving, the concept of rational conduct that satisfies the legitimate demands of intellectual and moral dignity? Will this be the society destined to create the closest approximation of the "perfect state"? Does the feverish restlessness that seems to magnify the activity and intensity of their lives have a truly worthwhile objective, and does that stimulus justify their impatience?

Herbert Spencer, voicing his sincere and noble tribute to American democracy at a banquet in New York City, identified this same unrestrainable restiveness as the fundamental characteristic of the lives of North Americans, an agitation manifest in their infinite passion for work and their drive toward material expansion in all its forms. And then he observed that such an atmosphere of activity exclusively subordinated to the immediate proposals of utility denoted a concept of life that might well be acceptable as a provisional quality of a civilization, or as the preliminary stage of a culture. Such a concept, however, demands subsequent revision, for unless that tendency is curbed, the result will be to convert utilitarian work into an end, into the supreme goal of life, when rationally it can be only one among numbers of elements that facilitate the harmonious development of our being. Then Spencer added that it was time to preach to North Americans "the gospel of relaxation." And as we identify the ultimate meaning of those words with the classic concept of *otium*, as it was dignified by the moralists of antiquity, we would include among the chapters of gospel that those tireless workers should heed everything concerned with the ideal, the use of time for other than selfish purposes, and any meditation not directed toward the immediate ends of utility.

North American life, in fact, perfectly describes the vicious circle identified by Pascal: the fervent pursuit of well-being that has no object beyond itself. North American prosperity is as great as its inability to satisfy even an average concept of human destiny. In spite of its titanic accomplishments and the great force of will that those accomplishments represent, and in spite of its incomparable triumphs in all spheres of material success, it is nevertheless true that as an entity this civilization creates a singular impression of insufficiency and emptiness. And when following the prerogative granted by centuries of evolution dominated by the dignity of classicism and Christianity we ask, what is its directing principle, what its ideal *substratum*, what the ultimate goal of the present Positivist interests surging through that formidable mass, we find nothing in the way of a formula for a definitive ideal but the same eternal preoccupation with material triumphs. Having drifted from the traditions that set their course, the peoples of this nation have not been able to replace the inspiring idealism of the past with a high and selfless concept of the future. They live for the immediate reality, for the present, and thereby subordinate all their activity to the egoism of personal and collective wellbeing. Of the sum of their riches and power could be said what Bourget said of the intelligence of the Marquis de Norbert, a figure in one of his books: that it is like a well-laid fire to which no one has set a match. What is lacking is the kindling spark that causes the flame of a vivifying and exciting ideal to blaze from the abundant but unlighted wood. Not even national egoism, lacking a higher motivation, not even exclusiveness and pride of nationhood, which is what in antiquity transfigured and exalted the prosaic severity of Roman life, can engender glimmers of idealism and beauty in a people in whom cosmopolitan confusion and the *atomism* of a poorly understood democracy impede the formation of a true national consciousness.

It could be said that when the Positivism of the mother country was transmitted to her emancipated children in America, it suffered a distilling process that filtered out the emollient idealism, reducing it to the harshness that previous excessive passion and satire had attributed to English Positivism. But beneath the hard utilitarian shell, beneath the mercantile cynicism, beneath the Puritanical severity, the English spirit masks—you must never doubt it—a poetic genius and a profound veneration for sensitivity. All this, in Taine's opinion, reveals that the primitive, the Germanic, essence of that people, later diluted by the pressures of conquest and commercial activities, was one of an extraordinary exaltation of sentiment. The American spirit did not inherit the ancestral poetic instinct that bursts like a crystalline stream from the heart of Britannic rock when smitten by an artistic Moses. In the institution of their aristocracy—as anachronistic and unjust as it may be in the realm of politics—the English people possess a high and impregnable bulwark against the attacks of mercantilism and the encroachment of the prosaic. This bulwark is so high and so impregnable that Taine himself states that, since the age of the Greek city-states, history has not seen an example of a way of life more propitious to heightening a sense of human nobility. In the ambience of American democracy, the spirit of vulgarity encounters no barriers to slow its rising waters, and it spreads and swells as if flooding across an endless plain.

Sensibility, intelligence, customs—everything in that enormous land is characterized by a radical ineptitude for selectivity which, along with the mechanistic nature of its materialism and its politics, nurtures a profound disorder in anything having to do with idealism. It is all too easy to follow the manifestations of that ineptitude, beginning with the most external and apparent, then arriving at those that are more essential and internal. Prodigal with his riches—because in his appetites, as Bourget has astutely commented, there is no trace of Molière's miserly Harpagon—the North American has with his wealth achieved all the satisfaction and vanity that come with sumptuous magnificence—but good taste has eluded him. In such an atmosphere, true art can exist only in the form of individual rebellion. Emerson and Poe, in that situation, are like plants cruelly uprooted from their natural soil by the spasms of a geologic catastrophe. Bourget, in *Outre mer*, speaks of the solemnity with which the word *art* trembles on the lips of the North Americans who have courted fortune. In such sycophancy, the hearty and righteous heroes of *self-help* hope to crown, by assimilating refinement, the labor of their tenaciously won eminence. But never have they conceived of the divine activity they so emphatically profess as anything other than a new way to satisfy their pervading restiveness, and as a trophy for their vanity. They ignore in art all that is selfless and selective. They ignore it, in spite of the munificence with which private fortunes are employed to stimulate an appreciation of beauty; in spite of the splendid museums and exhibitions their cities boast; in spite of the mountains of marble and bronze they have sculptured into statues for their public squares. And if a word may someday characterize their taste in art, it will be a word that negates art itself: the grossness of affectation, the ignorance of all that is subtle and exquisite, the cult of false grandeur, the *sensationalism* that excludes the serenity that is irreconcilable with the pace of a feverish life.

The idealism of beauty does not fire the soul of a descendant of austere Puritans. Nor does the idealism of truth he scorns as vain and unproductive any exercise of thought that does not yield an immediate result. He does not bring to science a selfless thirst for truth, nor has he ever shown any sign of revering science for itself. For him, research is merely preparation for a utilitarian application. His grandiose plans to disseminate the benefits of popular education were inspired in the noble goal of communicating rudimentary knowledge to the masses; but although those plans promote the growth of education, we have seen no sign that they contain any imperative to enhance selective education, or any inclination to aid in allowing excellence to rise above general mediocrity. Thus the persistent

North American war against ignorance has resulted in a universal *semicul-ture*, accompanied by the diminution of high culture. To the same degree that basic ignorance has diminished in that gigantic democracy, wisdom and genius have correspondingly disappeared. This, then, is the reason that the trajectory of their intellectual activity is one of decreasing brilliance and originality. While in the period of independence and the formation of their nation many illustrious names emerged to expound both the thought and the will of that people, only a half century later de Tocqueville could write of them, *the gods have departed*. It is true, however, that even as de Tocqueville was writing his masterpiece, the rays of a glorious pleiad of universal magnitude in the intellectual history of this century were still beaming forth from Boston, the *Puritan citadel*, the city of learned traditions. But who has come along to perpetuate the bequest of a William Ellery Channing, an Emerson, a Poe? The bourgeois leveling process, ever swifter in its devastation, is tending to erase what little character remains of their precarious intellectualism. For some time now North American literature has not been borne to heights where it can be perceived by the rest of the world. And today the most genuine representation of American taste in belle letters is to be found in the gray pages of a journalism that bears little resemblance to that of the days of the *Federalist*.

In the area of morality, the mechanistic thrust of utilitarianism has been somewhat regulated by the balance wheel of a strong religious tradition. We should not, nevertheless, conclude that this tradition has led to true principles of selflessness. North American religion, a derivation from and exaggeration of English religion, actually serves to aid and enforce penal law that will relinquish its hold only on the day it becomes possible to grant to moral authority the religious authority envisioned by John Stuart Mill. Benjamin Franklin represents the highest point in North American morality: a philosophy of conduct whose ideals are grounded in the normality of honesty and the utility of prudence. His is a philosophy that would never give rise to either sanctity or heroism, one that although it may—like the cane that habitually supports its originator—lend conscience support along the everyday paths of life is a frail staff indeed when it comes to scaling the peaks. And these are the heights; consider the reality to be found in the valleys. Even were the moral criterion to sink no lower than Franklin's honest and moderate utilitarianism, the inevitable consequence—already revealed in de Tocqueville's sagacious observation—of a society educated in such limitations of duty would not inevitably be that state of proud and magnificent decadence that reveals the proportions of the satanic beauty of evil during the dissolution of empires; it would, instead, result in a kind of pallid and mediocre materialism and, ultimately, the lassitude of a lusterless enervation resulting from the quiet winding down of all the mainsprings of moral life. In a society whose precepts tend to place the demonstration of self-sacrifice and virtue outside the realm of obligation, the bounds of that obligation will constantly be pushed back. And the school of material prosperity—always an ordeal for republican austerity—that captures minds today has carried the simplistic concept of rational conduct even farther. In their frankness other codes have surpassed even Franklin as an expression of the national wisdom. And it is not more than five years ago that in all of North America's cities public opinion consecrated, with the most unequivocal demonstration of popular and critical acclaim, the new moral law: from the Boston of the Puritans, Orison Swett Mardin wrote a learned book entitled *Pushing to the Front*, solemnly announcing that success should be considered the supreme goal of life. His "revelation" echoed even in the bosom of Christian fellowship, and once was cited as being comparable to Thomas a Kempis's *The Imitation of Christ*.

Public life, of course, does not escape the consequences of the spread of the germ of disorganization harbored in the entrails of that society. Any casual observer of its political customs can relate how the obsession of utilitarian interests tends progressively to enervate and impoverish the sense of righteousness in the hearts of its citizens. Civic valor, that venerable Hamiltonian virtue, is a forgotten sword that lies rusting among the cobwebs of tradition. Venality, which begins in the polling places, spreads through the workings of the institution. A government of mediocrity discourages the emulation that exalts character and intelligence and relates those qualities to the efficacy of power. Democracy, which consistently has resisted the regulator of a noble and instructive notion of human excellence, has always tended toward an abominable slavishness to numbers that undervalues the greatest moral benefits of liberty and nullifies respect for the dignity of others. Today, furthermore, a formidable force is rising up to emphasize the absolutism of numbers. The political influence of a plutocracy represented by the all-powerful allies of the trust, the monopolizers of production and masters of the economy, is undoubtedly one of the most significant features in the present physiognomy of that great nation. The formation of this plutocracy has caused some to recall, with good reason, the rise of the arrogant and wealthy class that in the waning days of the Roman republic was one of the visible signs of the decline of liberty and the tyranny of the Caesars. And the exclusive concern for material gain—the numen of that civilization—imposes its logic on political life, as well as on all other areas of activity, granting the greatest prominence to Alphonse Daudet's bold and astute *Struggle-for-lifer*, become, by dint of brutal efficiency, the supreme personification of national energy: a postulant for Emerson's representative *man*, or for Taine's *personage règnant* [leading personage].

There is a second impulse corresponding to the one that in the life of the spirit is speeding toward utilitarian egoism and the disintegration of idealism, and that is the physical impulse the multitudes and the initiatives of an astounding population explosion are pushing westward toward the boundless territory that throughout the period of independence was still a mystery hidden by the forests of the Mississippi. In fact, it is in this extemporaneous West—beginning to be so formidable to the interests of the original Atlantic states, and threatening in the near future to demand its hegemony—that we find the most faithful representation of contemporary North American life. It is in the West that the definitive results, the logical and natural fruits, of the spirit that has led this powerful democracy away from its origins stand out so clearly, allowing the observer to picture the face of the immediate future of this great nation. As a representative type, the Yankee and Virginian have been replaced by the tamer of the only-yesterday-deserted Plains, those settlers of whom Michel Chevalier said, prophetically, a half century ago, "the last shall be first." In that man of the West, a utilitarianism, void of any idealism, a kind of universal indefinition and the leveling process of an ill-conceived democracy will reach their ultimate triumph. Everything noble in that civilization, everything that binds it to magnanimous memories and supports its historic dignity—the heritage of the *Mayflower*, the memory of patrician Virginians and New England gentry, the spirit of the citizens and the legislators of the emancipation—will live on in the original states, there where in Boston and Philadelphia "the palladium of Washingtonian tradition" is still upheld. It is Chicago that now rears its head to rule. And its confidence in its superiority over the original Atlantic states is based on the conviction that they are too reactionary, too European, too traditional. History confers no titles when the election process entails auctioning off the purple.

To the degree that the generic utilitarianism of that civilization assumes more defined, more open, and more limiting characteristics, the intoxication of material prosperity increases the impatience of its children to propagate that doctrine and enshrine it with the historical importance of a Rome. Today, North Americans openly aspire to preeminence in universal culture, to leadership in ideas; they consider themselves the forgers of a type of civilization that will endure forever. The semi-ironic speech that Réné Lefebvre Laboulaye places in the mouth of a student in his

Americanized Paris to signify the superiority that experience has conceded to whatever favors the pride of nationalism would today be accepted by any patriotic North American as absolute truth. At the base of the Americans' open rivalry with Europe there is an ingenuous disdain, and the profound conviction that Americans will in a very brief time obscure the intellectual superiority and glory of Europe, once again fulfilling in the evolution of human civilization the harsh law of the ancient mysteries in which the initiate always killed his initiator. It would be futile to attempt to convince a North American that, although the contribution his nation has made to the evolution of liberty and utility has undoubtedly been substantial, and should rightly qualify as a universal contribution, indeed, as a contribution to *humanity*, it is not so great as to cause the axis of the world to shift in the direction of a new Capitol. It would be similarly futile to attempt to convince him that the enduring achievements of the European Aryans, who dwelt along the civilizing shores of the Mediterranean that more than three thousand years ago jubilantly displayed the garland of its Hellenic cities—achievements that survived until today, and whose traditions and teachings we still adhere to—form a sum that cannot be equaled by the formula *Washington plus Edison*. Given the opportunity, they would gladly revise Genesis, hoping to gain a place "in the beginning." But, in addition to the relative modesty of their role in the enlightenment of humanity, their very character denies them the possibility of hegemony. Nature has not gifted them either with a genius for persuasion or with the vocation of the apostle. They lack the supreme gift of *amiability*, given the highest meaning of the word, that is, the extraordinary power of sympathy that enables nations endowed by Providence with the gift and responsibility for educating to instill in their culture something of the beauty of classic Greece, beauty of which all cultures hope to find some trace. That civilization may abound—undoubtedly it does abound—in proposals and productive examples. It may inspire admiration, amazement, and respect. But it is difficult to believe that when a stranger glimpses their enormous symbol from the high seas—Bartholdi's Statue of Liberty, triumphantly lifting her torch high above the port of New York City—it awakens in his soul the deep and religious feeling that must have been evoked in the diaphanous nights of Attica by the sight of Athena high upon the Acropolis, her bronze sword, glimpsed from afar, gleaming in the pure and serene atmosphere.

I want each of you to be aware that when in the name of the rights of the spirit I resist the mode of North American utilitarianism, which they want to impose on us as the summa and model of civilization, I do not imply that everything they have achieved in the sphere of what we might call the *interests of the soul* has been entirely negative. Without the arm that levels and constructs, the arm that serves the noble work of the mind would not be free to function. Without a certain material well-being, the realm of the spirit and the intellect could not exist. The aristocratic idealism of Renan accepts this fact when it exalts—in relation to the moral concerns of the species and its future spiritual selection—the importance of the utilitarian work of this century. "To rise above necessity," the master adds, "is to be redeemed." In the remote past, the effects of the prosaic and self-interested actions of the merchant who first put one people in contact with others were of incalculable value in disseminating ideas, since such contacts were an effective way to enlarge the scope of intelligence, to polish and refine customs, even, perhaps, to advance morality. The same positive force reappears later, propitiating the highest idealism of civilization. According to Paul de Saint-Victor, the gold accumulated by the mercantilism of the Italian republics financed the Renaissance. Ships returning from the lands of the Thousand and One Nights laden with spices and ivory to fill the storehouses of the Florentine merchants made it possible for Lorenzo de Medici to renew the Platonic feast. History clearly demonstrates a reciprocal relationship between the progress of utilitarianism and idealism. And in the same way that utility often serves as a strong shield for the ideal, frequently (as long as it is not specifically intended) the ideal evokes the useful. Bagehot, for example, observed that mankind might never have enjoyed the positive benefits of navigation had there not in primitive ages been idle dreamers—surely misunderstood by their contemporaries—who were intrigued by contemplating the movement of the planets. This law of harmony teaches us to respect the arm that tills the inhospitable soil of the prosaic and the ordinary. Ultimately, the work of North American Positivism will serve the cause of Ariel. What that Cyclopean nation, with its sense of the useful and its admirable aptitude for mechanical invention, has achieved directly in the way of material well-being, other peoples, or they themselves in the future, will effectively incorporate into the process of selection. This is how the most precious and fundamental of the acquisitions of the spirit—the alphabet, which lends immortal wings to the word—was born in the very heart of Canaanite trading posts, the discovery of a mercantile civilization that used it for exclusively financial purposes, never dreaming that the genius of superior races would transfigure it, converting it into a means of communicating mankind's purest and most luminous essence. The relationship between material good and moral and intellectual good is, then, according to an analogy offered by Fouillée, nothing more than a new aspect of the old equivalence of forces; and, in the same way that motion is transformed into heat, elements of spiritual excellence may also be obtained from material benefits.

As yet, however, North American life has not offered us a new example of that incontestable relationship, nor even afforded a glimpse of a glorious future. Our confidence and our opinion must incline us to believe, however, that in an inferred future their civilization is destined for excellence. Considering that under the scourge of intense activity the very brief time separating them from their dawn has witnessed a sufficient expenditure of life forces to effect a great evolution, their past and present can only be the prologue to a promising future. Everything indicates that their evolution is still very far from definitive. The assimilative energy that has allowed them to preserve a certain uniformity and a certain generic character in spite of waves of ethnic groups very different from those that have until now set the tone for their national identity will be vitiated in increasingly difficult battles. And in the utilitarianism that so effectively inhibits idealism, they will not find an inspiration powerful enough to maintain cohesion. An illustrious thinker who compared the slave of ancient societies to a particle undigested by the social system might use a similar comparison to characterize the situation of the strong Germanic strain now identifiable in the Mid- and Far West. There, preserved intact—in temperament, social organization, and customs—are all the traits of a German nature that in many of its most profound and most vigorous specificities must be considered to be antithetical to the American character. In addition, a civilization destined to endure and expand in the world, a civilization that has not, in the manner of an Oriental empire, become mummified, or lost its aptitude for variety, cannot indefinitely channel its energies and ideas in one, and only one, direction. Let us hope that the spirit of that titanic society, which has until today been characterized solely by *Will* and *Utility*, may one day be known for its intelligence, sentiment, and idealism. Let us hope that from that enormous crucible will ultimately emerge the exemplary human being, generous, balanced, and select, whom Spencer, in a work I have previously cited, predicted would be the product of the costly work of the melting pot. But let us not expect to find such a person either in the present reality of that nation or in its immediate evolution. And let us refuse to see an exemplary civilization where there exists only a clumsy, though huge, working model that must still pass through many corrective revisions before it acquires the serenity and confidence with which a nation that has achieved its perfection crowns its work—the powerful ascent that Leconte de Lisle describes in "Le sommeil du condor" [The Dream of the Condor] as an ascent that ends in Olympian tranquility.

An Open Letter to the President of the United States

Manuel Baldomero Ugarte

Manuel Baldomero Ugarte (Buenos Aires, 1875–1951) was an Argentine writer and politician. Among his principal works are: *El porvenir de América Española* (1910, The Future of Spanish America), *La patria grande* (1922, The Nation), and *El destino de un continente* (1923, The Destiny of a Continent). This selection is from *La patria grande y otros textos*, introduction by Jorge Bolívar (Buenos Aires: Secretaría de Cultura de la Nación, 1994), 101–107. The following letter was addressed to Woodrow Wilson, who had just assumed the office of president and served in this capacity from 1913 to 1921. During his presidency the United States intervened in Latin America on numerous occasions: Mexico, Haiti, Cuba, and Panama. The United States also maintained troops in Nicaragua throughout his administration.

1913

Today, at the threshold of a new presidency and a new administration that has proclaimed its resolve to correct earlier injustices, I come to speak the truth to a great man and to a great people. Those who govern are sometimes distanced from public opinion by groups intent on influencing them in order to satisfy their own desires for dominance and wealth. For this reason it is imperative that the voice of those without personal ambitions for money or power, the voice of those who seek only a higher justice, which is the greatest good of our existence, rise up and confront such groups in order to establish a counterbalance.

Sir, the time has come to ensure justice in the New World; justice for certain Spanish American republics, which for years have suffered an odious treatment, and justice too for the United States, whose traditions are growing pale in the face of a policy that does not represent the true aspirations of Lincoln's and Washington's descendants.

I have just traveled throughout Spanish America; I have observed carefully the continent's current situation; and because I am well acquainted with the common sense of the American people, just as I recognize the respect they have for principle, I now embrace the certainty that, in order to put an end to the injustice that overwhelms us, it is sufficient to simply denounce it.

For many long years the United States, which has achieved within its borders the highest expression of freedom in our age, has been defending in our America a spirit that is contradictory and antithetical to its principles and laws. Private individuals and financial institutions from the United States have come to some of our lands, especially to Central America and the Caribbean Coast, only to falsify the principle of civil rights and violate the precepts of international law, reaching at times the extreme of forgetting even the most elementary rules of conduct. Many of our republics have become open season for the vilest of instincts that in the United States itself are not condoned since they violate notions of public responsibility and opinion. Failing to keep one's word, making a joke of contracts, threatening, robbing individuals, engaging in smuggling, bribing authorities, fomenting disorder have all been, to different degrees in several of our regions, everyday behaviors of those who, because they belong to a great nation, should exemplify more noble concepts of individual responsibility.

The local governments, at times timid, have not dared in the majority of cases to pursue these delinquents, afraid as they are by the size of English-speaking America or linked as they are to many unspeakable commitments. As a result of such behavior the United States has gradually become the most unpopular nation among us. Hostility is spreading among the masses and in some regions a North American citizen has to resort to disguising his nationality and passing himself off as an Englishman in order to escape the ill will surrounding him.

Our communities are hospitable and generous, Mr. President; within them exist numerous French, German, English, Belgian companies and for all these businessmen who are respectful of our customs a fraternal hand has always been extended. The fact that this hostility is centered on the North American is proof that it is not a question of an irrational and general antipathy for the foreigner, but rather a direct reflex action against specific behavior of which we are the victims.

In the United States these things go unknown, and I am sure that when this situation does become known, an even greater wave of censure will erupt than has already manifested itself among us.

You North Americans represent a civilization that emerged from a choice for moral law over brutish force; and which flourished in a world of new ideals, as a reaction against the former errors of the world. Therefore, it would be illogical for you to commit offenses against us as painful as those Europe has perpetrated in Asia or in Africa, because if you were to behave in this fashion you would be sending a message that your founding fathers were wrong when they sought to found a nation based on Justice and proclaiming, at the same time, the bankruptcy of mankind's perfectibility and God's will.

We are talking about men who violate the feelings of the foreign country where they operate: the construction companies who abuse the franchises granted them by contract and fraudulently flood the market with an array of products, thereby endangering local merchants and importers; the contractors who, in order not to have to pay overdue salaries to their workers, intimidate and harass them. These men cannot continue to pass themselves off as representatives of the genius and civilization brought to the New World by the immortal Puritans.

In this way, an era of mistrust has arisen between Latin America and Anglo-Saxon America that ultimately will be harmful to all of us. Those who view in a calm manner these issues know that what is happening is the work of isolated individuals. A great country instilled with a lofty historic mission cannot be responsible for this kind of duplicitous behavior. If a people who have risen so high were to employ such base conduct, it would be historical suicide for them; and it is impossible for a great force for renewal in the world and in life to become atrophied and withdraw before having completed its mission. But simple spirits, who make judgments based solely on what they see happening around them, are beginning to believe that the United States has two different notions of Justice: one that it applies to its fellow countrymen and another that it applies to foreigners; and that the United States sustains two moralities: one for national consumption and the other for export.

Furthermore, the kind of all too visible support given by official representatives of the United States to these men (often born in North America or naturalized there with the sole purpose of receiving protection) is something that surprises us and makes us very uneasy in Latin America.

All it takes is for one of these men to claim he has been mistreated in his business and U.S. consuls and ministers support them and even summon boats and soldiers, without first investigating the basis for such claims, or inquiring into the reasons that attend to such cases. I am well aware all great nations have the responsibility to protect the life and property of their citizens living abroad, but above that responsibility sits a sentiment for justice that prohibits the support of injustice and an even loftier statute that prevents a nation from becoming the accomplice to errors committed by some of its children.

The censurable political expansionism that has recently accompanied the legitimate commercial influence of the United States has often made use of these elements to create pretexts for attacks and interventions; just as it has taken advantage of the weakness of certain Spanish American governmental figures (or of the impatience of others who aspired to supplant them in power) in order to obtain concessions and advantages in some republics that harm citizens or compromise a country's autonomy.

For the moment the system has favored the development of businesses, the prosperity of specific financial groups, or the authoritarian drive of an overprotective nation, but the respectability of the United States has suffered a blow as harsh as that leveled at the independence of our republics, because when it assumes responsibility on a national scale for the offenses committed by a small number of its citizens, when it incites the basest of passions, and abuses its greatness, the United States becomes diminished in our eyes and identifies itself with the forces of corruption rather than with the elements of support that would enable us to perfect who we are.

The America of the North has many millions of inhabitants and an expansionist politics that favors only the smallest number of them; however, disapproval of the acts committed by the few affects the entire collective body, and it turns out that what individual citizens accrue in money, the national flag loses in prestige. Before, we thought the United States was strong and just, now we are beginning to believe you are only strong. And this is why public sentiment has become aroused, this is why there is a visible resistance to entrusting new projects to the companies of your country. We fear that within each proposal is hidden yet another deceit. Moreover, force is not enough to seduce and attract other nations if it is not accompanied by moral influence.

All of this is regrettable, Mr. President. The United States can be even greater because of its commerce and the spread of its spirit, without the need to humiliate our countries, without poisoning our political struggles or the rivalries between our republics, without harming itself.

By disseminating trust once again, the United States would bring about the rebirth of brotherhood, which at another time in our history existed between the two Americas.

This is why in these difficult times for the future of the New World, in these historical junctures that can give rise to new tendencies of incalculable consequences, leaving aside all affronts and justified anger, we come today openly, trusting in the nobility of the North American people, to issue a supreme call for justice. Latin America shares a common cause, we have the homogeneity that our past, our language, our religion bestow upon us. Above and beyond our local patriotism we cultivate a higher one, and even those regions that are far from feeling the weight of such harsh behavior are impressed more and more by the moral harm than by the material threat that such behavior entails.

We demand that the painful weight of the Platt Amendment be lifted from Cuba; we demand that the possibility of determining its own fate be returned to Nicaragua, allowing its people to depose, if it deems necessary, those who govern with the support of a foreign army; we demand that the situation in Puerto Rico be resolved in accord with the principles of law and humanity; we demand that the injustices committed in Colombia be corrected to the extent that it is possible; we demand that Panama, which today suffers the consequences, be able to exercise its rights in the port of Guayaquil; we demand that the archipelago of the Galápagos be respected; we demand that freedom be given to the heroic people of the Philippines; we desire that Mexico be free of the sword of Damocles, suspended always above its flag by the threat of intervention; we demand that the chaos of the Putumayo not serve as a pretext for diplomatic manipulations; we insist that companies who overstep their bounds not be supported; we demand that the republic of Santo Domingo not be suffocated by unjustifiable pressures; we demand that the United States abstain from intervening assiduously in the internal politics of our countries and that it not continue to make acquisitions of ports or bays on this continent; we demand that the health measures adopted not serve to diminish the autonomy of the nations of the Pacific; we demand equality, we demand respect; finally we demand that the star-spangled banner not become a symbol of oppression in the New World.

It cannot be said, Mr. President, that North Americans have abandoned the use of coercion and corporal punishment in public education only to use these same backward ways in the political education of our people; it cannot be possible that your ministers have in our small cities the special mission to threaten us; it cannot be possible that the fainthearted men who govern in some of our weak republics feel constantly the whip of their masters on their shoulders; it cannot be possible that having abolished the slavery of human beings in the nineteenth century, you would now allow it to be reintroduced in the twentieth century against our nations.

I do not wish to keep insisting on this point, nor do I want to cite specific cases because this letter is not one of attack but rather an attempt at reconciliation; but our America has great open wounds that must not become inflamed. We have suffered a great deal. What is emerging now is a clamor from people who do not wish to disappear. If it could be proved, as some contend, that the United States cedes, as it expands, to a higher need, that is independent of its personal desire, we would have to obey as we defend our legitimate instinct to survive. I am not ignorant of the fact you are strong and that you could squash any number of rebellions, but I insist that superior to the questions of material strength is that of moral strength. A boxer can hurt the child returning home from school, and the child may not even succeed in returning the punches. But this does not establish a right, nor does it assume the impunity of the aggressor. There is a supreme power called universal censure, and just as children are defended in the streets against bullies by public opinion, nations are defended in history by a supreme justice and the higher principles of humanity.

We love and respect the United States; we admire this great country that should serve as a model for us in many things; we wish to collaborate with it in the work of discovery and evaluation of the riches of this continent; and in order to avoid an ever growing distancing between us and the conflicts that surely will arise in the future, given the untenable nature of things, we now present ourselves loyally, without either pride or humility, conscious of our rights, to a man who, because of the will of his people, has been placed at the forefront of a great nation. We do not ask for favors; we claim what is ours, what our fathers conquered for us, what all peoples are willing to defend in whatever way possible, namely, their honor and dignity. We do not want the Monroe Doctrine, which has been badly interpreted, to create in America, for the benefit of the United States or for anyone else's benefit, new Egypts and Moroccos.

We will not accept the disappearance of our countries one after the other. We have confidence in our future. The best proof that Latin America is capable of an autonomous life is the surprising prosperity of its southern republics, curiously those who because of their size and relations with Europe find themselves safe from a decisive North American influence. In order for the regions that today are undergoing painful crises to enter a period analogous to those in the southern part, it is necessary for the financial institutions of the North to abstain from complicating our affairs and for the trade unions in New York and New Orleans to refrain from favoring revolutions and for the United States in a noble fashion to renew the work of *rapprochement* and of brotherhood that produced such great results for both sides in the early years of our relationship.

Spanish Americans have become aware of their destinies. The local quarrels, no matter how bitter they can be, are not enough to make them lose sight of their higher interests. The strongest countries that have already achieved a prosperous stability are beginning to feel historic responsibility weighing on them; and there is a visible movement, a profound agitation that cannot go unnoticed. Your presidency, sir, will mark a great transition in the politics of this planet if, in accord with the situation, you put an end to current selfish tactics and ensure a return to the healthy tradition of our origins. America will only be united, America will only be truly "for the Americans," giving this word its full meaning, when in the North it is remembered that there exist two varieties of Americans, and when without vain attempts at superiority and with scrupulous justice, the two groups develop independently in a different and cordial atmosphere.

I repeat that in America there is a great uneasiness, Mr. President. The entire continent hangs on your actions. If policies change, the campaign we have undertaken will cease immediately and we will once again be the most enthusiastic supporters of your great nation. If they do not change, a new cause for discord between men will emerge and it will strengthen an agitation that will be harmful to your commerce, because we will continue to defend, each time with greater energy, our own territory, just as you, placed in a similar situation, would have defended yours, convinced of fulfilling our duty and of being able to count on the support of others around the world.

The Infantilism of the North American

Gabriela Mistral

Gabriela Mistral (real name: Lucila Godoy Alcayaga) was born in Vicuña, Chile, on April 7, 1889, and died in New York on January 10, 1957. Poet, educator, diplomat, and feminist, she was the first Latin American to win the Nobel Prize for Literature, in 1945. She wrote extensively in poetry and prose and in the area of education was widely hailed in both Americas for her innovative teaching at the primary, secondary, and university levels. No stranger to the United States, she taught at Barnard College, Middlebury College, and Vassar College and served as Chilean consul in Los Angeles and New York. Among her most important works in poetry are *Sonetos de la muerte* (1914, Sonnets of Death), *Desolación* (1922, Desolation), *Ternura* (1924, Tenderness), *Tala* (1938), and *Lagar* (1954). The following selection is from Gabriela Mistral, *Recados para hoy y mañana*, vol. 2, compiled by Luis Vargas Saavedra (Santiago, Chile: Editorial Sudamericana, 1999), 43–46. By permission of Luis Vargas Saavedra.

1944

Europeans, Asians, and Hispanic Americans are equally surprised that the citizens of the United States, a nation of technocrats, stockbrokers, engineers, and industrialists, reflect in their facial expression, in the way they talk, and in their family life a remnant of mother's milk.

The tone of voice in which the word "infantile" is uttered, when applied to a Yankee, varies greatly from person to person. When used by the Japanese this qualifier contains an almost acidic, tart taste; in the case of the French, the tone used is somewhat mocking; among us it wavers between jest and ridicule. The trait is not just a bad one, we say, but it does reflect some silliness on the part of the North American.

I do not understand why Latins are prone to bequeath to the Anglo-Saxon the entire trait of infantilism, which is a treasure, and are proud and complacent in doing so, because they feel satiated by it. The Frenchman has dismissed it, the Spaniard has perhaps consumed it all in a feverish passion, but the Italian and the *mestizo* of America, we still carry it with us, even though we do not nourish it lovingly. And it is precisely the scratches on our fingers left over from childhood, like lumps of honey in the caldron, that create in us the constant spontaneity and circumstantial charm that adorns our character. But we are ashamed to take our childlike spirit along with us to the workplace, to the "meeting," to any official acts, and even to our informal social gatherings.

In this context, we are not talking about a fear of the intimate, because we Hispanics are essentially extroverts, and we like to express and manifest ourselves as freely as possible, much like a flowery tapestry. As we suppress the child in us there is at work an exchange of concepts: the confusion of infantilism with stupidity, the childlike with the disingenuous, and innocence with infantile behavior. As a result of our less than intelligent interpretation of all of this, the Spanish American has felt ashamed to recognize the child in him and, even more so, to give expression to this child in the presence of others.

The adult Anglo-Saxon, on the other hand, does not seek to sever his infancy completely; he is much the contrary; he knows that a maturity somewhat hastened quickly slides into the realm of the very old; he understands that preserving a segment of one's infancy is really about saving the solar plexus of life, and that losing the child in all of us is to embrace much too soon the cadaverine. It is almost like the person who has left his country, but does not know how to walk away completely and who keeps patrolling its coast furtively without being able to say good-bye once and for all. He distances himself as little as possible; he does not abandon the region; he acts craftily; he plays tricks, and you realize that he does achieve something by delaying his departure and by so doing he attains all that is offered in this interplay of corporal and spiritual mischievousness.

Having looked at this question in the rough and through the means at our disposal, it is obvious that the Anglo-Saxon has created a cult of the childlike, but we only see this cult as a ravenous appetite to avoid growing old, a stubborn and ridiculous kind of paganism. But if we look more closely, we discover that the Nordic or Yankee way of life owes to this love of the infantile some things that are more serious than a short skirt or the appropriate coloring for graying hair. A somewhat more subtle investigation of the topic would tell us that when the informal individual defends in his rational faculties certain imponderables about childhood, these faculties become something else, ones that are very different from those of the "adult," whose first dew produced by his senses he has allowed to dry up.

The popular inventor, so common in the United States, who springs up everywhere and each year offers from one thousand to two thousand minor inventions, is actually a childlike man whose hands remember the imaginative way in which they played when he was five years old and who in playing tricks, seeks and discovers new worlds mischievously. This mechanic, chemist, or amateur artisan dedicates his workday to a factory or workshop in which his soul is superfluous, but at night, alone in his room, he shakes out the industrial odors from his jacket and sits down to play at God's game, which is the game of creation, although in this case it may be minimal and may not go beyond making simple matchsticks and fibers of some kind. He may be thirty years old but he is really a young boy, sitting down, and rather than at his workbench, at the internal vertex of the work at hand, with his fantasy running wild and his head placed at the angle of interface.

Tired of the opera characterized by its pathetic shades, and unable to embrace the tangos of the South because he has not lived on Martin Fierro's *pampa*, the Yankee musician has paid special attention to the rhythms of his disdained black compatriots. He has become entranced by those dances precisely because of their playfulness, which while sexual in tone and whatever else you might say, are, nonetheless, a kind of game. And from those Sudanese solstices, from that carnal jungle, he has derived a bunch of sounds composed of both harmony and stridence, all of which are very exploitable and better than the original music it was becoming. If this musician had not had a living, childlike ability to hear, an entire reality of terrestrial folklore in the United States would have been lost. It is true that the white man, an opportunist who alters the nature of things, grasped this virgin material and manipulated it forcefully, in fact crumpling it into another shape. It is also true that from the hemispheres of black music, he retained a fundamental jazz and let go of the best piece: the inimitable black spirituals. At this same time, a rejuvenation, based on a childlike Africa, emerged.

Primary education also exists in the United States as something lightened by a puerile spirit. Prior to the wonderful Pestalozzi and Froebel, what was primary education if not a kind of Tutankhamenism? Following these two jovial personalities several Latins came on the scene to express their opinion on behalf of a return of childhood to childhood. María Montessori and Decroly pierced the dried-up tree bark of education until they found a fresh vein of sap. This great Italian woman once said to me that she undertook her work specifically for Latins but that it was the United States who received what she had to say with open arms and without complaint.

Here you have, then, in three brief sketches a few notes on infancy in adulthood, three darts that it launches from afar, or as the religious Yankee would say, three graces divinely postponed, launched upon a harsh and desert-like adulthood. But there exist thousands of new sprouts and small resurrections of the child in mature beings and each one of these seems like a return that God consents to, that even pushes us closer toward the Promised Land that was given to us only once and then suddenly slipped away. But it seems that we can get it back, when we ask for it with a burning humility. And we can experience it a second time, with our hair now gray, just like the elderly Nordic and American people.

The Culture of the Two Americas

Leopoldo Zea

Leopoldo Zea (Mexico, 1912–2004), a distinguished professor at the Universidad Autónoma of Mexico, was one of the most important Latin American philosophers and scholars of the past century. His fame began with his study of *Positivism* (1943), which became the seminal text on this philosophy's impact on Latin America in general and Mexico in particular. As one of the region's leading intellectuals, he strongly defended the integration of Latin America's republics while rejecting North American imperialism and the area's neocolonial past. In 1966 he founded the Colegio de Estudios Latinoamericanos, which has become one of the most distinguished research centers in the Americas. The essay included here is from "La cultura en las dos Américas." *Revista Nacional de Cultura*, vol. 31, no. 196 (January–March 1971), 2–12.

1971

I

As might be expected, the different cultures of Anglo-Saxon America and Ibero-America have given rise to several no less diverse attitudes with regard to the world, nature, and other human beings. This diversity of attitudes has become evident especially in the field of man's relationship to nature. With respect to the Anglo-Saxon, it is said that he is a practical man, concerned with dominating the natural world that surrounds him, unlike the Iberian, who seems to disdain such domination. While the Anglo-Saxon seems to have no other preoccupation than that of technology, which allows him to dominate the world around him, the Iberian seems to be more concerned with what we might call aesthetics.

This, of course, has given rise to the establishment of a series of errors such as believing that one America, the Iberian, represents the spiritual while the other, the Anglo-Saxon, embodies the material. This idea manifested itself in Ibero-America during the first decade of the twentieth century as a reaction against positivism. Foremost Ibero-American intellectuals made their way of thinking depend upon this thesis which, in one way or another, justified the backwardness of Ibero-America in the field of technology, especially with regard to what the United States represented in this same area. What is true is that there exists a Latin or Iberian spirit and an Anglo-Saxon spirit, that is to say, a special attitude with respect to the world. One cannot be so naïve as to think the Anglo-Saxon lacks a spiritual side because he has emphasized in his culture the domination of nature. Anglo-Saxon America has discovered, up to now, that happiness can be obtained by taking the road leading to the mastery of nature, a nature placed in the service of mankind. This is just the opposite of the Ibero-American, who has continued to view such predominance as useless, limiting it only to the essential, as he too searches for happiness in other areas that are closer to the aesthetic than to the material.

Once the political emancipation of Ibero-American peoples came to a close, an inquiry was initiated as to the causes preventing these peoples from acquiring the traits that characterized Anglo-Saxon peoples, especially those in the United States. The most prominent Ibero-American thinkers offered a range of explanations, the majority of which referred to the practical nature of the Anglo-Saxon contrasted with the imaginative, whimsical nature of the Ibero-American. The character of each group had much to do with the diverse cultural legacy they inherited. "The Yankee's civilization," Sarmiento would say, "was the direct outcome of the plough and the reading primer; the South American's civilization was destroyed by the cross and the sword. There in the North they learned to work and to read, here in the South to be idle and to pray." Likewise, Bilbao, in referring to the United States, would say: "There is no nation that reads more, that prints more, that has a greater number of schools and newspapers. Today it is the number one nation in agriculture, industry and commerce." The Ibero-American, the two men contended, has remained too devoted to concerns of a moralistic, religious, and aesthetic nature, overlooking those things that have produced and continue to produce today's great modern nations: practical things, things that have to do with a mastery of nature, things oriented more toward the technical, which is the foundation of this new eminence in the world. Nations are great because they have industry, because men make their greatness depend on the ability of their hands to create wealth, instead of depending on the contributions of the powerful and of their subordinates, which implies a mania for holding public office or being part of a bureaucratic system.

"I do not claim," said Juan Bautista Alberdi, "that ethics have been forgotten. I know that without them industry is impossible; but the facts prove that one reaches a moral level more quickly through the hardworking and productive habits of those honest nations than through abstract instruction." Ibero-America does not need any more lawyers or theologians, what it needs are geologists and naturalists. "Its development will be achieved with roads, artesian wells, immigration, and not with newspapers that either stir up people's emotions or are submissive to government, nor with sermons or the creation of legends. Can clerics," he asked, "give our youth the mercantile and industrial instincts that should characterize the South American? Will they extract from their hands that fever of activity and entrepreneurial skill that will make them the Yankee Spanish American? Our young people must be educated for industrial life, and to achieve this they must be educated in the arts and auxiliary sciences of industry. This type of South American must be someone who has been taught to conquer the great and oppressive enemy of our progress; the desert, material underdevelopment, the brutal and primitive force of nature on our continent."

The diversity between one America and the other is made to appear as an ability or lack of ability for technology. Using as a point of departure the idea that only those countries who have the talent for technology are countries at the height of progress, positivism was introduced in Ibero-America and its goal was to shape practical men, technical people who would create the greatness of Ibero-America just as these types of individuals had done in Anglo-Saxon America. The truth is that this positivistic education did not give rise to such practical men and technicians but rather plainly and simply to a new kind of justification for the social dominance of one group over another, a new kind of tyranny, new forms of oligarchy, all of which did little on behalf of Ibero-America's material advancement.

II

The differences, the diverse way of looking at the world in one America and the other, already anticipated by us, have their roots in the varied cultural formation of the men who conquered and colonized these areas. Both Anglo-Saxons and Iberians began the conquest of America incited for different reasons, guided by different motives, encouraged by the possible achievement of certain goals whose roots were in their own culture. One was the concern that animated the Iberians over the discovery, conquest, and colonization of America and another was the concern of the Anglo-Saxon colonizers and pioneers with the very process of colonization and expansion. In both groups religious fervor, viewed as the maximum expression of man's attitude toward the world and life, is what makes evident the underlying spirit that animated the meaning they gave the world and the way in which they attempted to take possession of it.

As far as Anglo-Saxon America is concerned, there has been a great deal of research carried out by contemporary sociologists such as Weber, Tawney, Troeltsch, and others who show the importance that Puritanism exercised in the colonization of America. Puritanism, derived from Calvinist doctrine, demonstrates as few expressions of modern culture do the spirit that animated the conquerors of the America that gave birth to what we know as the United States. The point of departure for this new church, like all expressions of modernism, was individualism. The new church in America, similar to Calvinism, was Puritan. Later on it opposed all authority that could not be justified rationally. It does not accept the existence of an ecclesiastic power that saves mankind, as does Catholicism. Salvation is something that each man must achieve through his own efforts. And salvation is achieved if one fulfills the mission God has imposed upon man on this earth. This mission is the dominance of nature. Man is destined to glorify God by imposing his stamp on the natural world through his work.

It is therefore through his action, his capacity for work and his mastery of nature, that his salvation or perdition becomes manifest. To master nature, transform it into culture, into great works, is to enhance God's glory. Hence, the necessity to take advantage of all of man's possibilities for actions that are geared toward such mastery. For this reason, everything that can contribute to the progress and prosperity of mankind and to the betterment of his community contributes to the greater glory of God. The greater the work, the greater the glory and honor. One does not work for the simply necessary, rather one engages in work for something that also transcends man himself. It is not enough to work in order to obtain what is needed; it is imperative to do something else: to accumulate, to *capitalize*. Work, action for the sake of action, accumulation, becomes one of man's ends.

It is for this reason that the triumph on earth of the man who works comes to be one of the best indicators that he is pleasing to God. Success in this life, then, is a sign of salvation in heaven. The one who acquires more things, greater wealth, the one who has better demonstrated his capacity for dominating the natural world, is the one who is closer to achieving the salvation of his soul. He is a chosen one. The Puritan is the man who has received grace, which becomes evident in his works. The success achieved is nothing else but the indication of his character as a chosen one, as preordained. This individual, for the same reason, finds himself in a situation that is superior to men who have not fulfilled their mission. Hence his right to the expansion carried out over abandoned or virginal lands; his right to establish his dominance over territories whose nature has not been cultivated and placed in the service of man.

An expression of this attitude is to be found in the expansion carried out by the Anglo-Saxon pioneer in the West, in lands that the natives did not work. First, in the name of the God of Puritanism, then in the name of civilization and progress, the Anglo-Saxon settlers and pioneers extended their dominance throughout North America. Their mission was to work the lands, master the rivers, make the fields produce by bringing nature under control in areas where only the Indian lived, a being incapable of creating for the greater glory of God. The mission of these men was to take away America's lands from the hands of incapable men who had forgotten their mission in the world. The expansion of the frontier is viewed as an expansion of the good, of the good over the bad, however one wishes to call this. Within such a conception of the world and life, idleness has no meaning except in a negative sense: passivity will be viewed as something diabolic along with all of its consequences. Work is at the center of this entire interpretation of life.

Contrasted with these men who have made work the crux of their existence, there emerges another group of men who conceive of the world and of life in a very different way. Other peoples. In America they are the peoples of Iberian origin who are little concerned with controlling nature beyond what their most urgent needs might require. They are people who, in the opinion of the first group, have done very little to demonstrate that their mission, like the first group's, is to master nature. People who have not collaborated in the invention of technology for bringing nature under control. People who are incompetent regarding industry, inept as far as new technologies are concerned; people without a pragmatic sense of life: rhetorical, conservative, absolutists. People who continue to maintain antiquated formulas of absolute government that they inherited from Spain, independent of the names they may give these formulas. The men who have made the dominance of nature the center of their activity, thought and still think that in these countries the riches enclosed within their natural world still remain in a kind of virgin state. Thus, for them, nature waits and continues to wait for man to harvest its fruits. Forests of precious woods, jungles with exquisite fruits, lands whose innermost recesses still contain precious metals for exchange and industry, lands in which rich sources of black gold are still hidden upon which depends the work that produces the wealth of great nations.

III

The peoples to the south of those colonized by Anglo-Saxons appear, contrary to the latter, more inclined toward work of an aesthetic nature and toward contemplation and religious or metaphysical abstraction. There is something to this assertion without it indicating an incapacity for manual labor and industry, as many of them have come to believe as they examine their conscience. Much of this attitude has to do with those who have called their intellectuals Iberian peculiarities. The "arrogance" in these countries, Buarque de Holanda tells us, has been a sign of struggle and emulation; but also the source of many of their weaknesses. The Iberians, influenced by this concern for the seignorial, began to disdain any concern that did not signify the enhancement of one's personality independent of his material situation. Material, matter, could not be anything other than an instrument for the realization of more ennobling actions. Manual work could not be appreciated except as a function of the purpose for which it is an instrument. The Iberian never accepted manual work as an end in itself. To support the greatness of the individual based on material wealth was to diminish that very greatness. Amérigo Castro shows in a confidential document that he discovered, the lack of interest Castilians had in the fifteenth century for becoming wealthy, which, to a certain extent, had diminished their arrogant sense of self. In that period it was said that Castile possessed fertile land and men with a strong sentiment for bellicose undertakings. The men of these lands had no talent for technology: but this ineptitude was due to the fact that the riches of their lands were sufficient for them.

The Iberian, unlike the Anglo-Saxon, does not seek, in a material sense, more than what he needs to meet his most pressing daily necessities. There exists, of course, ostentation, that is, the display of wealth; but in the most useless sense, as a way of exhibiting one's personality. Such personality and arrogance could not manifest themselves in other ways as successfully as through the expression of heroic deeds. This is the case, for example, of our creoles in Spanish America and the *mazambos* in Brazil who, not being able to repeat the great deeds of their grandfathers, searched for the compensation of their personality through extravagance and an exhibition of a wealth they had not even created. Their wealth, in this context, is at the service of their own personality; it does not have a function that transcends the individual as it does in the case of the Anglo-Saxon. It becomes an accumulation, whose uselessness is evident in that same ostentatious display and extravagance. For this reason, the Iberian who works does not seek in manual work anything other than what serves his idea of the self. There is nothing that transcends it. There is nothing beyond what the self needs. The *campesino* or the great Castilian landowner does not seek any other wealth than what satisfies his most immediate and daily needs. That is why he does not have to make an effort to invent instruments that will permit him to produce more than he needs. The land with its riches was more than enough. "The fertility of the land," says the aforementioned document, "makes them to a certain extent proud and idle men and not inventive and hardworking." And this is not considered a defect. Their ineptitude for technology is not a defect for these men. This can be nothing else but an indicator that they are destined to realize works superior to material ones. "If Spain is not great because of its ability and industrial and commercial wealth," the document states, "it is, on the other hand, because of its spirit of greatness." From this land have emerged great men, emperors, captains, conquerors, and saints. Men of heroic feats, seekers of glory, for whom a good and fertile land was more than sufficient so that they could dedicate their time to other tasks. Technology and commerce only debase man, distancing him from his true goals. These men, like the Anglo-Saxons, also seek to give God greater glory on earth, but a glory that is attained and sought after through other means. These men also feel like the chosen: their mission, to bring other men and other peoples the true religion, the true formula for salvation. The difference is that among Anglo-Saxons it is something that only the individual can attain through his own efforts, and is the reason for which they disdain men who are not capable of doing anything by themselves. The Iberians believe that they are the ones, as individuals, who can take salvation to others who do not possess this ability. Hence, the diversity of forms of evangelization in one America and the other; and the very different treatment of the natives. In one America, perceiving them as strange entities, alien, almost like animals; in the other, as individuals whom it is absolutely necessary to incorporate into society, no matter the cost of such integration. Therefore, some make of their own ability for salvation, which is manifest in the success of their works, the center of their existence, their mission in life; while others make of their ability to incorporate other men and other peoples the crux of their mission on earth.

Iberians are men with a lofty imperial sense who seek immortality through the incorporation of other men and other peoples into what they take to be the objectives of man, which they represent. Anything that deviates from this sense is not considered worthy of being taken seriously. The subsequent failure of this imperial intention does not have to change the habits and customs that this very intention implies. Among these are the disdain for work in the sense it is understood by Anglo-Saxons, the almost negative regard for industry, and that same zeal of our mental emancipators to endow Iberians with a capacity for technology, invention, and mechanical work. Buarque de Holanda speaks about the repugnance the Iberian felt for any work that implied the submission of those ends considered belonging to the individual.

> The action taken on things, on the material universe, implies a submission to an external object, the acceptance of a law that is strange to the individual. This action is not demanded by God; it does not increase His glory in any way nor does it augment our dignity. It can be said, on the contrary, it endangers and debases it. Manual and mechanical work seeks an end that is external to man and claims to achieve the perfection of a work that is distinct from man. . . . In this sense, one can understand why the modern religion of work and the appreciation for practical activities have never taken root among Hispanic peoples. A dignified idleness was always better or more ennobling in the eyes of a Portuguese or Spaniard than the arduous struggle for daily bread. What both admired as an ideal is the life of the grand *señor* who excludes all worry, and all stress from his existence.

Hence we find a lack of solidarity for work that is evident among the Anglo-Saxons, a lack of spirit that has made possible the associations I spoke about at the beginning. Men do not come together to make the land more productive, or to start businesses whose benefits are profitable to all. They do not come together to apportion among themselves the tasks of material work, that inevitable something necessary for other ends, but something that, for them, not all men are obligated to realize. Rather it is something that must be realized by the least apt for the principal mission of the Iberian spirit, something more typical of farm laborers in the Peninsula, of servants where there are masters; of Indians or blacks in America. Solidarity is not to be found in material work, in a task that tends simply toward the domination of nature. Solidarity among gentlemen as well as among gentlemen and servants, solidarity among men who are independent of differences in cast because of manual labor, is to be found on another level, on the level of the community's own mission. It is a valid mission for all its members, regardless of their social situation. "Solidarity only exists," Buarque de Holanda says,

> where there is a linking of sentiments, rather than a relationship based on interests, in the home for example, or among friends. They are circles that are necessarily restricted, more antagonistic toward than supportive of associations established on a level that is broader, more like a guild or like a nation. . . . The individual who forms these limited and narrow circles accepts only one form of rejection of that concrete self, and it is what allows him to make his persona grow. . . . The autarchy of the individual, [Buarque de Holanda continues] the extreme exaltation of the individual self, a fundamental passion that does not tolerate commitments, accepts only one alternative: the renunciation of that same self in light of a greater good. For the same reason that it is rare and difficult, obedience appears sometimes to Iberian peoples as the supreme virtue among all the rest. And it is not strange that this obedience—obedience that is blind and differs profoundly from medieval and feudal principles of loyalty—has been, up to now, for the Iberians, the only truly strong political principle. The will to command and the disposition to carry out orders are equally characteristic.

IV

The different attitudes of Iberians and Anglo-Saxons toward the world and life has become evident, as one would have assumed, in the diverse expressions of the culture of theses peoples in America. The meaning of the university is different in one America from the other. In the United States universities are nothing more than an instrument for preparing its individuals. In these universities, as in all other forms of education, individuals are endowed with the means to allow them to triumph in life. Within them are individuals trained to lead the country in the fields of expertise that have produced the country's greatness. North American universities, unlike the Ibero-American, do not have a political function even though the individuals they educate may become politicized. In Ibero-American countries just the opposite occurs. There the universities are political entities, entities that have to be controlled by political goals. For this reason, universities in the United States are generally supported by private entities, by institutions or individuals who seek in them the preparation of talented individuals for their industries, businesses, and the internal and external politics that serve their purpose. In Ibero-America, on the contrary, universities depend, in general, on the governments that control the public life of the country. They are centers of support or resistance to governmental policies that must be controlled or at least neutralized. In these universities are prepared the men who dream, in one way or another, of the opportunity to become part of the government that leads the nation. Hence the tendency, very characteristic of Ibero-American university students, to view the University as the highest expression of the nation, as the creator of the spirit whose path the nation must follow. In Vasconselos's motto "the spirit will speak through my race" is manifested this sense of the Ibero-American university as the spiritual rector of the nation. This does not happen in North American universities, independent of the fact that each university student recognizes how much he owes his personal formation to his "alma mater." North American universities educate individuals, but not the nation; the nation is the product of individuals, whether university people or not. Not even for a moment is the question of university hierarchy raised. This hierarchy is created on the basis of aptitude, which can be, although not necessarily, improved by the university. North American universities do nothing else than educate capable individuals for a specific field, for those needed by society. Hence we have a certain orientation toward the technical, which is so necessary for its goals. In Ibero-American universities, only up until the last few years have they attended to the ever-increasing demands for a technical education. This does not mean, however, that the orientation toward the liberal professions such as law, medicine, architecture, and fine arts has disappeared because of these demands. These are professions that are not always pursued because of the preparation they may offer, but rather for the degree they award, for what they may add to the makeup of the degree holder. Degrees, in this case, are sometimes simple ostentation, forms of social or political worth independent of the training that one assumes has been received. They become titles that are pursued now just as years ago titles of nobility were pursued. "Lawyer," "doctor," "architect" are reflections of what in yesteryears were "baron," "marquis," "count," or "duke." A reflection of this attitude would have to be the university institutions of scientific, philosophical, historical, and literary investigation and the organization of libraries as instruments of research that appeared to lag behind and be completely disorganized when compared to equivalent institutions in the North American university system. In the latter everything seems ready to facilitate the work of the researcher, no matter who he may be. In Ibero-American universities the organization of libraries and research institutions has been in the majority of cases the work of specific individuals who have made every effort to realize this goal. It has not been the product, as in the North American universities, of a previous social order, but rather of something undertaken even against a social order, against a specific form of understanding the world and life. In other words, it has been the work of individuals equivalent to those great Ibero-American teachers who have striven to transform their countries and make them more prepared for a world that, from the sixteenth century on, was beginning to be governed by other values.

These are individuals, specific, personal, specific and personal like those men who created their own greatness by creating that of Spain and Portugal. They were individuals who persisted in making their countries modern nations, like those who persisted in making their countries great empires. We are talking about individuals who dedicated themselves to the task of reeducating their countries in order to make them nations ready for a struggle in which independence was at stake and that minimum of happiness to which all peoples have a right. Individuals who, without renouncing the meaning that the world and life have for the Iberian, made every effort to assimilate for their own use the technology and the skill that made the Anglo-Saxon nations the leaders of the modern world. To these specific individuals is owed the reeducation of the peoples of Ibero-America. To them is owed the emergence nowadays of institutions of scientific, philosophic, historical, and literary research that have nothing to be ashamed of with regard to many of the North American universities, despite a lack of material means. It is a lack that has been compensated for by an Iberian ability to adapt them to the circumstances no matter how impoverished they may be. Little by little centers of scientific research of great importance were formed thanks to the talents of their members. They included centers for philosophic research whose importance is already recognized by the great research centers of the United States and Europe. Our libraries are likewise being reorganized in a variety of centers dedicated to Ibero-American culture. In our America there are also emerging centers of culture that are truly models of organization that, being products of our countries, have nothing to envy as far as those created in Anglo-Saxon America are concerned. The *Casa de Cultura* of Ecuador is, among others, an example of cultural organization, which by uniting the best qualities of Anglo-Saxon centers of culture has brought together the best of countries like ours. The fruits of this same spirit that tries to assimilate the best of Anglo-Saxon culture without, as a consequence, rejecting the best of Iberian culture can also be found in the university cities that are emerging in different countries throughout Ibero-America. Centers in which the Ibero-American intellectual is slowly acquiring the material means that have allowed his counterparts in the United States to achieve a minimum of comfort and security so necessary to continue one's research, study, and creativity within the dimensions of cultural expression.

As a result of all of these efforts there is emerging in Ibero-America a new type of man: a man who is going to deny the legend that made of him an individual lacking the aptitude for other work and professions that were not artistic or aesthetic in nature. This man is proving himself; he can be a good technician; he can also be a scientist capable of collaborating in the progress of his country in accord with the most up-to-date ways of bringing nature under control. This man, without giving up what we have come to call his peculiarities, is becoming assimilated with great facility by that world of Anglo-Saxon culture that used to seem alien to him. Nowadays, for example, one often speaks of man's subordination to machines because of technology. Technology, it seems, far from serving mankind is gradually taking control of him; it is turning him into just another part of its complicated mechanisms. In this sense it appears the Ibero-American has succeeded in keeping his self intact, making machines subordinate to him. Machines still serve him to produce what he most needs or what he needs at the moment, while trying to avoid the moment in which production as a goal subordinates the man who realizes this production. The breakdown of a machine, its paralysis, still does not break the rhythm that the Ibero-American considers crucial for its work. The Ibero-American does not demand from a machine anything other than a minimum of daily well-being. He stores up wealth but without that wealth becoming an end in itself. He even contents himself with a certain necessary squandering of it, but without becoming subordinate to it. Today's Ibero-American, like his ancestors, continues to consider life as something to be lived each day. He lives each day as an expression of his specific personality, both in poverty as in wealth. Life for him is always circumstantial, troublesome, and independent of material circumstances. While in other countries the accumulation of possessions is an accumulation for the sake of accumulation, a hoarding for the sake of hoarding, a pure and constant capitalization, in Ibero-America such wealth continues to be an instrument in the service of other ends. Man is still not a slave to his wealth, but someone who uses it for ends that he considers his own. Can this be a defect? A fault? Only time will tell.

Chile

Address to the United Nations General Assembly (December 1972)

Salvador Allende

Salvador Allende Gossens (1908–1973) was president of Chile from November 1970 until his death on September 11, 1973, when La Moneda, the executive seat of government, was attacked by forces under the leadership of General Augusto Pinochet during a military coup d'état. Allende, a member of the Socialist Party, had participated in the political life of Chile for more than forty years. During that time he had served as senator, deputy, and cabinet minister. He was also a candidate for the presidency in 1952, 1958, and 1964, finally winning election in 1970. The following may be found in *Salvador Allende Reader: Chile's Voice of Democracy*, edited with introduction by James D. Cockcroft, translated by Moisés Espinoza and Nancy Nuñez (Melbourne: Ocean Press, 2000), 200–221. By permission of Ocean Press.

1972

I am very grateful for the high honor of being invited to speak from this rostrum, the most representative in the world and the most important forum in all matters concerning mankind. I should like to greet the secretary-general of the United Nations, whom we were honored to welcome to our country during his first few weeks in office, the representatives of more than 130 countries composing the General Assembly, and you, Mr. President, who come from a country with which we have friendly ties, and whom we have known personally since you presided over the delegation of the People's

Republic of Poland at the third session of the United Nations Conference on Trade and Development (UNCTAD).

I come from Chile, a small country, but one where every citizen is free to express himself as he sees fit, where there is unlimited cultural, religious, and ideological tolerance, and where racial discrimination has no place; a country whose working class is united in a single trade-union federation, where universal suffrage and the secret ballot are the cornerstones of a multiparty system; a country whose parliament has been active without interruption since its creation 160 years ago, whose judiciary is independent of the executive, and whose Constitutional Charter, which has practically never ceased to be applied, has been amended only once since 1833. I come from a country where public life is organized around civic institutions, a country whose armed forces have demonstrated their professional vocation and profound democratic spirit; a nation of close to 10 million people which, in one generation, has produced two Nobel Prize winners for literature, Gabriela Mistral and Pablo Neruda, both children of modest workers; a land whose history, soil, and people have merged in a great sense of national identity.

Chile, however, is also a country whose backward economy has been subjected to, even taken over by, foreign capitalist enterprises, and whose external debt has swollen to over $4 billion, the annual service of which represents more than 30 percent of the value of its exports; a country with an economy sensitive to outside events, chronically stagnant and inflationary, where millions of people have been forced to live in circumstances of exploitation, misery, and open or covert unemployment.

I come here today because my country is confronted with problems that, because of their universal importance, are the object of the permanent concern of this Assembly of nations: namely, the fight for social liberation, the struggle for well-being and intellectual progress, and the defense of national identity and dignity.

The prospect that faced my country, as in the case of so many others of the Third World, was the familiar model of adopting an alien pattern of modernization, which technical studies and tragic reality have both shown to have the inevitable effect of excluding more and more millions of people from all possibility of progress, well-being, and social liberation and relegating them to a subhuman existence—a pattern destined to lead to still greater housing shortages and to condemn an ever-increasing number of citizens to unemployment, illiteracy, ignorance, and physical want.

In a word, this same prospect before us has kept us in a state of colonization or dependency and exploited in times of Cold War as well as in times of open conflagration and of peace. We, the underdeveloped countries, are asked to agree to being condemned to a second-class, eternally subordinate status.

This then is the pattern, which the working class of Chile, upon becoming arbiter of its own future, has decided to reject, striving instead for a rapid, self-determined, and independent development and the revolutionary reorganization of traditional structures.

The Chilean people has won for itself the reins of government, after a long period of noble sacrifice, and it is now fully engaged in the task of establishing economic democracy so that the country's productive activities will meet its social requirements and expectations and not be exploited for private gain. Through a well-planned and coherent program, the old structure based on the exploitation of the worker and the domination of the principal means of production by a minority is being superseded. Its place is being taken by a new structure directed by the workers which, in serving the interests of the majority, is laying the foundations for a pattern of growth which spells genuine development, which involves all the inhabitants of the country, and which does not relegate vast sections of the people to poverty and social banishment.

The workers are replacing the privileged groups politically and economically, both in the centers of work and in the communes and the state itself. This is the revolutionary content of the process being experienced by my country today: the rejection and replacement of the capitalist system and the opening of a way toward socialism.

The need to place all our economic resources at the service of the people's tremendous unsatisfied requirements had to go hand in hand with the recovery by Chile of its national dignity. We had to put an end to the situation where we Chileans, struggling against poverty and stagnation, were forced to export huge amounts of capital for the benefit of the most powerful market economy in the world. The nationalization of our basic resources constituted a historic act of reclamation. Our economy could no longer tolerate the state of subordination implied in the concentration of more than 80 percent of its exports in the hands of a small group of large, foreign companies that have always placed their own interests before the needs of the countries in which they were making exorbitant profits. Neither could we accept the vicious effects of the *latifundio*, of the industrial and commercial monopolies, of credit restriction in favor of only a few, or of brutal inequalities in income distribution.

The change we are effecting in the power structure, the progressive management role which the workers are assuming, the nation's recovery of its basic resources and the freeing of our country from its subordination to foreign powers constitute the culmination of a long historic process of efforts to win political and social freedoms and of heroic struggle by several generations of industrial and rural workers to organize themselves as a social force in order to conquer political power and oust the capitalists from economic power.

The Chilean people's traditions, personality, and revolutionary consciousness have enabled them to push forward toward socialism while strengthening civic freedoms, both collective and individual, and respecting cultural and ideological pluralism. Ours is a continuing struggle for the institution of social freedoms and economic democracy through the full exercise of political freedom.

Our nation's democratic will has taken up the challenge to carry through this revolutionary process within the framework of a state of highly institutionalized legal precepts, which has been flexible to change and today faces the need to adapt to the new socioeconomic reality.

We have nationalized our basic resources. We have nationalized copper. We have done so by a unanimous decision of Parliament, in which the government parties are in the minority. We want everybody to understand this clearly: we have not confiscated the great foreign copper-mining companies. In accordance with constitutional law, however, we have put right a long-standing injustice by deducting from the amount of compensation the profits over 12 percent per annum which those companies have obtained since 1955.

The profits which some of the nationalized companies had obtained over the previous fifteen years were so exorbitant that, in applying the limit of a reasonable profit of 12 percent per annum, the companies were affected by significant deductions. Such was the case, for example, with a branch of the Anaconda Company, whose annual profits in Chile between 1955 and 1970 averaged 21.5 percent on its book value, while Anaconda's profits in other countries were only 3.6 percent per annum. The same applied in the case of a branch of the Kennecott Copper Corporation, which over the same period made an average annual profit of 52.8 percent in Chile, even reaching such incredible rates as 106 percent in 1967, 113 percent in 1968, and over 205 percent in 1969. Kennecott's average profits in other countries during that period amounted to less than 10 percent per annum. In other cases, however, the application of the rules established in line with the Constitution has meant that other foreign copper companies have not been subject to deductions under the heading of excessive profits since the reasonable limit of 12 percent per annum had not been exceeded.

It should be stressed that in the years immediately preceding nationalization the large copper companies initiated expansion plans. However, those plans—which were unsuccessful for the most part—were not financed from their own resources, despite their huge profits, but by means of external credits. In accordance with legislative provisions, Chile has had to take over responsibility for those debts, which amount to the enormous sum of more than $727 million. We have begun to pay those debts, including one which one of those enterprises had contracted with Kennecott, its own parent company in the United States.

Those same enterprises exploited Chile's copper for many years, in the last forty-two years alone taking out more than $4 billion in profits although their initial investment was no more than $30 million. In striking contrast, let me give one simple and painful example of what this means to Chile. In my country there are 600,000 children who will never be able to enjoy life in a normal human way because during their first eight months of life they did not receive the minimum amount of protein. Four billion dollars would completely transform Chile. A small part of that sum would ensure proteins for all time for all children of my country.

Copper mining has been nationalized not only with scrupulous regard for domestic legislation but also with respect for the norms of international law—which does not exist, of course, simply to serve the interests of the great capitalist enterprises.

That, in brief, is the process through which my country is living and which I have thought it appropriate to describe to this Assembly—a process backed by the authority we enjoy by virtue of the fact that we are complying strictly with the recommendations of the United Nations and basing our economic and social development on our own internal efforts. This Assembly has advocated transforming outmoded institutions and structures, mobilizing national resources both natural and human; redistributing income, allocating priority attention to education and health and also to special treatment for the poorer sectors of the population. All these are essential components of our policy and are being implemented to the full.

In view of what I have said, it is all the more painful for me to have to come here to this Assembly to denounce the fact that my country is the victim of serious aggression.

We had foreseen that there would be external difficulties and opposition when we began to make changes, particularly as regards the nationalization of our natural resources. Imperialism and its cruelties have had a long and ominous history in Latin America; and the dramatic and heroic experience of Cuba is still fresh in our minds, as is that of Peru, which has had to suffer the consequences of its decision to exercise its sovereign rights over its petroleum.

After all the innumerable agreements and resolutions adopted by the world community, recognizing the sovereign rights of each country to dispose of its natural resources for the benefit of its people; after the adoption of the International Covenant on Economic, Social and Cultural Rights [resolution 2200 A (XXI)] and the International Development Strategy for the Second United Nations Development Decade [resolution 2626 (XXV)], which solemnly confirmed all these instruments, here we are, well into the 1970s, suffering from yet another manifestation of imperialism, one that is more subtle, more cunning, and more terrifyingly effective in preventing us from exercising our rights as a sovereign state.

From the very day of our electoral triumph on 4 September 1970, we have felt the effects of a large-scale external pressure against us which tried to prevent the inauguration of a government freely elected by the people, and has attempted to bring it down ever since. An attempt has been made to cut us off from the world, to strangle our economy and paralyze trade in our principal export, copper, and to deprive us of access to sources of international financing.

We are aware of the fact that, when we denounce the financial and economic blockade applied against us, it is somewhat difficult for world public opinion, and even for some of our fellow citizens, to understand what we mean. This aggression is not overt and has not been openly declared to the world; on the contrary, it is an oblique, underhand, indirect form of aggression, although this does not make it any less damaging to Chile.

We are having to face forces that operate in the half-light, that fight with powerful weapons, but that fly no identifying flags and are entrenched in the most varied centers of influence.

There is no embargo against trading with us. No one has stated an intention to fight us face to face. On the surface it would appear that the only enemies we have are our natural political adversaries at home. But this is not true. We are the victims of virtually imperceptible activities, usually disguised with words and statements that extol the sovereignty and dignity of my country. We know in our own hearts, however, the distance that separates these words from the specific activities that we have to face.

I am not talking about vague matters; I am referring to specific problems that burden my people today and that will have even more serious economic repercussions in the coming months.

As is the case with most of the developing countries of the Third World, the external side of Chile's economy is highly vulnerable. Chile's exports amount to a little over $1 billion a year, but over the last twelve months the slump in the price of copper on the world market has meant a loss to my country of income of about $200 million, whereas the products which the country has to import—both industrial and agricultural—have risen sharply in price, in some cases by as much as 60 percent. Thus, as nearly always, Chile is obliged to sell cheap and buy dear.

Moreover, at this very time, which is itself so difficult for our balance of payments, Chile has had to face, among others, the following concerted actions apparently designed to take revenge on the Chilean people for its decision to nationalize its copper.

Until my government took office, Chile received a net inflow of resources of approximately $80 million per year in the form of loans granted by international finance organizations, such as the World Bank and the Inter-American Development Bank. This source of finance has now been cut off abruptly.

In the last decade, Chile was granted loans worth $50 million by the Agency for International Development of the United States government. We do not expect that these loans will be continued. The United States in its sovereignty may grant or withhold loans with respect to any country it chooses. We only wish to point out that the drastic elimination of these credits has resulted in sharp restrictions in our balance of payments.

When I became president my country had short-term credit facilities from private United States banks amounting to about $220 million to finance our foreign trade. Within a short space of time, however, these credits were suspended and about $190 million of this total credit was withdrawn and we had to pay this sum as the credit was not renewed.

Like most Latin American countries, Chile is obliged, for technological or other reasons, to acquire substantial amounts of capital goods from the United States. Now, however, both the supplier credits and those normally granted by the Export-Import Bank in respect to this type of transaction have also been denied to us, so that we are in the anomalous position of having to pay in advance to obtain such goods. This places our balance of payments under extraordinarily severe pressure.

Disbursements under the terms of loans contracted with United States public sector agencies, and already in operation before my government came to power, have likewise been suspended. Consequently, in order to go ahead with the projects concerned—for which it had been confidently expected that financing would be provided by United States government bodies—we have been obliged to make cash purchases of goods on the United States market, since it is impossible to change the source of the imports in question in the middle of the execution of the projects.

As a result of the actions directed against the copper trade in the countries of Western Europe, our short-term transactions with private banks of that area, mainly involving the collection of payment from sales of copper, have been very seriously obstructed. Thus, credit facilities in respect of over $20 million have not been renewed, financial negotiations involving over $200 million which were on the point of coming to a favorable conclusion have been broken off, and a climate has been created which hampers the normal course of our purchases in Western Europe and seriously distorts all our activities in the field of external financing.

This financial strangulation, which has had an immediate and a violent effect because of the nature of the Chilean economy, has led to the severe limitations on our ability to secure the equipment, spare parts, manufacturing inputs, foodstuffs, and medicines which we need. Each and every Chilean is suffering from the consequences of these measures, because they affect the daily life of each citizen, and naturally his internal political life.

What I have just described to the Assembly amounts to a perversion of the fundamental nature of international agencies, the utilization of which as tools of the policies of individual member states is legally and morally unacceptable, no matter how powerful such states may be. Such misuse represents the exertion of pressure on an economically weak country, the infliction of punishment on a whole nation for its decision to recover its own basic resources, and a premeditated form of intervention in the internal affairs of a sovereign state. In a word, it is what we call imperialist insolence. As members are well aware and are scarcely likely to forget, that kind of action has been repeatedly condemned by United Nations resolutions.

We not only are enduring a financial blockade, but also are the victims of downright aggression. Two companies belonging to the hard core of the great transnational enterprises, namely, the International Telephone and Telegraph Company (ITT) and the Kennecott Copper Corporation, which had driven their tentacles deep into my country, proposed to manage our political life.

A gigantic corporation whose capital is larger than the national budgets of several Latin American countries put together, and bigger even than that of some of the industrialized countries, the ITT launched a sinister plan to prevent me from acceding to the presidency just as soon as the people's triumph in the September 1970 elections became known.

Between September and November of that year terrorist activities took place in my country, which were planned outside our frontiers in collusion with internal fascist groups. Those activities culminated in the assassination of the commander-in-chief of the Army, General René Schneider

Chereau, who was a just man, a great soldier, and a symbol of the constitutional attitude of Chile's armed forces.

In March 1972, documents revealing the link between those dark designs and the ITT came to light. The ITT has admitted that in 1970 it even suggested to the United States government that it should intervene in the political events in Chile. The documents are authentic, and no one has dared gainsay them.

In July the world was shocked to learn the details of a new plan of action which the ITT itself presented to the United States government, a plan aimed at overthrowing my government within a period of six months. I have in my briefcase the document, dated October 1971, which contains the eighteen points of that plan. Its objectives included strangling the economy, diplomatic sabotage, sowing panic among the population, and fomenting social disorder so that the government would, it was hoped, lose control of the situation and the armed forces would be impelled to break the democratic system and impose a dictatorship.

At the very moment when the ITT was putting forward that plan, its representatives were pretending to negotiate with my government a formula for the purchase by the Chilean state of the ITT's share in the Chilean Telephone Company. From the earliest days of my administration we had, for reasons of national security, started conversations to purchase that telephone company controlled by the ITT. I myself had two interviews with senior executives of the enterprise. My government acted in good faith in those discussions, but the ITT refused to accept a price fixed on the basis of an assessment made by international experts. It placed difficulties in the way of a rapid and fair solution, while surreptitiously it tried to bring about a chaotic situation in Chile.

The refusal of the ITT to accept a direct agreement, and the knowledge of its sly maneuvers, have compelled us to place a nationalization bill before Congress.

The determination of the Chilean people to defend the democratic system and the progress of the people's revolution, and the loyalty of the armed forces to their country and its laws, foiled the sinister designs of the ITT.

Before the conscience of the world I accuse the ITT of attempting to bring about civil war in my country, the greatest possible source of disintegration of a country. That is what we call imperialist intervention.

Today Chile is threatened by another danger, the removal of which depends not only on the national will, but also on a wide range of external elements. I refer to the action taken by the Kennecott Copper Corporation. The Chilean Constitution provides that nationalization disputes should be resolved by a tribunal, which, like all tribunals in my country, has complete independence and sovereignty in the adoption of decisions. Kennecott accepted that jurisdiction and for a year it pleaded its case before that tribunal.

When its appeal was rejected, however, it then decided to use its great power to rob us of our copper export earnings and to bring pressure to bear against the government of Chile. It was so bold, in September last, as to request the courts in France, the Netherlands, and Sweden to place an embargo on payments for those exports. It will no doubt attempt that in other countries too. The grounds for this action could not possibly be less acceptable, from whatever legal or moral standpoint they are viewed.

Kennecott wants the courts of other nations which have nothing to do with the problems or affairs between the Chilean state and it to declare invalid a sovereign act of my government undertaken by virtue of the highest mandate, namely, that given by the country's Constitution and backed by the unanimous will of the Chilean people.

Such pretensions run counter to fundamental principles of international law, according to which a country's natural resources—particularly when they are its very lifeblood—belong to it and can be freely utilized by it. There is no generally accepted international law or, in this case, any specific treaty that can justify Kennecott's action. The world community, organized in accordance with the principles of the Charter of the United Nations, does not accept that international law can be interpreted in a manner which subordinates it to capitalist interests so as to induce the courts of law of any foreign country to protect a structure of economic relations designed to serve capitalism. Were it to do so, it would be undermining a fundamental principle of international life, that of nonintervention in the domestic affairs of states, as explicitly recognized by the third session of UNCTAD. We are governed by the principles of international law that have been reaffirmed repeatedly by the United Nations, particularly in General Assembly resolution 1803 (XVII), and were recently restated by the Trade and Development Board specifically in relation to the denunciation which my country formulated against the Kennecott Copper Corporation. In addition to reaffirming the sovereign right of all countries to dispose freely of their natural resources, the board's resolution states in paragraph 2 that:

> in the application of this principle, such measures of nationalization as States may adopt in order to recover their natural resources are the expression of a sovereign power in virtue of which it is for each State to fix the ... procedure for these measures, and any dispute which may arise

in that connection falls within the sole jurisdiction of its courts, without prejudice to what is set forth in General Assembly resolution 1803.

General Assembly resolution 1803 (XVII) provides that, in exceptional circumstances, disputes may be settled through international adjudication provided there is "agreement by sovereign states and other parties concerned."

This is the sole thesis acceptable to the United Nations. It is the only one that conforms to its philosophy and principles. It is the only one that can protect the rights of the weak from the abuse by the strong. As is only right in view of the foregoing, we have succeeded in the Paris courts in securing the lifting of the embargo affecting the proceeds of the sale of a consignment of our copper.

Notwithstanding, we shall continue with undiminished determination to maintain that only the Chilean courts are competent to pass judgment in any dispute concerning the nationalization of our basic resources.

For Chile, this is not merely an important problem of juridical interpretation; it is a question of sovereignty. Indeed, it is far more than this—it is a question of survival.

The aggression perpetrated by Kennecott is causing serious damage to our economy. The direct difficulties that it has posed for the marketing of copper alone have meant the loss of many millions of dollars for Chile in two months. But that is not all. I have already referred to the effect that it has had in obstructing my country's financial operations with Western European banks. Quite clearly, there is also a desire to create a climate of uncertainty among the purchasers of our principal export product, but that shall not happen.

Such are the designs of that imperialist enterprise at the present time. It cannot hope, however, that any political or judicial power will in the long run deprive Chile of what is legitimately its own. It is trying to force our hand, but it will never succeed.

The aggression of the great capitalist enterprises is intended to prevent the emancipation of the working classes. It represents a direct attack on the economic interests of the workers, in this specific case, leveled against Chile.

Chile is a nation that has attained the political maturity to decide by majority vote to replace the capitalist economic system by the socialist. Our political system has shown that it possesses institutions that are sufficiently open to have brought about the expression of this revolutionary will without violent upheavals. It is my duty to inform this Assembly that the reprisals and economic blockade that have been employed in an attempt to produce a chain reaction of difficulties and economic upsets represent a threat to domestic peace and coexistence. But they will not achieve their evil intention. The vast majority of the Chilean people can resist this threat with dignity and patriotism. What I said at the beginning will always be true: the history, the land and the people of Chile have combined to produce a great feeling of national identity.

At the third session of UNCTAD I referred to the phenomenon of the transnational corporations and drew attention to the staggering increase in their economic power, political influence, and corrupting effect. It is not surprising, therefore, that world opinion should react with alarm in the face of this reality. The power of these corporations is so great as to transcend all frontiers. The foreign investments of United States companies alone, which today amount to $32 billion, grew by 10 percent annually between 1950 and 1970, while United States exports rose by only 5 percent. The profits of such companies are fabulous and represent an enormous drain on the resources of the developing countries.

In one year, those enterprises repatriated profits from the third world representing net transfers in their favor of $1,723 million: $1.013 billion from Latin America, $280 million from Africa, $366 million from the Far East, and $64 million from the Middle East. Their influence and sphere of action are rudely transforming traditional practices in international trade, transfer of technology, transmission of resources among nations, and labor relations.

We are witnessing a pitched battle between the great transnational corporations and sovereign states, for the latter's fundamental political, economic, and military decisions are being interfered with by worldwide organizations that are not dependent on any single state and which, as regards the sum total of their activities, are not accountable to or regulated by any parliament or institution representing the collective interest. In a word, the entire political structure of the world is being undermined.

"Merchants have no country of their own. Wherever they may be they have no ties with the soil. All they are interested in is the source of their profits." Those are not my own words: they were spoken by Jefferson.

The great transnational enterprises are not only undermining the genuine interests of the developing countries, but their overwhelming and uncontrolled force is felt too in the industrialized countries in which they are based. This fact has been denounced in recent months in Europe and the United States; it has in fact given rise to investigations in the United States Senate. In the face of this danger the developed countries can feel no more secure than the developing world. This disturbing phenomenon has already prompted the growing mobilization of organized labor, including the world's great trade unions. Once again international solidarity among the workers of the world must face a common adversary: imperialism.

This is basically why the Economic and Social Council of the United Nations, as a result of the complaint submitted by Chile, unanimously adopted in July of last year resolution 1721 (LIII) calling for the convening of a study group of eminent persons to study "the role of multinational corporations and their impact on the process of development, especially that of the developing countries, and their implications for international relations, and to submit recommendations for appropriate international action."

Ours is not an isolated or unique problem: it is simply the local manifestation of a reality that goes beyond our frontiers and takes in the Latin American continent and the whole Third World. In varying degrees of intensity and with individual differences, all the peripheral countries are exposed to something of this kind.

As for the developed countries, the concept of human solidarity should cause them to feel repugnance at the fact that a group of corporations can with impunity interfere in the most vital workings of the life of a nation, even going so far as to disrupt it completely.

When the spokesman of the African group of states in the Trade and Development Board announced the position of the African countries a few weeks ago regarding Chile's complaint about the aggression of the Kennecott Copper Corporation, he said that the group was in complete solidarity with Chile because the issue was one that did not affect only one country but represented a potential threat to the entire developing world. Those words are highly significant, for they indicate that a whole continent recognizes that what is happening in Chile is opening up a new stage in the battle between imperialism and the weaker countries of the Third World.

The battle to protect their natural resources is part of the broader struggle being waged by the countries of the Third World to overcome underdevelopment. There is a clear-cut dialectical relationship: imperialism exists because underdevelopment exists; underdevelopment exists because imperialism exists. The aggression that we are suffering makes it seem illusory to give any credence to the promises that have been made in recent years regarding large-scale action to bring the nations of Africa, Asia, and Latin America out of their backwardness and want. Two years ago this General Assembly, celebrating the twenty-fifth anniversary of the founding of the United Nations, solemnly proclaimed the International Development Strategy for the Second United Nations Development Decade. Under it, all states members of the organization pledged themselves to spare no effort to change, through specific measures, the existing inequitable international division of labor and to bridge the enormous economic and technological gap separating the affluent countries from the developing nations.

It is now clear that none of those pledges has become a reality. On the contrary, we have moved backward. Thus the markets of the industrialized countries have remained as firmly closed as ever to the commodities of the developing world—especially agricultural commodities—and the level of protectionism is on the rise. The terms of trade continue to deteriorate; the system of generalized preferences for our exports of manufactures and semimanufactures has not been implemented by the nation whose market, given its volume, offered the best prospects; and there is no indication that the country concerned will implement it in the immediate future.

The transfer of public financial resources, far from reaching 0.7 percent of the developed nations' gross national product, has dropped from 0.34 to 0.24 percent. The indebtedness of the developing countries, already enormous at the beginning of this year, has risen in a few months from $70 to $75 billion. The heavy debt-service payments, which are an intolerable drain on those countries' resources, are largely attributable to the types and terms of the loans. Those payments increased by 18 percent in 1970, and by 20 percent in 1971, which is more than twice the average rate for the 1960s.

That is the tragedy of underdevelopment and the tragedy of our countries, that we have not yet been able to claim our rights and, through vigorous concerted action, protect the prices of raw materials and commodities and withstand the threats and aggressions of neoimperialism.

We are potentially rich countries; yet we live in poverty. We go from place to place seeking credit and help; yet—a true paradox in keeping with the capitalist economic system—we are major exporters of capital.

Latin America, as a component of the developing world, forms part of the picture I have just described. Together with Africa, Asia, and the socialist countries, Latin America has fought many battles over the last few years to change the structure of economic and trade relations with the capitalist world and to replace the unjust and discriminatory economic and monetary order created at Bretton Woods at the end of World War II.

It is perfectly true that there are disparities in national income between many countries in our region and those of the other developing continents, and such disparities exist too within our region—a region which includes several countries which may be considered as relatively less developed among the developing nations. But these disparities—which become almost insignificant in comparison with the national product of the industrialized world — do not exclude Latin America from that immense sector of humanity that is underprivileged and exploited.

The Latin American Consensus of Viña del Mar, approved in May 1969, affirmed these common characteristics and typified, defined, and quantified the region's economic and social backwardness and the external factors responsible for it, stressing the tremendous injustices committed against our region under the guise of cooperation and help. For the much-admired great cities of Latin America conceal the tragedy of hundreds of thousands of people living in shantytowns, the result of fearful unemployment and underemployment, hiding the gross inequalities between small privileged groups and the broad masses, whose nutrition and health standards are no higher than in Africa, and who have practically no access to culture.

It is easy to understand why Latin America has such a high infant mortality rate and such a low life expectancy when it is realized that it lacks 28 million dwellings and 56 percent of its population is undernourished, that there are more than 100 million illiterate and semi-illiterate persons, 13 million unemployed, and over 50 million underemployed. More than 20 million Latin Americans do not even know what money is, even as a medium for trade.

No system, no government, has been capable of making good the dramatic deficiencies in housing, work, food, and health. On the contrary, these get worse year by year with the natural growth of population. If this situation continues, what will happen at the end of the century when the population will be over 600 million?

The situation is even worse in Asia and Africa, with their lower per capita income and weaker development process.

It is not always realized that the Latin American subcontinent, with its enormous potential resources, has become the main field of action of economic imperialism in the past thirty years. Recent data from the International Monetary Fund reveal that for Latin America the private investments account of the developed countries showed a deficit of $9 billion between 1960 and 1970. In other words, this amount represents a net capital contribution to the richest countries in one decade.

Chile feels a deep sense of solidarity with all the countries of Latin America, without exception. It therefore advocates and strictly observes the policy of nonintervention and self-determination, which it applies at the world level. We ardently promote closer economic and cultural relations. We support greater dovetailing and integration of our economies. Hence, we are working enthusiastically within the Latin American Free Trade

Association and, as a first step, we are striving for the formation of a common market for the Andean countries, linking us with Bolivia, Colombia, Peru, and Ecuador.

Gone are the days when Latin America simply protested. Statistical data and the continent's needs contributed toward strengthening a sense of awareness. Ideological barriers have been broken down by realities. Plans designed to divide and isolate us have not succeeded. What has come to the forefront is a desire to coordinate the defense of the interests of all nations of the hemisphere and of those of all developing nations. "Those who stand in the way of peaceful revolution make violent revolution inevitable." Again, those are not my words; I agree with them. They were spoken by John F. Kennedy.

Chile is not alone. No one has succeeded in isolating it from Latin America or from the rest of the world. On the contrary, it has received infinite demonstrations of solidarity and support. The growing repudiation of imperialism, the respect merited by the efforts of the Chilean people, and the response to our policy of friendship with all nations of the world have combined to defeat the attempts to erect a hostile barrier around us.

In Latin America all the systems of economic and cultural cooperation and of integration to which Chile belongs at the regional and subregional levels have continued to gain vigor at a rapid pace, and within this context our trade, particularly with Argentina, Mexico, and the countries that were parties to the Andean Pact, has increased considerably.

There has been no split in the concerted stand adopted by Latin American countries at world and regional meetings in support of the principles of self-determination in respect of their natural resources. In the face of the recent threats to our sovereignty we have received fraternal demonstrations of complete solidarity. To all we offer our sincere thanks.

Socialist Cuba, which is enduring a rigorous blockade, has always unreservedly given us its revolutionary support.

At the world level, I must say in particular that right from the start the socialist countries of Europe and Asia have been at our side in an attitude of absolute solidarity. The large majority of the world community honored us in choosing Santiago as the site for the third session of UNCTAD, and it has displayed interest in our invitation—which I hereby repeat—to hold in Chile the forthcoming United Nations Conference on the Law of the Sea.

In September, the Conference of Foreign Ministers of the Non-Aligned Countries in Georgetown, Guyana, publicly expressed its firm support for us in our fight against the aggression practiced by the Kennecott Copper Corporation.

The Intergovernmental Council of Copper Exporting Countries, the coordinating body established by the main copper exporting countries, Peru, Zaire, Zambia, and Chile, recently met at the ministerial level in Santiago at the request of my government to take up Kennecott's aggression against my country. At that meeting the council adopted various resolutions and recommendations of great significance. These constitute unreserved support for our position and an important step taken by Third World countries to defend the trade in their raw materials.

No doubt there will be an important debate in the second committee on those resolutions. I merely wish to stress the categorical assertion that any action likely to hinder or curtail the exercise of a nation's sovereign right freely to dispose of its natural resources entails an act of economic aggression. The action of Kennecott Copper Corporation against Chile indeed constitutes economic and trade aggression. Furthermore those resolutions call for the suspension of all economic or trade relations with Kennecott, and provide that disagreements on questions regarding compensation for nationalizations are within the sole jurisdiction of the very states exercising such rights. But of paramount importance is the decision taken by CIPEC to establish a "permanent mechanism for protection and solidarity" regarding copper. Such a mechanism, together with that of OPEC on oil, leads the way to what should be an organization of all third world countries to protect and defend all their commodities, mineral and hydrocarbons as well as agricultural.

The vast majority of the countries of Western Europe, from the Scandinavian countries in the north to Spain in the south, have increased their cooperation with Chile, and their understanding has been of great support to us. Thanks to that, we have renegotiated our external debt.

Lastly, we have been touched to see the solidarity of the workers of the world, expressed through their major federations and trade unions and made manifest in such deeply significant acts as the refusal of the stevedores of Le Havre and Rotterdam to unload Chilean copper, payment for which had been arbitrarily and unjustly placed under embargo.

I have concentrated my statement on the aggression against Chile and on Latin American and world problems which are connected with the origin or effects of that aggression. I now wish to refer briefly to other matters of interest to the international community.

I shall not mention all the world problems on the agenda of this session. I do not pretend to have solutions for them. This Assembly has been working hard for over two months in defining and adopting appropriate measures, and I am confident that this work will bear fruitful results.

My comments will be of a general character and will reflect some concerns of the Chilean people.

The picture of the international political scene in which we have lived since the last world war has changed very rapidly, and this has resulted in a new correlation of forces. Centers of political and economic power have grown in number and strength. The socialist world, whose influence has increased significantly, is playing an ever more important role in the adoption of vital international policy decisions. I am convinced that the reform of world trade relations and the international monetary system—a change that is desired by all nations of the world—will be impossible unless all countries in the world, including those in the socialist area, participate fully in the process. The People's Republic of China, which contains nearly one-third of the world's population, has finally, after a long period of unjust ostracism, recovered its place in the forum of multilateral negotiations and has initiated diplomatic and trade relations with most countries of the world.

The European Economic Community has been enlarged with the entry of the United Kingdom and other countries, which now have a bigger say in decision making, particularly in the economic field. Japan's economic growth rate has reached prodigious proportions.

The developing world is daily becoming more conscious of the realities that surround it and of its own rights. It demands justice and equal treatment and recognition of its rightful place on the world scene.

As always, the motivating force behind these changes has come from the people, who are making history in their progressive struggle for freedom. Man's intelligence has pushed science and technology forward at a giddy pace. The persistence and vigor of the policy of peaceful coexistence, economic independence, and social progress, which the socialist nations have promoted, has helped decisively to ease the tensions that divided the world for more than twenty years, and it has been a determining factor in the acceptance of new values in international relations and society.

We welcome the changes that bring promises of peace and prosperity to many nations, but we demand that the whole of mankind be able to share in them. Unfortunately, these changes have brought only meager benefits to the developing world, which continues to be as exploited as before and indeed is becoming increasingly remote from the civilization of the industrialized world. The noble aspirations and the just rebellion now seething in it will continue to find expression in an increasingly forcible manner.

We are gratified to see the virtual end of the Cold War, and other heartening developments: the negotiations between the Soviet Union and the

United States on both trade and disarmament; the conclusion of treaties between the Federal Republic of Germany and the Soviet Union and Poland; the imminence of the European Security Conference; the negotiations between the two German states and their almost certain entry into the United Nations; and the negotiations between the governments of the Democratic People's Republic of Korea and the Republic of Korea, to name some of the most promising. There is no doubt that the international situation is now marked by truces, agreements, and an easing of the previously explosive situation.

There are still too many unresolved conflicts, however, that call for a stronger will by the parties to reach agreement and for collaboration between the world community and the major powers. Aggression and friction continue unabated in several parts of the world: the Middle East conflict, the most explosive of all, for which it has not yet proved possible to find the peaceful settlement advocated in resolutions of the principal organs of the United Nations, among which is resolution 242 (1967) of the Security Council; the blockade and persecution of Cuba; colonial exploitation, the ignominy of racism and apartheid; the widening of the economic and technological gaps between rich and poor countries.

There is as yet no peace in Indochina. But it has to come. There shall be peace for Vietnam. It must be so, because nobody now has any doubt regarding the futility of this monstrously unjust war that is still pursuing the totally unobtainable objective of imposing on peoples with a revolutionary consciousness policies which they cannot accept because they run counter to their national interests, their genius, and their personality.

Peace will come. But what will this war—so cruel, so long, and so unfair—leave behind it? After all these years of bloody fighting, the only outcome is the torture of a remarkably dignified people, millions of dead and orphaned, entire cities wiped out, the ecological destruction of hundreds of thousands of acres of land, devastated without any possibility of future vegetation. The people of the United States themselves are touched by grief; thousands of homes have been plunged into sorrow by the absence of their loved ones. The path that was laid out by Lincoln has not been followed.

This war has also taught many lessons. It has taught the world that the abuse of power saps the moral fiber of the country that misuses it and produces profound doubts in its own social conscience; whereas a people defending its independence can be raised to heroic heights by its convictions and rendered capable of resisting the physical violence of the world's mightiest military and economic machine.

The new political framework offers favorable conditions for the community of nations, in coming years, to make a major effort to give the world order a new lease of life and a new dimension.

That effort must be founded on the principles of the Charter, and on others such as those of the third session of UNCTAD, which the world has added to it. As we have already said, the United Nations should be guided by three concepts that are fundamental to the responsibilities entrusted to it: collective political security, collective economic and social security, and universal respect for basic human rights, including economic, social, and cultural rights, without any discrimination whatsoever.

We attach particular importance to the need to ensure collective economic security, on which Brazil and the United Nations secretary-general have recently placed so much stress.

As a major step in this direction, the world organization should implement as soon as possible the Charter of Economic Rights and Duties of States, a valuable proposal which the president of Mexico, Luis Echeverría, brought before the third session of UNCTAD. Like this great leader of a fraternal country, we too believe that a just order and a stable world are impossible so long as no set of commitments and rights has been established to protect the weaker states.

Future action by the community of nations must place emphasis on a policy in which all nations will play an active part. After all, the United Nations Charter was conceived and presented in the name of "We, the peoples of the United Nations."

International action must be directed toward serving the man who enjoys no privileges but who suffers and toils: the miner in Cardiff and the *fellah* in Egypt; the cocoa farmer in Ghana or the Ivory Coast, and the peasant of the plateaus of South America; the fisherman in Java and the coffee farmer in Kenya or Colombia. International action must reach the 2 billion underprivileged, those whom the community has the obligation to bring up to the level of the modem world and to reaffirm the "dignity and worth of the human person," to use the words of the Preamble to the Charter.

The international community must not wait a moment longer to secure the implementation of the Strategy for the Second Development Decade and to bring that instrument into line with the new realities of the Third World and the burgeoning awareness of its peoples.

The slackening of tension in international relations and the progress of cooperation and understanding make it not only possible but essential to divert all the enormous efforts that have been devoted to making war to activities that will try to cross new frontiers and meet the truly vast and varied needs of more than two-thirds of mankind. Thus, the more developed countries must increase their production and employment in line with the real interests of the less developed countries. Only when that is done will it be possible to say that the international community really exists.

This Assembly is to decide upon the arrangements for holding the United Nations conference which is to establish what is termed the Law of the Sea—namely, a set of standards to regulate, on a worldwide basis, everything connected with the use and exploitation of the vast areas represented by the sea and the seabed, including the subsoil thereof. This is a major task of great promise for the United Nations, for the problem is one of which mankind in general has only recently developed an awareness, and even many existing situations may be perfectly compatible with the general interest. I should like to recall that just twenty years ago the countries in the southernmost part of Latin America—Ecuador, Peru, and Chile—were responsible for beginning that process which will culminate in the adoption of a treaty on the law of the sea. It is essential that the treaty include the principle approved at the third session of UNCTAD on the rights of coastal states over the resources of the seabed and the subsoil thereof coming within the limits of their national jurisdiction, and that instruments and machinery be established to ensure that the seabed area beyond the limits of national jurisdiction is the common patrimony of mankind and is exploited for the benefit of all by an international authority.

I should like to reaffirm our confidence in the mission of the United Nations. We know that its successes and its failures depend on the political will of the states of the world and on its ability to interpret the wishes of the vast majority of mankind. Whether the United Nations is simply a forum for debates or an effective instrument depends on the will of those states.

I have brought to this Assembly the voice of my country, a country united in the face of pressure from outside, a country that asks for and deserves understanding, for it has always respected the principles of self-determination and complied strictly with the principle of nonintervention in the internal affairs of other states. My country has never failed to comply with its international obligations and is now actively cultivating friendly relations with all the countries of the world. Admittedly, we have differences of opinion with some of them, but there is no country with which we are not prepared to talk matters over, using the framework of the multilateral and bilateral instruments to which we are parties. Our respect for those treaties is unswerving.

I have tried to reaffirm most emphatically that a desire for universal peace and cooperation is one of the dominant characteristics of the

Chilean people. That is why they will resolutely defend their political and economic independence and the implementation of their collective decisions, which have been democratically adopted in the full exercise of their sovereignty.

Events that have taken place within less than a week strengthen our conviction that soon victory will be with us in the struggle to attain these objectives: the candid, direct, and friendly exchange of views with the distinguished president of Peru, General Juan Velasco Alvarado, who publicly restated the full solidarity of his country with Chile in the face of the hostile actions I have already exposed, the resolutions of the Intergovernmental Council of Copper Exporting Countries I have mentioned, and my visit to Mexico.

It is difficult, indeed almost impossible, to describe the depth, the force, the spontaneity, and the eloquence of the support given us by the government of Mexico and the Mexican people. I received such expressions of support from President Luis Echevarria, the Parliament, the universities, and the people, all speaking with one voice, that I am still under the spell of their boundless generosity.

I come here reassured, for after such an experience I am absolutely certain that the awareness of the Latin American peoples of the risks facing us all has acquired a new dimension and that they are convinced that only by unity can they defend themselves from this grave peril.

When one has witnessed, as I have in the past few days, the enthusiasm and warmth of hundreds of thousands of men and women crowded in the streets and squares and crying slogans such as, "We are all for you; do not give up," all our doubts are dispelled and all our anxieties are erased. It is the peoples, all the peoples south of the Río Bravo, that stand up to shout, "Enough—no more dependence," "an end to intervention"; to affirm the sovereign right of all developing nations freely to dispose of their natural resources. This is something that is embodied in the conscience and determination of more than 250 million human beings who demand that they be listened to and respected.

Hundreds of thousands of Chileans wished me Godspeed with fervor and warmth when I left my country and gave me the message which I have offered to this world assembly. I am convinced that you, representing the nations of the world, will understand and assess my words. It is our faith in ourselves that increases our confidence in the great values of humanity and our confidence that those great values will prevail. They cannot be destroyed.

U.S. Hegemony on the American Continent

Irene Zea

Irene Zea, the daughter of Leopoldo Zea, is professor of international relations and Latin American studies at the Center for International Relations in Mexico. She is the author of numerous essays on Latin American politics and history. This essay appeared originally as "La hegemonía estadounidense en el continente Americano," *Revista de Relaciones Internacionales*, vol. 3, nueva epoca, no. 10 (July–September, 1975), 27–43. By permission of *Revista de Relaciones Internacionales*, Universidad Autónoma de México.

1975

Introduction

Two peoples, diverse in their origins and each with not only a different view of the world but also one that is contrary to the other, meet face to face on the same continent. It is a continent too small for Americans of Anglo-Saxon origin and too big for those of Latin origin. Both are nationalistic, but while the nationalism of one is expansive in nature, that of the other is essentially defensive. In the clash of these two nationalisms, the North American variety will be triumphant and by the beginning of the twentieth century U.S. hegemony on the American continent will become an established fact.

The history of Latin America is, thus, determined by that of the United States. The link between the two Americas is expressed in terms of underdevelopment, exploitation, and dependency. There have been several attempts on the part of Latin American nations to break with this link, but with the exception of Cuba, all of these efforts have not gone beyond mere attempts. The very contradiction in Latin America's attitude toward the United States to a certain extent impedes such efforts. On the one hand, North America is admired, but, on the other, it is rejected. It is needed and at the same time hated. It is accepted and it is something repudiated. In any case, the interests of Latin American nations are subordinated to those of North America and as a function of the latter the relations between the two Americas thus develop.

North American expansionism and its predominance in Latin America vary according to the determinants of its internal evolution and according to the nature of the dangers threatening its hegemonic position. This threat is defined as all that may imply a limitation on its interests, from an open challenge on the part of an extracontinental power (the missile crisis) to the attempts of some Latin American countries to free themselves economically and recover control of their own natural resources (the case of Chile). Thus the predominance of North American interests, particularly economic ones, will constitute above everything else the essential element of U.S. policy toward Latin America. The Monroe Doctrine, the Big Stick, Dollar Diplomacy, the Good Neighbor, the Alliance for Progress, and the Mature Relationship are nothing more than expressions of the same policy adapted to different circumstances and to different realities. Some, more flexible than others, some less or more effective, but the result is always the same: Latin America was and is a zone of exclusive influence of the United States.

The Monroe Doctrine

During the war for independence of the Spanish colonies, Latin American rebels tended to view the young republic to the north as their natural ally: the United States was emerging as a worthy model to follow because of its freedom and democracy. But very soon these young rebels became disillusioned. In the face of the Spanish American Revolution the government in Washington would not take a step beyond what suited its own interests. Thomas Jefferson, the admired North American paladin, when he learned of the uprising in the South, which was a consequence and reflection of his own country's independence, would advise the following: "delay this independence until such time as the United States can benefit from it and not England" (Medina Castro, p. 26). North American opportunism is reflected very clearly in this statement and it becomes obvious when the United States declares itself neutral in this contest. This neutrality will become one of its favorite policies, whether faced with the revolution for Spanish American independence or French intervention in Mexico, and each and every time when its own personal interests are not at stake. The policy was a convenient one since, as in the case of the struggle for Latin American independence, it did not prevent the United States from continuing to negotiate with the Old World the territories needed by its expansionism while it awaited calmly the outcome of the struggle in order to pronounce itself in favor of the victorious party. In fact, in 1819 a transcontinental treaty was signed with Spain and as a result it obtained the territory of Florida. The Old World, already in decline, ceded Florida in an attempt to stem U.S. expansion because it was already claiming the province of Texas as part of Louisiana. Now, with a clear and perfectly delineated border, it was hoped that its claims would cease. Everything was futile; the struggle was already decided in favor of the Spanish colonies and the United States at this point decided to take sides. It recognized the independence of the new colonies and in 1825 sent Joel R. Pointsett to Mexico with precise instructions to negotiate a new borderline and obtain, through the payment of five million pesos, the territory of Texas.

At the beginning of the second decade of the twentieth century the overall outlook for Latin America was not very attractive. Instability and uncertainty were the principal characteristics. Although it was true the emancipation of the former Spanish colonies opened an economic market to the United States and facilitated its territorial expansion, it nonetheless found itself at a disadvantage with Great Britain, which had already established its economic dominance in Latin America. In addition, there was the shadow of the Holy Alliance that hoped to recover the territories lost by Spain. These were territories that were still very far from assuming the typical characteristics of a nation and which wasted away in internal struggles.

The presence of another European power on the American continent represented for the United States a potential danger to its security and a limitation to its expansion. On the basis of these two considerations, national security and expansion, the United States issued its famous Monroe Doctrine in December of 1823 (Petras, p. 234).

For some authors the Monroe Doctrine is the manifestation of U.S. inferiority with regard to Europe (Bosch, p. 17). North Americans had not yet undergone the Industrial Revolution which gave England and France an instrument of power typical of the nineteenth century: the world of finance and commerce. For this reason, when the language of the land (the United States was still a typically agrarian nation) came face to face with the language of high finance, the former was at a disadvantage and the United States found itself compelled to undertake a decisive intervention in Latin America to clear the continent of its European presence and prepare the way for its future expansion (Bosch, p. 23). The political intrigues in the internal process of Latin American nations would from that moment on play a very important role.

If, on the one hand, the United States rejected European intervention in Latin America, it left open the question of its right to intervention. In fact, this doctrine was founded on three postulates that become the basis of U.S. foreign policy toward Latin America. The first of these is that of noncolonization by European powers on the continent; the second is the abstention of these same powers from intervening in the affairs of American nations, with the corresponding promise from the United States that it would not interfere in European affairs; and the third is the rejection of any imposition or extension of Europe's political system on the American continent (Bemis, p. 59). In synthesis, America for the Americans but for the Americans of Anglo-Saxon origin.

When the independence of the New World was declared from the Old, the United States not only cut Latin America's links to the rest of the world, abrogating its right to regulate its hemispheric relations with extracontinental powers, but it also incorporated Latin America definitively within its exclusive sphere of influence (Petras, p. 236). Moreover, the doctrine was essentially a unilateral decision made by the United States that at no time took into account the opinion of Latin America's nations. The latter naively interpreted it as an instrument of protection when in fact the one defended by the doctrine was the United States.

In any case, the efficacy of the doctrine did not go beyond being an official declaration. The United States had neither the means nor the possibility of carrying it out. It was still an agrarian nation well beneath the power of England. In this sense the doctrine implied a simple act of daring by a young capitalist nation that was making known its hegemonic aspirations for control over the new republics (Medina Castro, p. 64). The United States, in order to apply this doctrine, would have had to consolidate first its internal market and achieve its national unity. Thus, in 1838 the French intervened in Argentina, in 1861 the Spaniards in Santo Domingo, from 1862 to 1867 a type of monarchic government was established in Mexico headed by a European prince, and the Americans did not convert their words into actions. However, the Monroe Doctrine was not forgotten, it was placed on file for the time being with only slight allusions made to it (Polk in 1845), and then dusted off when the United States possessed sufficient means to carry out its provisions.

The Big Stick

After the Civil War the United States entered a period of rapid industrialization. Monopolistic capitalism made its boisterous appearance and the need for markets became a fundamental imperative of U.S. foreign policy. Imperialism took a different form. From an imperialism of the territorial type it moved to one of an economic type in which control is less direct, transforming even the role of the army, from a conquering one to a kind of policeman whose task was to establish conditions favorable to commerce and investment (Bosch, p. 7). Latin America became the experimental field of this new modality of imperialism. The Monroe Doctrine was suddenly brought to life because of the border problem between Venezuela and British Guyana, after almost half a century of silence. In fact, the Monroe Doctrine was resuscitated in 1895 when the United States practically imposed upon England the negotiation of the Venezuela–Guyana problem. Statements made by Secretary of State Olney only strengthened and amplified the meaning of the doctrine when he announced that "the United States is practically sovereign on this continent and its mandate is law in the affairs in which it chooses to intervene." The hegemonic position of the United States was reaffirmed as well as its prerogative to regulate extrahemispheric relations. But, even more importantly, North American intervention in the internal affairs of Latin American states became justified. Roosevelt will fine-tune this interventionist protectionism later on in his famous corollary to the Monroe Doctrine.

In the meantime, the United States continued to test the reach of its power. The question of the Venezuelan–Guyanese border dispute turned out to be a success and London accepted implicitly the Monroe Doctrine and all that it implied. Still there were two bothersome issues and two countries were still very much present on the continent. We are referring to Cuba and Panama. Both are strategically important for the security of the American Union. Cuba was still part of decadent Spain and Panama was in the hands of a French contractor and at the same time coveted by England. Unfortunately for the North Americans, in neither of the two cases are the provisions of the Monroe Doctrine applicable. Nonetheless, the United States intervened, eliminated its European rivals, and established its predominance in these areas.

The justification for the intervention in Cuba had to do with humanitarian and altruistic motives. One has to recall that all interventions by the United States have some kind of justification. In this particular case President McKinley was moved by what was happening on the island. Ten years of civil war had decimated the population, destroyed property, and, above all, affected North American interests. Intervention, then, was absolutely necessary "to assure a stable government on the island that was capable of maintaining order and of fulfilling international obligations offering guarantees of peace, tranquility and security to its citizens *as well as to ours*" (Bosch, p. 89). War, therefore, was declared against Spain. It was a ridiculous war that lasted barely three months. The United States achieved its goal. It did not take control of Cuba but by means of the Platt Amendment it assured a stable government that guaranteed the situation of privilege enjoyed by foreign interests.

With Panama it is a different story. First, England was eliminated from the equation by repealing the Clayton-Bulwer Treaty by which the United States and Great Britain had to agree to share mutually the rights over any interoceanic passage that might be built in Central America. Next the United States bought from the French contractor the rights over the canal and finally negotiated with Colombia the acquisition of the Canal Zone. Colombia showed itself to be stubborn. The United States did not give up and fabricated the independence of a new Spanish American republic. The struggle was not at all a bloody one. The final settlement: a mere pittance. The result: the United States obtained in perpetuity rights over the zone, in which it conducted itself as a sovereign in the area.

But Cuba and Panama weren't enough. Monopolistic capitalism continued to grow and it needed natural resources and markets. The United States is a powerful nation and one that had decided to establish its hegemony over the entire continent. The Caribbean was the next step in this process, but here once again the Monroe Doctrine didn't apply. It had to be reworked and President Theodore Roosevelt performed this task perfectly. Santo Domingo presented him with a great opportunity. A backward nation, continually involved in uprisings, it found itself unable to meet its international obligations, setting in motion a possible intervention by creditor nations whose motive was to get their money back. Before Europe intervened, the United States did and the Roosevelt Corollary emerged as the magic formula to eradicate all excuses for intervention on the part of Europe on the

American continent: "If a nation knows how to act and fulfills its obligations, it has no reason to fear interference from the United States. But if it is incapable of this and strays from the path of civilized nations, the United States, to its great distress, will nonetheless be obliged to exercise the role of policeman." The United States in a definitive way became the judge of the conduct and obligations of all Latin American nations. European intervention was prohibited, but it sanctioned North American intervention to prevent such occurrences (Gil, p. 64). The "big stick" made its appearance in North American diplomacy, fulfilling the prophecy of Simón Bolívar, who said: "The United States seems destined by Providence to plague Latin America with all sorts of misery in the name of freedom" (Zea, p. 17). In the name of freedom and order, to avoid anarchy, preserve stability, and avoid intervention, the United States manifested over and over again its presence in these tiny republics, provoking a deep resentment that ultimately will nourish Latin American nationalism and give rise to figures like Sandino against the creations of North America: the Trujillos, the Somozas, and the Batistas.

Dollar Diplomacy

The succeeding American administration broadened the Roosevelt Corollary and added to the phenomenon of military interventions the purpose of promoting and extending the banking and financial interests of the United States in the Caribbean area. Washington's political support for foreign investors gave rise to dollar diplomacy (Gil, p. 70). Up until then, the investment of capital abroad had been carried out independently of its political implications. Risk and speculation were part of the attractiveness of this game. But to the extent that external capital started forming special interests, the demand for privileges and concessions from the host governments also increased. In this context the government in Washington ended up supporting these demands, whether through diplomatic pressures or, in the final analysis, through military interventions. One of the principal theorists of this new modality was Woodrow Wilson, who explained better than anyone else the ideas about economic expansion and the strategic needs imposed by the new frontiers of self-interest and ambition:

> Since commerce ignores national borders and the manufacturer insists on having the world as a great marketplace, the flag of his nation has to follow him and the doors of nations that are closed to him will have to

be knocked down. The concessions obtained by financiers should be safeguarded by the ministers of the State, even when the sovereignty of nations who are not disposed to do it is violated in the process. . . .

Given this point of view, the natural resources and markets of Latin American countries should be at the service of the United States, who assumes the right and duty to act as a policeman in the area with the intention of assuring that order, stability, and, of course, the appropriate conditions of preference and privilege prevailed for foreign investors (Freeman-Smith, p. 53). The notion of "extraterritoriality" became the common rule. Foreigners now enjoyed not only exemptions but also protections, subsidies, and preferences in countries where they found themselves. The North American came to be "the first class citizen" in Latin American cities and Latin Americans themselves became "second class citizens" in their own countries. According to a popular Mexican refrain: "The government is the mother of foreigners and the stepmother of Mexicans."

During this period the United States intervened in five Latin American nations: Cuba, Haiti, the Dominican Republic, Nicaragua, and Panama. In all five, intervention had its dual justification: to restore the economic order of the country affected and to train police or military forces in order to maintain political stability. Altruistic ends, no doubt, but they didn't benefit whatsoever the nations of Latin America. The restructuring of the economic order served to benefit U.S. development; a determinant of Latin American underdevelopment and political power was placed in the hands of the military, who made themselves invincible and who, in the long run, ended up producing the most repulsive of dictatorships (Matthews and Silvert, p. 224).

The passage from European interventionism to North American tutelage with the corresponding economic penetration of the United States in Latin America followed a pattern that was repeated with slight variations almost throughout the American continent. Foreign creditors were eliminated, public debt was consolidated, the control of the national banks was assured, the most important sectors of the national economy were invaded, and the Department of State was pressured so that it would safeguard those investments whether through political pressures or armed intervention (Petras, Erisman, and Mills, p. 243). This pattern was combined with some economic or political incentives for "friendly" governments who during the Second World War became the principal allies of democracy and freedom: dictators who killed and repressed democratic groups in the name of freedom.

The Good Neighbor

With the administration of Franklin D. Roosevelt there was a change in direction in the foreign policy of the United States, which is indicative of the manner in which the United States adapted to a new historical moment.

On the one hand, it had to deal with internal problems derived from the Great Depression. On the other, on an international level, it had to face the danger of the growth of fascism.

The Depression of 1929 had repercussions on a world order that were reflected particularly in Latin America. When exports from the metropolis to the periphery became contracted, Latin America faced the need to produce goods previously exported, which was reflected in the emergence of an economic nationalism and the establishment of a series of populist regimes characterized by their anti-imperialist politics. The economic crisis brought with it social tensions that sensitized Latin America's people regarding the impact of Nazi-fascist doctrine. The "Good Neighbor Policy" was the imperialist's reply to Latin American nationalism and the danger of fascist inroads on the continent. The "Good Neighbor," however, signified more of a change in form than in content. U.S. hegemony not only continued but was also reinforced through new mechanisms centered fundamentally upon veiled formulas like multilateralism and cooperation (Petras, Erisman, and Mills, p. 247).

The policy of the "Good Neighbor" implied a rejection of armed intervention and a growing support for the economic demands of Latin American countries. The sacrifice was worth the price and the United States soon found itself richly compensated for it. Nothing was free. In exchange for certain economic concessions and for rejecting a part of its imperialist politics, Latin America's unconditional political support for the United States in the case of an open confrontation with the Axis powers was expected.

Two important considerations made this change possible by 1930: the hegemony of the United States on the continent had been fully established and in the case of war, it was expected that the United States could count on the natural resources of Latin America, principally those of a strategic nature from the point of view of wartime needs. It shouldn't surprise us, then, that a policy unquestionably aggressive in nature becomes one that is more conciliatory, based principally on consultation and collaboration.

In 1934 the United States renounced its right to intervene in Central America and the last of its soldiers left Haiti; the Platt Amendment was repealed and the United States agreed to revise the Panama Canal Treaty. The United States undertook this withdrawal because it had managed to organize, in the zones previously occupied by its own military forces, local armed forces that remained loyal to the United States. They were politically stable regimes and devoted to the interests of the metropolis. "Internal colonialism" was the link that guaranteed its union with the center (Halperin Dongue, p. 368). Of course, there were regimes not so devoted to the interests of the United States who took advantage of this international period to carry out a series of nationalizations. Mexico, with Cárdenas at the helm, was just one of these. But in the final analysis it was a question of renegotiating the terms of dependency and not of breaking with the capitalist system. It was really about an independent capitalism under the direction of the state. North Americans showed themselves to be prudent and did not intervene. They appeared to be sincere. Actions spoke louder than words and this attitude moved many Latin Americans to entertain the possibility of realizing Bolívar's dream of Pan-Americanism. However, it was a Pan-Americanism very different from the one conceived of by the great liberator, for whom the unity of Latin America was to be imposed as a necessary defense in a world in which only the powerful counted: "Divided, we will end up being weaker, less respected by our enemies and those who remain neutral" (Zea, p. 93). Unity, yes, but not in the sense presented by the North Americans through the euphemism of "big brother." In the union of the weak with the strong the latter is always the one who benefits. Several years later, a Latin American author would describe Pan-Americanism as the "union of twenty sardines with a shark." However, at the time no one saw or wanted to see what a union of Latin America and the United States might imply.

When the Second World War broke out the "good neighbor" policy had fulfilled its mission and left a very favorable balance. Latin America followed the United States and participated on the side of the Allies, contributing indirectly to the war effort. Extensive programs of technical, economic, and military assistance were developed, strengthening the critical sectors of the economy that were necessary for the war industry. Besides primary resources, Latin America contributed soldiers and workers who migrated to the United States to offset the reduced working force in agriculture. The war from an economic point of view brought a bonanza to Latin America, but during the postwar period the programs of economic assistance were suspended, provoking a fall in the price of natural resources during a period in which the price of industrial products rose with an incredible rapidity (Ojeda, p. 514).

One could assert that during the Second World War the doctrine of "hemispheric security" started to develop. It was a doctrine that supposedly protected continental solidarity against foreign interests, but in the final analysis, the only ones protected were North American interests (Ianni, p. 24). Even the second military conflict of great external threat was represented by "European despotism." But after the war, at a time in which two great superpowers emerged with political and economic systems diametrically opposed to one another, the great danger was now represented by "Communist despotism" (Zea, p. 78). Both in the past as well as at this moment the doctrine of hemispheric security consolidated the economic, military, and political supremacy of the United States on the continent, creating a relationship of dependence. But if in the past the task of protecting the continent from foreign interference had been uniquely and exclusively in the hands of the United States, it was now a shared responsibility: the responsibility of everyone. The Rio de Janeiro Accord was the concrete expression of this new conception of hemispheric defense.

In effect, the Rio Accord turned out to be the first military agreement of the Cold War (Parkinson, p. 11). In accordance with its signers, it was a treaty of collective defense against the armed attack or threat to peace in any American republic. However, in this period the United States was very confident and sure of the loyalty of Latin American nations and didn't consider it necessary to keep spending money on economic aid programs to keep these nations on its side. The policy of the "Good Neighbor" had done its work and the areas that were sensitive to the Cold War were located outside the continent. The United States, already acting like a real power, with international responsibilities, tended to look toward Europe and Asia, neglecting its traditional sphere of influence. Latin Americans began to complain bitterly but to no avail. The pullback in price for raw materials began to make itself felt until a new occurrence attracted the attention again of the United States toward Latin America. It was now the Korean War that raised again the question of Latin American cooperation. Political support is offered in exchange for economic support. "International Communism" is defined as the common enemy, subversion as its principal symptom, and the Organization of American States as the mechanism of inter-American solidarity that was to coordinate the political and military defense against this danger (Mitchell, p. 182).

The Rio Accord and the Organization of American States are the two instruments that will legitimate the imperialistic actions of the United States in Latin America. Thus in 1954 the Organization of American States condemned the administration of Arbenz in Guatemala, branding him a

Communist. He was so called because he had the audacity to go against North American interests when he nationalized some of United Fruit's lands that weren't even under cultivation and for having dared to establish relations with some of the Eastern European countries. Or, in other words, the definition of Communist resulted a bit peculiarly when it implied, more than anything else, going against the interests and hegemony of the United States. A tyrant, a dictator was welcomed, they were called friends and were protected if they were against this supposed Communism, because in this way the rights of foreign investors were protected and their properties guaranteed. It became clear how the United States disguised its interventionism by collective actions. It could no longer be accused of arbitrary aggression since its action was justified by a regional organization in terms of self-defense against an external danger (Petras, Erisman, and Mills, p. 255). After the incident of Guatemala no crisis seemed to threaten U.S. hegemony and by 1960 Latin America was practically excluded from the map of the Cold War (Ojeda, p. 514). The Cuban Revolution would disabuse the North Americans of their error: Latin America could not be taken for granted.

The Alliance for Progress

In January 1959 a guerrilla revolution triumphed in Cuba. In opposition to the contrast between capitalism and Communism, a humanist alternative was offered. A third way that within a short time would be viewed as unfeasible, because when North American interests were affected by agrarian reform, which was going to be carried out at any price, it met with the decided opposition of the United States. Pressure did not take long to manifest itself: the quota of imported Cuban sugar was suppressed, the marketplace was closed off to Cuba, and the island's economy began to turn toward the Eastern bloc. This posed a great problem for a hegemonic power that could not accept a dissident country within the inter-American system. Given the experience of Guatemala, it was expected that the same deeds would be repeated and in April 1961 the Kennedy administration invaded the Bay of Pigs with exiled Cuban refugees supported, trained, and armed by the United States. The undertaking failed and the island, besieged economically and attacked militarily by its powerful neighbor, became a socialist country (Halperin Donghe, p. 452).

The conflict between Latin America and the United States that derived from the Cuban Revolution presented itself on two levels: (1) the basic conflict between Cuba and the United States over control of raw materials and the type of economic and political development considered to be suitable for the island and (2) the conflict between the United States and the rest of Latin America, whose nationalism had been exacerbated by the Cuban model, which offered a new alternative for escaping the underdevelopment determined by the same hegemonic position of the United States on the continent. To put it another way, the first was a conflict of a structural, ideological nature that basically represented a struggle for power since it was not only a question of a revolutionary experiment that affected North American interests but also the implantation of a rival member in an area considered under the indispensable hegemonic umbrella of the United States (Halperin Donghe, p. 450). The second was a conflict of a formal type that only required an adjustment of mechanisms and that at the same time permitted a certain independence of action on the part of Latin American countries with respect to the control exercised by the United States. Since the conflict with Cuba represented a priority for the United States, the United States during this period permitted the establishment of certain liberal reformist regimes such as that of Quadros or Goulart in Brazil, who nationalized some foreign companies and established relations with several Communist bloc nations but did not inhibit the authority of the United States in the region (Petras, p. 195).

The Cuban conflict determined to a great extent the United States' Latin American policy. When the Bay of Pigs invasion failed, the Kennedy administration fell back on a series of offensive strategies that have as their goal two fundamental objectives: isolate Cuba politically and economically and avoid the exportation of the island's revolution to other parts of the American continent.

To achieve the first objective the forum of the Organization of American States was utilized in which through a series of meetings Castro was condemned and expelled from the Organization at the same time that an economic blockade was imposed upon him with the obligatory breaking of diplomatic relations by all members with the exception of Mexico. The attempt was also made to reduce Cuba's military ties to the Soviet Union through an open confrontation between the two superpowers created by the missile crisis that forced the Soviet Union to withdraw its atomic warheads and for the United States to recognize the existence of a socialist regime on the continent. Lastly, a campaign to discredit the Cuban Revolution was waged, emphasizing the weak points in the socialist system and highlighting the virtues of the capitalist system of free enterprise (Ojeda, p. 616).

The Bay of Pigs, Punta del Este, and the missile crisis were all attempts on the part of the United States to recover its power over the island. All of these, in one form or another, failed and the United States found itself for the first time in many years faced with a heretofore inexperienced impotence. The Cuban Revolution came to express in a very special way the most profound sentiments of Latin Americans. The power and influence of North America were resented and felt. Castro had demonstrated that yes, it was indeed possible to struggle against the presumed superiority of the United States and limit its influence. Optimism ran through the whole American subcontinent and pockets of guerrillas, encouraged by the Cuban model, began to emerge everywhere. The United States reacted in a frenetic manner. The fear of another Cuba, of another popular movement that would endanger the foundations of its preeminence forced it to revise its Latin American policy, as it initiated a series of programs specifically geared to curtail the emergence of new pockets of rebellion and to eliminate the support of the masses for these movements (González Aguayo, p. 6). It was clearly demonstrated that the most serious threat to U.S. hegemony on the continent did not stem from foreign powers but rather from internal forces encouraged by Cuban nationalism. A dual strategy was designed against these internal, revolutionary elements that was to control and direct the domestic events of all Latin American nations. The Alliance for Progress and counterinsurgency efforts were two sides of the same coin. A program of economic assistance was one side; a program of military assistance was the other. Both were complementary.

Until the implementation of the Alliance for Progress the United States had been almost totally indifferent to the social and political consequences provoked by Latin American underdevelopment and to the "revolution of aspirations" proposed by the sale of the "American way of life." Televisions, refrigerators, the latest model cars had rapidly invaded the Latin American market and the dreams of many on the American subcontinent, dreams that tended to become frustrated because the economic capacity of many of these people did not allow them to realize such dreams. These new aspirations, which at any moment threatened to become social tensions that could lead to revolutionary explosions, were linked to the old problems of extreme poverty and injustice. The Alliance for Progress found the way to prevent this: it would turn the great, dispossessed masses into consumers. The promotion of social and economic reforms became an issue of foreign relations. Great sums of money in the form of loans would end up in Latin America. The attempt was made to increase the rate of Latin America's growth, elevate its standard of living, and, of course, increase its capacity to buy. The plan was simple. It was really a question of an alliance between the two Americas. That is to say, rich America would give money and advice to poor America and the latter would contribute with its additional funds, reforms, and, above all, the intense desire to follow the United States in the most important aspects related to socioeconomic development (Petras, Erisman, and Mills, p. 248). Thus, changes in the agrarian system, the tax system, education, and political organization were all suggested. This broad field of activities gave the United States a greater hand in the basic scheme of Latin America's political and administrative decision making. All of this was added to the important economic benefits obtained through the Alliance for Progress. Economic assistance was in no way free of charge. No matter how small it might be, it came with strings attached and in the majority of cases it was not offered in cash but rather in merchandise, provided the commitment was made to promote conditions propitious to a greater foreign investment in the area. As far as social reforms were concerned, they did not go far, just enough to create a social structure capable of resisting revolutionary propaganda. These were short-term palliatives offered to the masses to keep them quiet. This explains the existence of governments like Goulart's or Estenssoro's that managed to survive until another military-styled government replaced them, one that was not so anxious to carry out social reforms beyond the indicated limit. The exploitation and manipulation of the region by the United States proceeded in a more sophisticated fashion.

The concept of hemispheric security adapted to new circumstances. From a defensive situation toward the external, it came to be an offensive strategy toward the internal (González Aguayo, p. 32). The emphasis on the internal was especially evident in the counterinsurgency efforts that Kennedy, a great admirer of the Green Berets, established as the military counterpart of the Alliance for Progress. The United States did not intervene directly to suppress popular uprisings, rather this task was left in the hands of local regimes previously furnished with military equipment and technical advisers on the subject (Petras, Erisman, and Mills, p. 261). Military assistance for Latin America increased noticeably, facilitating the buildup of military forces that little by little started to play a more active role in the internal political process. By 1965 it was clear the United States was not going to finance for Latin America the social revolution planned by several economists and that supporting the forces of order became the preferred policy (Halperin Donghe, p. 448). Moderate liberal governments began to lose support and to see the social reforms demanded by the Alliance obstructed by the United States itself. Interest was being directed toward a new "modern" military class that better safeguarded and was more loyal to North American interests. The United States not only supported military coups but also encouraged them, allowing the establishment of dictatorships whose function was to eliminate all types of "subversion," repressing any popular movement that threatened to alter the "status quo."

Thomas Mann, the coordinator of the Alliance, concretized in four points the new direction adopted by the United States toward Latin America: (1) take a neutral position regarding internal social reforms; (2) protect and promote private investment in the hemisphere; (3) show no preference for institutions of a democratic, representative type; and (4) oppose Communism categorically (Mitchell, p. 190). The intention was quite clear: the cause of social reform was being abandoned and that of ideological security was being embraced. Anti-Communism became the principal theme of foreign policy. The struggle against the Red menace was undertaken, but not openly, and in favor of democracy, embracing as allies all those who supported this same cause without worrying about whether these people were dictators, tyrants, or as totalitarian as those governments against which they fought. The important thing was no longer democracy, social justice, or economic development but rather that Latin America not become a fertile ground for the implantation of a socialist system. Not for anything in the world could a "second Cuba" be tolerated.

The Mature Association or a Discreet Presence

By the beginning of the decade of the seventies Latin America had practically disappeared from the map of the Cold War. A progressive militarization of Latin American political life had led to the creation of pro-American regimes while guerrilla movements were almost completely eliminated. The Alliance for Progress was on its deathbed due to its own inaction, and the two great rivals of the Communist world, China and the Soviet Union, had reached an agreement with the United States. Once the crisis had passed there was no longer any need to pay special attention to Latin America and U.S. interest in the region fell to the lowest level on its scale of priorities (González Aguayo, p. 32).

As economic aid programs were being reduced, Latin Americans began to lose faith in the Organization of American States and to limit its power and importance. This organization had been one of the principal instruments of political control during the critical period of the Cold War, but now, to a certain extent, there was little justification for its existence. Latin

Americans tended to regroup within organizations of a regional nature, such as the Andean Pact, without seeking the permission of the United States and often against what might be construed as the interests of the United States. The nations of the American subcontinent began to act on their own, apparently annoying the United States, who from time immemorial had assumed the right to regulate Latin America's relations with the outside world. The fear that Communism might be exported to another area of Latin America was now a thing of the past and the Nixon administration initiated a new policy, which in its early years produced more ambivalence than anything else. It was not a clear or precise policy and resembled a "no policy," which is what many people called it. Little by little it began to define itself and was designated the "mature association", the "blurred profile," and even the "discreet presence."

The United States, concerned with its internal racial conflicts, unemployment, inflation, etc., seemed to ignore what was happening around it. On the continent regimes were established with different political and economic systems, such as Allende's in Chile and Velasco Alvarado's in Peru. These set in motion a series of nationalistic measures and established relations with the countries of Eastern Europe, the Soviet Union, and China while at the same time manifesting a profound anti-Americanism. The United States did not become overly concerned and left the control of Latin American affairs in the hands of North American corporations and their private investors, who were advised and helped by the CIA. Washington at the time exercised only an indirect supervision through its control of commerce and international institutions like the Inter-American Development Bank. This institution repeatedly refused loans for Chile and Peru.

Furthermore, the nationalizations undertaken by Chile and Peru had an impact that was quite relative. Both oil and copper, as well as other natural resources, were part of international oligopolies that were structured vertically. This implied that not only the production phase was controlled by the multinational but that this control also extended to the refining, manufacturing, commercialization, and distribution of the final product. Anaconda'a slogan, "From the mine to the consumer," explained the entire process very well. Therefore, when a nationalist government takes control of its country's production phase it finds the entry of its product to an external market blocked and has to come to terms once again with multinational corporations who impose their conditions. These forms of dependency and control made it completely unnecessary for Washington to confront directly the nationalistic economic theorists of Latin America.

Its hegemonic position was so firmly established that neither anything nor anyone could alter it.

It was only when Chile went too far that the United States determined the moment had arrived to bring it back into the fold. On this occasion the United States did not send marines nor did it utilize an inter-American peacekeeping force. Rather it intervened through a clandestine involvement in the internal politics of the country that led to the fall of the Allende government and his death. This was one of the saddest and darkest episodes in the history of U.S. relations with Latin America and would leave a very bitter taste in the mouths of Latin Americans and reinforce their feeling of pessimism at the impossibility of ever escaping the tight control exercised by the United States over the region.

On one occasion a North American statesman said: "The United States seems destined by Providence to extend itself beyond its own borders, and to reach as far as Patagonia." Such is in general terms what has been the evolution of relations between the two Americas. The battle of Latin America will have to be a battle for national liberation, a quest for an identity that will grant it a form of being, a way of living its own life, without being a mere reflection and dependent upon that other America.

Bibliography

Bemis, Samuel T. *The Latin American Policy of the United States*. New York: Alfred Knopf, 1943.

Bosch García, Carlos. *La base de la política exterior estadounidense*. México: UNAM, 1969.

Connell-Smith, Gordon. *The Inter-American System*. New York: Oxford University Press, 1966.

Freeman-Smith, Robert. *Los Estados Unidos y el nacionalismo revolucionario*. México: Editorial Extemporáneos, 1973.

Gil, Federico. *Latin American–United States Relations*. New York: Harcourt Brace Jovanovich, 1971.

González Aguayo, Leopoldo. "La política latinoamericana de Estados Unidos: Notas para un possible ensayo de teoría." In *Revista del Centro de Relaciones Internacionales* no.6.

Halperin Dongue, Tulio. *Historia contemporánea de América Latina*. Madrid: Alianza Editorial, 1969.

Ianni, Octavio. "Imperialism and Diplomacy in Inter-American Relations," in Julio Cotler and Richard R. Fagen, eds., *Latin America and the United States: The Changing Political Realities*. Stanford, California: Stanford University Press, 1974.

Matthews, Herbert, and K. Silvert. *Los Estados Unidos y la América Latina: de Monroe a Fidel Castro*. Mexico: Editorial Grijalbo.

Medina Castro, Manuel. *Estados Unidos y América Latina: Siglo XIX.* Havana, Cuba: Casa de las Américas, 1968.
Mitchell, Christopher. "Dominance and Fragmentation in U.S. Latin American Policy." In Julio Cotler and Richard R. Fagen, eds., *Latin America and the United States: The Changing Political Realities.* Stanford, California: Stanford University Press, 1974.
Ojeda, Mario. "The United States–Latin America Relationship since 1960." In *The World Today* December 1974, pp. 513–522.
Parkinson, F. *Latin America, the Cold War and the World Powers 1945–1973.* Beverly Hills, California: Sage Publications, 1974.
Petras, James. *Politics and Social Structure in Latin America.* New York: Modern Reader, 1973.
Petras, James, H. Michael Erisman, and Charles Mills. "The Monroe Doctrine and United States Hegemony in Latin America." In James Petras, ed., *Latin America: From Dependence to Revolution.* New York: Wiley and Son, 1973.
Zea, Leopoldo. *Latinoamérica y el mundo.* Caracas: Universidad Central de Caracas, 1959.

Mexico and the United States
Positions and Counterpositions

Octavio Paz

Octavio Paz (Mexico, 1914–1998) is considered one of the leading Latin American intellectuals of the twentieth century. Poet, essayist, literary and art critic, editor, diplomat, he was the author of countless books that are read and admired throughout the world. Some of his most significant works include: *El laberinto de la soledad* (1950, The Labyrinth of Solitude), *¿Aguila o sol?* (1951, Eagle or Sun?), *El arco y la lira* (1956, The Bow and the Lyre), *Libertad bajo palabra: Obra poética, 1935–1957* (1960, Freedom beneath the Word: Poetic Work 1935–1957), *Salamandra* (1962, Salamander), *Corriente alterna* (1967, Alternating Current), *Viento entero* (1965, Full Wind), *Postdata* (1970, Postscript), *El mono gramático* (1975, The Monkey Grammarian) *El ogro filantrópico* (1979, The Philanthropic Ogre), *Tiempo nublado* (1983, One Earth, Four or Five Worlds), and *Los hijos del limo* (1993, Children of the Mire). Paz was awarded the Nobel Prize for Literature in 1990. The following was the keynote address given by him in Spanish at a symposium entitled "Mexico Today," held in Washington, D.C., September 29, 1978. It was later published in *Tiempo Nublado* (Barcelona: Seix Barral, 1983), 139–159. The following selection is from *Obras Completas, 8, El peregino en su patria: Historia y política de México,* by Octavio Paz (México: Fondo de Cultura Económica, Círculo de Lectores, 1994), 437–453. By permission of Marie José Tramini de Paz.

1978

Poverty and Civilization

If man is not the king of creation, he certainly is the exception of nature, the singularity that defies all rules and definitions. Scientists react amazed in the face of unexpected behavior and, to a certain degree, in a capricious way, to the phenomenon of elementary particles, but what really are such physical eccentricities in the face of the psychological and moral extravagances of a Nero or a Saint Francis of Assisi? The history of societies is no less rich in irregularities and peculiarities than the biographies of individuals: what is anthropology if not the description of unusual customs and delirious rituals? Societies are unpredictable like individuals and hence the catalogue of failed prophecies made by sociologists, without excluding the most important ones, is bigger and more impressive than that of astrologists and clairvoyants. History accumulates incoherencies and contradictions with a kind of humor that is both involuntary and perverse. When I was in India, witnessing the spectacle of endless disputes between Hindus and Muslims, I would ask myself why, by what accident or historical fatality, two manifestly irreconcilable religions like Hinduism and Islam were compelled to live with one another. The presence of the most pure and intransigent monotheism in the interior of a civilization that has elaborated the most complex and perfect polytheism seemed to me to verify the indifference with which history perpetrates its cruel paradoxes. At the same time, I must admit that the contradictory pairing that Hinduism and Islam form in India does not surprise me: how could I forget that I was (and am) part of a paradox that is no less strange: namely, that of Mexico and the United States?

Our countries are neighbors and are condemned to live alongside one another. However, more than because of physical and political borders, the two are separated by social, economic, and psychic differences that run very deep. These differences are obvious and a superficial look could simply reduce them to the well-known dichotomy of development versus underdevelopment, of wealth versus poverty, of power versus weakness, and of domination versus dependence. But the really essential difference is invisible and it may also be insurmountable. To prove that it does not belong to the domination of the economy or to the realm of political power, all we have to do is imagine a Mexico suddenly converted into a prosperous and powerful country, a superpower like the United States. The differences, far from disappearing, would become clearer and more pronounced. The reason: these differences are not only exclusively quantitative but also belong to the realm of civilization.

What separates us is precisely that which unifies us: we are distinct versions of Western civilization.

Ever since Mexicans became conscious of their national identity, around the middle of the eighteenth century, they also became interested in their neighbors. At first it was with a mixture of curiosity and disdain; later on, it was one of admiration and enthusiasm, and it was not long before their attitudes were colored by fear and envy. The idea that the Mexican people have of the United States is contradictory, passionate, and impervious to criticism; more than an idea, it is really a question of a mythical image. The same can be said of the vision of our intellectuals and writers. Something similar occurs with North Americans, whether they are writers or politicians, businessmen or just simple travelers. I cannot forget the existence of a handful of admirable studies done by several North American specialists, particularly in the field of archeology and in the ancient and modern history of Mexico. Unfortunately, as worthy as these studies are, they do not make up for what we need the most: a vision that is both comprehensive and penetrating. True, the observations of novelists and poets who have written on Mexican themes have frequently been brilliant and, at times, have hit their target. But their perceptions have been fragmentary and as one critic says, who has dedicated a book to the topic (Drewey Wayne Gunn, *American and British Writers in Mexico*) they reveal less of Mexican reality than the personality of their authors. In general, North Americans have not looked for Mexico in Mexico; they have sought its obsessions, its enthusiasms, its phobias, hopes, interests—and that is what they have found. In summary, the history of our relations is one of a mutual and persistent deception, generally—although not always—involuntary.

The differences between Mexico and the United States are not, of course, imaginary projections but rather objective realities. Some are of a quantitative character and can be explained by the social, economic, and historical development of the two countries. Others, the most permanent ones, even though they are also the product of history, are not so easily definable or measureable. I have already pointed out that they belong to the order of civilizations, that fluid zone of indecisive contours, in which are fused and confused ideas and beliefs, institutions and techniques, styles and moralities, fashions and religions, material organization and that evasive reality we call, quite inexactly, "the genius of peoples." The reality that the word "civilization" names is not easily defined. It is the world's vision of each society but at the same time it is the experience of time: there are those peoples who are launched toward the future while the eyes of others are fixed upon the past. Civilization is the style, the way in which a society has of living, living together and dying. It comprises the erotic and culinary arts; dance and burial; courtesy and insult; work and leisure; rites and celebrations; punishments and awards, how we deal with the dead and with the ghosts who fill our dreams; our attitudes in the presence of women and children, the elderly and strangers, enemies and allies, eternity and the instant, the here and now and the other world.... A civilization is not only a system of values, it is a world of forms and behaviors, of rules and exceptions. It is the visible part of a society—institutions, monuments, ideas, works, things—but above all it is the submerged, invisible part: the beliefs, desires, fears, repressions, dreams.

North and South

The cardinal points have served to orient us not only in space but also in history. The duality East/West soon acquired a much more symbolic meaning than geographic and it became the emblem of opposition between civilizations. The same occurred with North/South. The opposition East/West has always been seen as the basic and primordial one; it alludes to the movement of the Sun and thus it is an image of the direction and sense of our living and dying. The relationship East/West symbolizes two directions, two attitudes, two civilizations. When they cross each other, there is a warlike collision or, more infrequently, that miraculous conjunction that we call "the attraction of opposites." The duality North/South refers to the opposition of ways of life and sensibility. The differences between North and South can be oppositions within the same civilization.

It is clear that from both the geographic and the symbolic point of view, the opposition between Mexico and the United States belongs to the duality North/South. This opposition is very old and it begins to unfold during pre-Columbian America, which is to say that it is prior to the existence of the United States and Mexico. The north of the continent was populated by nomadic and warlike nations. Mesoamerica, on the other hand, knew an agricultural civilization that was the mistress of complex social and political institutions, dominated by bellicose theocracies that invented refined and cruel rituals, a great art, and vast cosmogonies inspired by a very original vision of time. The great opposition of pre-Columbian America—in the territory now occupied by Canada, the United States, and Mexico—was not, as in the ancient world, between distinct civilizations but rather between different modes of living: nomadic and sedentary, hunters and farmers. This division had an enormous influence in the later development of the

United States and Mexico. The politics of the English and Spanish regarding the American Indian was determined in great part by this fact: it was not unimportant that the English founded their settlements in the territory of nomads and the Spanish in the lands of sedentary indigenous peoples.

The differences between the Spanish and English who founded New Spain and New England were no less prominent and decisive than those that distinguished nomadic Indians from sedentary ones. Again, it was a contrast within the same civilization. In the same way that the vision of the world and the beliefs of the American Indians sprang from a common source, independently of their way of life, the Spanish and the English shared the same principles and the same intellectual and technical culture. However, the difference between them, although of another type, was very profound, similar to that which divided an Aztec from an Iroquois. Thus, the new opposition between the English and Spanish was grafted onto the ancient opposition between nomads and sedentary peoples. The distinct and divergent attitudes of the Spanish and English have been often described. All of them can be summarized by a fundamental difference in which, perhaps, may be found the origin of the distinct evolution of our respective countries: in England the Reformation triumphed while Spain was the champion of the Counter-Reformation.

As we all know, the reformist movement had political consequences in England that were decisive in the formation of Anglo-Saxon democracy. In Spain the evolution came about in quite a different way. Once the last Moorish rebellion was finally put down, Spain achieved its precarious political unity, not its national unity, by means of dynastic alliances. At the same time the monarchy suppressed regional autonomies and municipal freedoms, shutting off the possibility of a subsequent modern democracy. Spain was deeply marked by Arabic domination and in this there persisted the dual inheritance of Christianity and Islam, the notions of Crusade and Holy War. In Spain, juxtaposed, without completely fusing, could be found the traits of the modern period that was just beginning, and those of the former society. The contrast with England could not be more notable. The history of Spain and that of its former colonies, from the sixteenth century on, is one of our ambiguous relationship—attraction and repulsion—with the modern era. Right now, at the twilight of modernity, we are still not modern.

The discovery and conquest of America are events that inaugurate modern history, but Spain and Portugal carried them out with the sensibility and temperament of the Reconquest. Cortés's soldiers, amazed by the pyramids and temples of the Mayas and Aztecs, could think of nothing better than to compare them with the mosques of Islam. Conquest and evangelization: these two words, profoundly Spanish and Catholic, are also deeply Muslim. The Conquest not only meant the occupation of foreign territories and the submission of its inhabitants, but also the conversion of the vanquished. In other words, it was legitimized by this process of conversion. The political-religious philosophy was dramatically opposed to that of English colonization: the notion of evangelization occupied a secondary role in English colonial expansion.

The areas dominated by the Spanish were never really colonies, in the traditional sense of the word: New Spain and Peru were vice-royalties, kingdoms subject to the Crown of Castile like all other Spanish kingdoms. However, the English settlements in New England and in other parts were colonies in the classical sense of the word, that is to say, communities set up in a foreign territory that preserved their cultural, religious, and political ties to the mother country. This difference in attitude was combined with the difference in cultural context that the English and Spanish found: nomadic and sedentary Indians, primitive and urban societies. The Spanish policy of submission and conversion would not have been able to be applied to the bellicose indigenous nations of the North with the same facility with which it was applied to the sedentary populations of Mesoamerica, as could be seen when, one century later, the Spanish Conquest extended to the nomadic territories, represented today by the northern part of Mexico and the South of the United States. The results of this dual and contradictory set of circumstances were decisive: without them our countries would not be what they are today.

The Spanish exterminated the ruling classes of Mesoamerica, especially the clerical caste, that is to say, the memory and understanding of the vanquished. The bellicose aristocracy who escaped this destruction was absorbed by the nobility, the church, and the bureaucracy. Spanish policy toward the Indians had dual consequences: on the one hand, as they were reduced to the realm of servants, they became a cheap work force and were the foundation of the very hierarchical New Hispanic society. On the other hand, having been Christianized, they survived both epidemics and their servitude and became, therefore, a constitutive part of the future Mexican nation.

Indians are the spine of Mexico, its first and its last reality.

To racial mestizaje must be added the religious and cultural aspects. The Christianity brought by the Spanish to Mexico was a Roman syncretistic Catholicism that had assimilated pagan gods, making them into saints and devils. The phenomenon was repeated in Mexico: idols were baptized and in popular Mexican Catholicism the ancient beliefs and divinities are present, barely coated by a thin film of Christianity.

The indigenous world impregnates not only the popular religion of Mexico but also the entire life of Mexicans: the family, love, friendship, attitudes toward the father and mother, popular legends, forms of courtesy and living with one another, the cuisine, the image of authority and political power, the vision of death and sex, work and celebration. Mexico is the most Spanish country in Latin America; at the same time it is the most Indian. The civilization of Mesoamerica died a violent death, but Mexico is Mexico thanks to its indigenous presence. Even though the language and religion, the political institutions and the culture of the country are Western, there is an aspect of Mexico that looks toward another side: the Indian side. We are a people between two civilizations and between two pasts. In the United States the indigenous dimension does not appear. This is, in my judgment, the greatest difference between the two countries. The Indians who were not exterminated were confined to "reservations." The Christian horror at the "fallen nature of man" extended to Native Americans: the United States was founded on a land without a past. The historical memory of North Americans is not American but rather European. Hence, one of the most powerful and persistent tendencies in North American literature, from Whitman to William Carlos Williams and from Melville to Faulkner, has been the search for (or invention of) American roots. It is the desire for incarnation, an obsession to establish roots in the American soil: to this impulse we owe some of the fundamental works of the modern period.

The situation in Mexico, a land of superimposed pasts, is precisely the opposite. The city of Mexico was built on the ruins of México-Tenoctitlán, the city of the Aztecs, which in turn was built like Tula, the Toltec city constructed like Teotihuacán, the first great city of the American continent. This continuity of two millennia is present in every Mexican. It does not matter that this presence is an unconscious one nor that it assumes ingenuous forms of legend and even of superstition. It is not so much knowledge as it is a *personal experience*. The presence of the Indian means that one of the facets of Mexican culture is not Western. Is there anything similar in the United States? Each one of the ethnic groups that form the multiracial democracy that is the United States possesses its own culture and tradition and some of these—for example: the Japanese and the Chinese—are not Westerners. These traditions coexist with the central North American tradition without any fusion occurring. They are strange bodies within North American culture. Even in some cases—the most notable is that of the Chicanos—minorities defend their traditions when faced with North

American tradition. The resistance of the Chicanos is not only political and social but also cultural.

Inside and Outside

If the distinct attitudes of Hispanic Catholicism and English Protestantism could be summarized in two words, I would say that the Spanish attitude was *inclusive* while the English was *exclusive*. In the first, the notions of conquest and domination are allied to those of conversion and absorption; in the second, conquest and domination do not imply the conversion of the vanquished but rather their separation. An inclusive society, founded on the dual principle of domination and conversion, had to be hierarchical, centralist, and respectful of the uniqueness of each group: a strict division of classes and groups, each one governed by laws and special statutes with everyone believing in the same faith and obeying the same master. An exclusive society had to separate itself from the natives, whether by physical exclusion or extermination. At the same time, since each community was an association of pure men, and separated from others, it tended toward an egalitarianism between them and to assuring the autonomy and freedom of each group of believers. The origins of North American democracy are religious and in the first communities of New England this dual and contradictory tension between freedom and equality, which has been the leitmotif of U.S. history, is already present.

The opposition I have just outlined is expressed with great clarity in two religious terms: communion/purity. This opposition deeply underscored attitudes toward work, celebration, the body, and death. For the society of New Spain work was neither redemptive nor valuable for its own sake. Manual work was *servile*. The superior man neither worked nor engaged in business: he waged war, gave orders, legislated. He also thought, contemplated, loved, courted, and enjoyed himself. Leisure was noble. Work was good because it produced wealth but wealth was good because it was destined to be used and consumed in those holocausts that are wars, in the construction of temples and palaces, and in ostentation and celebrations. There are distinct forms of the dissipation of wealth: gold glistens on altars or it overflows in *fiestas*. In Mexico, still, at least in the small cities and villages, work is the vestibule of *fiesta*. The year spins around the dual axis of work and celebration, accumulation and expenditure. The fiesta is simultaneously sumptuous and intense, lively and gloomy; it is a vital and multicolored frenzy that dissipates into smoke, ashes, and nothingness. The aesthetics, then, of perdition: the fiesta is inhabited by death.

The United States has really never known the art of the fiesta, with the exception in recent years of the triumph of hedonism over the former Protestant morality. This is natural: a society that affirmed so energetically the redemptive value of work had to reject as a kind of depravity the cult of the fiesta and the fascination for expenditure. This Protestant condemnation was more religious in nature than economic. But the Puritan conscience could not see that the value of the fiesta was precisely a religious value: communion. In the fiesta the orgiastic element is fundamental: it represents a return to one's origins, a going back to the primordial state in which one is joined to the great whole. Every true fiesta is religious because every fiesta entails communion and purity. For the Puritans and their heirs, work is redemptive because it liberates man and that liberation is a sign of divine selection. Work is a purification, that is, at the same time, a separation: the chosen one ascends, breaks his bonds to the earth, which are the laws of the fallen. For Mexicans, the notion of communion represents completely the opposite: not the separation but rather participation, not rupture but union, the great universal mixing, the great bath in the waters of the beginning, a state that is beyond purity and impurity.

The position of the body is inferior in Christianity. But the body is always an active power and its explosions can destroy a civilization. For this reason, the church undoubtedly made an agreement from the beginning with the body. If it did not restore it to the place it occupied in Greco-Roman society, it did indeed try to restore its dignity: the body is "nature fallen," but in itself, it is innocent. After all, Christianity, unlike Buddhism, is the religion of a god made flesh. The dogma of the resurrection of the body is contemporary with primitive Christianity; much later, in the medieval period, there appeared the cult of the Virgin. Both beliefs are the two highest expressions of this desire for incarnation in Christian spirituality. The two were transported to Mesoamerica by Spanish culture and they fused immediately, the first with the funereal cults of the Indians and the second with the adoration of goddesses of fertility and war.

The perception of death held by modern Mexicans, which at the same time is the hope of resurrection, is impregnated by both Catholic eschatology and Indian naturalism. Death for a Mexican is corporal, exactly the opposite of death for a North American, for whom it is abstract and disembodied. For Mexicans, death can be seen and touched: it is the body uninhabited by the soul, a pile of bones that, in some way, as in the Aztec poem, will again flourish. For North Americans, death is what you cannot see: the absence, the disappearance of a person. In the Puritan consciousness death was always present but as a noncorporal presence, a moral entity, an idea. Later, the rationalist and social-scientific criticism of Christianity evicted death from the consciousness of North Americans. Death evaporated and became unmentionable. Finally, rationalism and progressive idealism have been replaced in vast sectors of the North American population these days by a neohedonism. But this cult of the body and pleasure implies the recognition and acceptance of death. The body is mortal and the realm of pleasure is the instant, according to Epicurus, who understood this better than anyone. North American hedonism shuts its eyes to the reality of death and it has been unable to imagine the destructive power of the instant with a wisdom like that of the Epicureans of antiquity. Today's hedonism ignores moderation: it is a recourse of the anxious and desperate, an expression of nihilism that is consuming the West.

Capitalism exalts activities and behaviors traditionally called *virile*: aggression, a competitive and emulative spirit, and combativeness. North American society made these its values and glorified them. This explains, perhaps, why nothing similar to Mexican devotion to the Virgin of Guadalupe has appeared in any of the different versions of Christianity that North Americans profess, without excluding from this comment the Catholic minority. In the Virgin are linked Mediterranean and Mesoamerican religiosity, both with ancient cults to feminine deities. Guadalupe-Tonantzin is the mother of all Mexicans—Indians, mestizos, whites—but she is also a bellicose virgin who often has figured in the standards of uprisings among *campesinos*. In the Virgin of Guadalupe is embodied a very old version of femininity, which similar to other pagan goddesses does not exclude a heroic disposition.

Let me pause for a brief parenthesis: when mentioning the *masculinity* of North American capitalist society, I am not ignoring the fact that in this society women have achieved rights and positions that in other parts of the world are still denied to them. But they have obtained these as "subjects of law," that is to say, as neutral or abstract entities, as citizens and not as women. Our civilization needs more than just equal rights between men and women; we need a "feminization" similar to what occurred in medieval Europe's mentality by way of "courtly love." Or we need an influence like the feminine irradiation of the Virgin of Guadalupe upon the imagination and sensibility of Mexicans.... Let me continue: the social situation of the Mexican woman, because of her Hispanic-Arab and Indian legacy, is deplorable, but what I want to underscore here is not so much the character of relationships between men and women as much as the intimate relationship of the female with those elusive symbols we call "femininity" and "masculinity." For reasons I have mentioned above, Mexican women have a very intense awareness of the body. For them the body, theirs and that of the male, is a concrete and palpable reality. It is not an abstraction nor a function but rather an ambiguous and magnetic power in which pleasure and pain, fecundity and death are intertwined.

Past and Future

Pre-Columbian Mexico was a mosaic of nations, tribes, and languages. Spain, for its part, despite the fact it had achieved its political unity, was also a conglomerate of nations and peoples. The heterogeneity of Mexican society was the other face of Spanish centralism. The political centralism of the Spanish monarchy had as its complement, and even as its foundation, religious orthodoxy. The real, effective unity of Mexican society has been achieved slowly during the course of several centuries, but its political and religious unity was established from on high as the joint expression of the Spanish monarchy and the Catholic Church. We had a state and a church before we had a nation. Also, our evolution has been very different from that of the United States, in which small colonies of settlers had, from the very beginning, a notable and belligerent awareness of their identity vis-à-vis the state. Among North Americans, the nation was prior to the state.

Let us look at another difference: in those communities there occurred a fusion between religious convictions, the emerging national consciousness, and political institutions. Thus between the religious convictions of North Americans and their democratic institutions there was no contradiction but rather harmony. In Mexico, however, Catholicism identified itself with the regime of the vice-royalty, that was its orthodoxy. For this reason, when Mexican liberals tried to introduce democratic institutions after independence, they had to confront the Catholic Church. The installation of republican democracy in Mexico meant a radical break with our past and led to the civil wars of the nineteenth century. Those wars produced the militarism that, in turn, resolved itself in the dictatorship of the military caudillo Porfirio Díaz. The liberals defeated the church, but they could not establish a true democracy, only an authoritarian regime disguised as a democracy.

A third and no less profound difference: the opposition between Catholic orthodoxy and Protestant reformism. In Mexico, Catholic orthodoxy had adopted the philosophical form of neo-Thomism, a school of thought that was quite defensive in confronting the emerging modernity and, in fact, it was more apologetic than critical. In New England communities were often composed of religious dissidents or, at the very least, by believers in a free reading of scripture. So, on the one hand: orthodoxy, dogmatic philosophy, and a cult to authority; on the other, a free reading and interpretation of doctrine.

Both societies were religious, but their religious attitudes were irreconcilable. I am not thinking only of dogmas and principles but also of the way in which they practiced and understood religion. In the one case, for example: we have the complex and majestic conceptual edifice of orthodoxy, an ecclesiastical hierarchy equally complex, wealthy militant religious orders like the Jesuits, and a ritualistic conception of religion in which the sacraments occupied a central place. In the other: a free discussion of scripture, a poor clergy reduced to the minimum, a tendency to erase the hierarchical limits between the simple believer and the priest, a religious practice founded not on ritual but on morality and not on the sacraments but on an internalization of faith.

The basic difference, from the point of view of the historical evolution of the two societies, resides, in my opinion, in the following: the modern world begins with the Reformation, a religious critique of religion and the necessary antecedent of the Enlightenment. With the Counter-Reformation and neo-Thomism, Spain and its possessions closed themselves off from the modern world. We did not have an Enlightenment because we never had a Reformation or an intellectual and religious movement like French Jansenism. Hispanic American civilization is admirable because of many of its concepts, but it makes one think of an edifice of immense solidity—at one and the same time it is a convent, a fortress, a palace—destined to endure but not change. In the long run, the edifice became an enclosed world, a prison. The United States is the offspring of the Reformation and the Enlightenment. It emerged under the sign of criticism and self-criticism. And this we already know: he who embraces criticism embraces change. The transformation from critical philosophy to progressive ideology was achieved and reached its zenith in the nineteenth century. Rationalist criticism swept away the ideological heavens and cleansed them of myths and beliefs. At the same time, the ideology of progress displaced the atemporal values of Christianity and transplanted them to the earthly and linear time of history. Christian eternity became the future of liberal evolutionism.

The difference that I have just outlined is the final contradiction, and in it culminate all the divergences I have already mentioned. A society defines itself essentially through its attitude toward time. By reason of its origins and its intellectual and political history, the United States is a society oriented toward the future. The extraordinary spatial mobility of the North American people has been frequently pointed out, a nation viewed as constantly on the move. To this physical and geographic displacement corresponds, in the field of beliefs and mental attitudes, this movement in time. The North American lives at the extreme point of the present moment, always ready to jump into the future. The foundation of the nation is not in the past but in the future. Better said: its past, its birth certificate, was a promise of the future and every time the United States returns to its origins, to its past, it rediscovers the future.

Mexico's orientation, as we have seen, was just the opposite. In the first place, its ideal was to persist in the image of divine immutability. Secondly, a plurality of pasts, all of them present and competing within the soul of every Mexican. Cortés and Montezuma are alive and well in Mexico. At the moment of that great crisis called the Mexican Revolution, the most radical faction, that of Zapata and his *campesinos*, was unable to postulate new forms of social organization and offered only a return to the principle of communal ownership of the land. The rebellious campesinos demanded the return of the land; in other words, they wanted to return to a form of pre-Columbian property that had been rejected by the Spanish. The instinctive image that the revolutionaries created of the Golden Age was situated in the remotest of pasts. Utopia, for them, did indeed consist of building the future but in going back to their origins, to the beginning. The traditional Mexican attitude toward time has been ably expressed by Ramón López Velarde in this way: "Beloved country, stay always the same, faithful to the image in your daily mirror."

In the seventeenth century Mexican society was richer and more prosperous than the United States. This situation continued up to the first half of the eighteenth century. To confirm this, all we have to do is take a look at the monuments and buildings of the cities of that period: Mexico City and Boston, Puebla and Philadelphia. In less than fifty years everything changed. In 1847 the United States invaded Mexico, defeated it, and imposed terrible and onerous conditions for peace. A century later, the United States became the number one power in the world. An unusual set of circumstances of a material, technical, political, ideological, and human type explains the prodigious development of the United States. Among these conditions, the mix of attitudes that I have summarily described was no less decisive than the existence of an immense and rich territory, a population that was enterprising, and an extraordinary scientific and technical development. Again, in the small communities of New England the seeds of the future were already sprouting: namely, political democracy, capitalism, and social and economic development. The American Revolution was not a break with the past; the separation from England did not come about in order to change the original principles for different ones but rather to fulfill these principles in a more complete way. In Mexico the opposite occurred. At the end of the eighteenth century the governing classes of Mexico—especially the intellectuals—discovered that the principles on which their society was founded condemned it to a state of immobility and backwardness. They attempted a dual revolution: to separate themselves from Spain and to modernize the country through the adoption of new republican and democratic principles. Their models were the American Revolution and the French Revolution. They achieved their independence from Spain, but the adoption of new principles was rendered ineffective because Mexico changed its laws, but not its social, political, and economic reality.

During the first half of the nineteenth century Mexico underwent an endemic civil war and two foreign invasions, the North American and the French. In the second half of the century order was reestablished but at the expense of democracy. The worst part of all of this was the deception, a plague of all Latin American societies: in the name of liberal ideology and the positivism of Comte and Spencer a dictatorship was established that lasted thirty years. It was a period of peace and appreciable material development, and of increasing penetration by foreign capitalism, particularly English and North American. The Revolution of 1910 proposed to rectify the direction in which the country was headed. In part, it achieved this. I say "in part" because Mexican democracy is still not a reality and because the advances obtained in certain sectors have been nullified or find themselves endangered by the excessive political centralization, the unrestrained increase in population, social inequality, the collapse of higher education, and the actions of economic monopolies, among them, North American. The development of the Mexican state, like that of all states in the twentieth century, has been enormous, even monstrous. There is a curious contradiction in this: the state has been the agent of modernization but it has not been capable of modernizing itself completely. It is a hybrid of the Spanish patrimonial state of the seventeenth and eighteenth centuries and of the modern bureaucracies of the West. As far as our relationship is concerned: it continues to be the same old relationship between the strong and the weak, oscillating between indifference and abuse, deception and cynicism. The majority of Mexicans maintain, justifiably, the conviction that the treatment we receive as a nation is unfair.

The Dual Opposition

Beyond the topic of achievements and failures, contemporary Mexico confronts the same question that, since the end of the eighteenth century, most lucid Mexicans have not ceased asking themselves and it has to do with modernization. In the nineteenth century it was thought that the mere adoption of new liberal and democratic principles was enough. Now, after almost two centuries of stumbling, we have come to realize that nations change very slowly and that for those changes to be fertile ones they must agree with the past and the tradition of each nation. Thus, Mexico has to find its own road on the way to modernity. Our past must not be an obstacle but rather a point of departure. This is very difficult given the kind of tradition we have; difficult but not impossible. That was actually the profound sense of the Mexican Revolution: much before we did, Zapata's campesinos criticized *à outrance* the process of modernization. They did this through taking up arms. In order to avoid new disasters we must reconcile ourselves with our past. Only in this way will we succeed in finding a way toward modernity. The search for our own model of modernization is a theme that is directly linked to another: today we know that modernity, in its two versions, the capitalist and the pseudosocialist of totalitarian bureaucracies, is fatally flawed at its very core, namely, the notion of continuous and unlimited progress. The nations that had inspired the liberals of the nineteenth century—England, France, and, above all, the United States—today have grave doubts, are hesitant and unable to find their own way. They have ceased to be universal models. Mexicans of the nineteenth century turned their eyes toward the great democracies of the West: today we have nowhere to turn.

During more than thirty years, between 1930 and 1960, the majority of Mexicans were sure of the road chosen. Such certainties have disappeared and some wonder if it is not time to start all over again. But the question is not limited only to Mexico: it is universal. As unsatisfactory as the situation of our country may appear to us, it is not desperate, especially when compared with what is happening in other places. Latin America, with just a few exceptions, lives under military dictatorships protected if not funded by the United States. Cuba escaped the tutelage of the United States only to become the peon of the Soviet Union's policy of military aggression in Africa. A large percentage of the nations of Asia and Africa who achieved independence after World War II suffer under native tyrannies that often are more cruel and despotic than those of their former colonial powers. In the so-called Third World, with distinct names and attributes, there reigns a ubiquitous Caligula.

In 1917 the October Revolution in Russia ignited the hopes of millions; in 1978, the word *Gulag* had become synonymous with "Soviet socialism." The founders of the socialist movement firmly believed that socialism would not only put an end to the exploitation of men and women but also to war. In the second half of the twentieth century totalitarian "socialisms" had not only enslaved the working class, depriving it of its basic rights — those of free assembly and the right to strike — but they also covered the entire planet with the threatening clamor of their disputes and quarrels. In the name of distinct versions of "socialism" the Vietnamese and Cambodians decapitated one another. The ideological wars of the twentieth century are no less ferocious than religious wars. In my youth, it was popular to say that we were witnessing the final crisis of capitalism. Now we understand that the contemporary crisis is not one of a socioeconomic system but of all of civilization. The crisis is general, involving the entire world; its most extreme, acute, and dangerous expression is to be found in the Soviet Union and its satellites. The contradictions of totalitarian socialism are more profound and irreconcilable than those of capitalist democracies.

The infirmity of the West, more than social and economic, is a moral one. It is true that the economic problems are serious and have not been resolved: quite the contrary, inflation and unemployment continue to rise. It is also true that in spite of abundance, poverty has not disappeared. Vast groups — women, racial, religious and linguistic minorities — continue to be or continue to feel excluded. But the real and deepest discord is to be found in each individual soul. The future has turned into a region of horror and the present has become a desert. Liberal societies rotate tirelessly: they do not advance; they simply repeat each other. If they do change, they do not become transfigured. The hedonism of the West is the other face of its desperation; its skepticism is not wisdom, but a rejection; its nihilism leads to suicide and to inferior forms of credulity, such as political fanaticism and the illusions of magic. The vacant place that Christianity has left in modern souls is not occupied by philosophy but by the most vulgar superstitions. Our eroticism is now a technique, not an art, nor a passion.

I will not insist on this point: the description of the West's ills has already been presented many times. The latest, a few months ago, was that of Solzhenitsyn. He is a man of admirable courage. However, I must say that although his description seems to me accurate, his judgment about the causes of the infirmity and the remedy he proposes do not seem so. We cannot renounce the critical tradition of the West; nor can we go back to the medieval theocratic state. The dungeons of the Inquisition are not the answer to the camps of the Gulag. It is not worth substituting for the state-party the state-church, that is, simply, one orthodoxy for another. The only effective weapon against orthodoxies is criticism; in order to defend ourselves from intolerance and fanaticism we have no other recourse than to exercise, with firmness and lucidity, the opposing virtues: tolerance and freedom of spirit. I do not disown Montesquieu, or Hume or Kant.

The crisis in the United States affects the very foundation of the United States, the very principles on which it was founded. I have already said that there is a leitmotif that runs throughout U.S. history, from the period of New England's Puritan colonies up to the current moment: it is the tension between freedom and equality. The struggles of blacks, Chicanos, and other minorities are nothing more than an expression of this dualism. To the internal contradiction corresponds another that is external: the United States is a republic and also an empire. In an essay I wrote some years ago I pointed out that the first of these contradictions (the internal, between equality and freedom) was resolved in Rome with the suppression of freedom. Caesarism was, in the beginning, an egalitarian solution that, like all solutions implemented by force, led to a suppression of equality. The other contradiction caused the ruin of Athens, the first imperial republic in history.

It would be presumptuous of me to propose solutions to this double contradiction. I believe that every time a society finds itself in crisis, it looks instinctively to its origins and seeks in them, if not an answer, then a sign, an indication. North American colonial society was a free and egalitarian society, but also an exclusive one. Faithful to its origins, both in its internal policy as well as external, the United States has always ignored the *other*. In its domestic politics: the black, the Chicano, the Puerto Rican; in its external politics: all marginal cultures and societies. Today the United States confronts very powerful enemies, but the fatal danger comes not from outside but from within: it is not Moscow but a certain mixture of arrogance and opportunism, a blindness and a short-term Machiavellianism, a volubility and stubbornness that have characterized its foreign policies for the past few years and that recall, strangely, the Athenian state in its dispute with Sparta. In order to defeat its enemies the United States must first conquer itself: and return to its origins. But not for the sake of repeating them, rather to rectify them: the *other* and the others—the minorities inside its borders as well as the marginal peoples and nations outside—exist. We are not only the majority of the species, but each marginal society, no matter how poor it may be, represents a unique and precious version of humanity. If the United States is to recover its integrity and its lucidity it will have to recover itself and in order to recover itself it will have to recover all the *others*: those excluded from the West.

The First New Days
A Conversation with Roberto Fernández Retamar (Selection)

Sergio Marras

Roberto Fernández Retamar (1930–) is a Cuban poet, literary critic, essayist, and important spokesman for Fidel Castro and his government. For years he has served as the director of Casa de las Américas in Havana. While his poetry is highly regarded, it is in the area of the cultural essay that he has achieved his greatest acclaim. Among his most important works are: *Poesía reunida* (1966, Collected Poetry), *A quien pueda interesar* (1970, To Whom It May Concern), *Cuaderno paralelo* (1973, Parallel Notebook), *Revolución nuestra, amor nuestro* (1976, Our Revolution, Our Love), *Ensayo de otro mundo* (1967, An Essay of Another World), *Calibán* (1971), *Para una teoría de la literature hispanoamericana y otras aproximaciones* (1975, Toward a Theory of Spanish American Literature and Other Approximations), and *Nuestra América y el occidente* (1978, Our America and the West).

Sergio Marras is a Chilean journalist and former director of the political magazine *Apsi*. His works include *América Latina: Marca registrada* (1992, Latin America: A Registered Trademark), *Carta apócrifa de Pinochet a un siquiatra chileno* (1998, An Apocryphal Letter from Pinochet to a Chilean Psychiatrist), *Chile, ese inasible malestar* (2001, Chile, That Intangible Malaise) and *¿Por qué lloran los hombres?* (2003, Why Do Men Cry?). The following selection is from *América Latina: Marca registrada* (Buenos Aires: Grupo Editorial Zeta, 1992), 303–336. By permission of the author.

1991

It's cold in Havana, but those of us, the generation who dreamed, can't imagine it ever being cold in Havana. That's why we say it's warm on this night in Havana, at the José Martí International Airport.

He appears at the door to his office very early in the morning. He has a deep voice, strong enough to weaken all of the hurricanes in the Caribbean. He is the incarnation of Don Quixote. We've been told both good and bad things about him. For this reason, as we begin our conversation with him our potential prejudices find themselves in balance. Shortly after meeting him I realize he belongs to a class of epic individuals, to the Numantians, to that group of men who will die with their boots on, those who will be the last ones to leave the playing field. He is one of those who are capable of dying for a cause, even lost ones. A warrior, an Amadís.

Why are lost causes "lost"?

"Look, maybe what we know as real socialism has failed but I don't doubt for a second that real capitalism has also failed. What will come afterwards, no one knows."

He doesn't stop talking, defending, insisting on defending all those things that for everyone else probably seem indefensible: the uncontainable nature of limit situations for example.

"How can that guy Fukuyama believe that history has come to an end when we still haven't succeeded in putting an end to prehistory? That's what it's all about, my dear friend."

Who dares contradict him?

There are only a few armchairs, a desk, and a picture of Che in the room. He continually rocks in his chair almost as if he were pumping all the oil necessary to fulfill his role as a revolutionary intellectual.

Outside the revolution seems to be on its deathbed and at the same time this seems not to be the case. The Cubans are still standing and apparently they are relaxed.

How do you explain that since Martí the world has turned upside down? How do you explain beginning with Fidel, that what was yesterday is no longer today? What questions should I be asking on a day of high seas as I look at the *Malecón* of my youthful illusions!

"The truth is never sad, what it is is unavoidable," Joan Manuel Serrat sings on the radio.

"We are heaven's past," Silvio Rodríguez hums on the TV.

The problem is that it's cold in Havana for those of us whose generation dreamed. But, perhaps just as I never dreamed that it could be cold in Havana, I cannot help but feel the warmth of Don Quixote striking blows against the windmills of an implacable history. A dignified warmth, of course, that will succeed in melting more than just the ice.

The New First Days

Do you believe that in Latin America it has been writers who from the nineteenth century, perhaps even earlier, have shaped ideologically our republics and imposed an enlightened plan on our reality that did not always correspond to the European?

Yes, but only up to a certain point. We writers, I suppose, in all parts of the world, give voice to silence. We are spokesmen, as literary figures, of the communities in which we live. On the other hand, as you are very well aware, undoubtedly in our America the writer has fulfilled a role that goes much further than in other societies. Bergson[1] stated that Spain had no philosophy, only a collection of maxims. Perhaps the anecdote is false but it points to something I want to insist upon: philosophy, in the way in which it was understood by the Greeks and the great German philosophers of the nineteenth century, has been relatively underdeveloped in Spain and above all in Latin America. Here writers, in general, have invaded the philosopher's turf. It isn't possible to do a history of Latin American thought limiting it solely to philosophers and their peers, without including those who are traditionally called writers. If we're talking about Latin American thought we can't exclude Martí, Vallejo, Neruda, Sarmiento, Darío, Gabriela Mistral, Carpentier, Alfonso Reyes, and, finally, all of those colleagues you have interviewed for this book. In this sense, to return to your question, the fact that it has been writers, which is actually the case, who have managed concepts like those you mention does not mean that they have necessarily done this with their backs to their respective communities. I believe that they have done this giving voice to their societies.

But don't you think that sometimes these writer-politicians are wishful thinkers who mix a cocktail containing a certain amount of enlightenment and a certain romanticism and impose this mixture on others through a vertical institutionality, apparently libertarian, but at the same time with a good dose of Napoleonic pragmatism?

I'm going to be a bit brutish, because the situation is much more complex. There are thinkers who in effect have attempted to impose criteria that do not correspond to our realities. A classic example of this, because of his greatness, his talent and constant travels, is Sarmiento. There's no doubt that Sarmiento, who was an admirable writer, reflects that point of view you have described, that consists of trying to impose what he calls civilization, that is to say, the outline of a developed capitalist society upon our region, by which he ends up converting our area of the world, to the extent that he is successful in imposing his ideas, into what he himself calls a subsidiary. What an awful word! But, at least in the nineteenth century, unlike the twentieth, people were less deceitful and they spoke with more clarity. These thinkers tried to make of our countries a mere subsidiary of their respective metropolis, only not through a plan for equality but rather nourishing exclusively the seat of government.

In other words, you still believe that the development of a few countries is possible at the expense of the underdevelopment of others?

Yes. Some time ago I proposed to speak about underdeveloping countries in order to give a correct binary sense to the pairing underdeveloped-underdeveloping and not to the pairing of underdeveloped-developed as one is prone to do. Africa did not emerge underdeveloped. As a matter of fact, in the fifteenth century there were many levels of civilization in Africa, just as there were on other continents. The arrival of the European, of the emerging Western states and the furious depredation implied by all of this for the rest of the planet, has, up until today, disarticulated Africa in the most brutal way. As in the case of America, it destroyed its great cultures. When Sarmiento and thinkers like him proposed the imposition of civilization, what they did was simply to become spokesmen for the exploitation of underdeveloping countries. But not all Latin American intellectuals were like this. It was not the case of Bolívar. It is often said, and not without reason, that Andrés Bello was the one who, with his *Allocution to Poetry*, inaugurated what could be called the cultural independence of our America. However, I believe it was Bolívar who initiated that cultural independence. Bolívar's literary texts, which are prior to the corresponding texts of Andrés Bello, evidently set in motion that cultural independence. In his *Letter from Jamaica* he saw with great clarity our cultural specificity and the need to adhere to that specificity. There was also a brilliant figure in Chile: Francisco Bilbao. Even today it seems incredible to me that the work of a figure like Bilbao does not enjoy the diffusion it deserves since its author is truly indispensable. Bilbao assumed the point of view of the aboriginal inhabitants of this region and he gave voice to those people until these same communities acquired this voice on their own, something that has not been easy to do up to now.

I've been told on several occasions that I have counterposed Martí and Sarmiento and that this really makes no sense because it's a question of two different historical periods. But Sarmiento and Bilbao are from the same epoch and many of Bilbao's texts are anti-Sarmiento. Bilbao called him, ironically, the "civilized one."

For the majority of Chileans the name Bilbao is nothing more than a street...

The ignorance that I had at forty years of age concerning Bilbao and the ignorance, in general, that characterizes our continent regarding Bilbao, a figure that would greatly honor any community of human beings on this Earth, is only a part of a much larger problem that we are raising. There are many other figures we don't know in Venezuela, Colombia, in Central America who do not correspond to the type of intellectual that Sarmiento was, but rather to the type of intellectual who sought to interpret the reality of a country without imposing foreign models.

Martí would certainly be a model of this for you, no?

Of course, the archetypal model of this tendency is Martí. "Our America comes neither from Washington nor Rousseau, but rather from itself," he states. But even though Martí is as big a figure as you can imagine, he is not the only one. There is an enormous cohort of Latin American thinkers, even during the nineteenth century, who place their intellectual talents, generally developed in the great metropolises, at the service of their people. Not in a demagogic sense but rather in an organic, intellectual sense.

But in spite of this, don't you think that no matter how well intentioned these thinkers may have been, no matter how open they may have been toward their respective realities, in the final analysis what prevailed was a rationalistic, enlightened model, adorned with epic, romantic impulses, which, although they did not impose them by force, they did impose capriciously without concerning themselves about whether they were functional or not?

I believe that just as the mission of a carpenter is to build furniture and only a carpenter and not a fireman, nor an astronomer, nor a shaman can do it, so too the mission of a thinker is to produce thought. But that doesn't mean that the furniture a carpenter makes be used exclusively by a carpenter, nor that the thoughts produced by a thinker serve solely for consumption by other thinkers. To think is to give structure to reality. You can't scold a thinker for thinking.

The European and North American examples are very different. Although there are intellectuals who continue organizing and systematizing thought, the latter emerges from below, from the experiential, through successive contradictions, encounters, and struggles of all types. I have the sense that in Latin America this thought from below never moves in an upward direction, rather it remains within an elite, and from this vantage point norms of behavior and the rules of the game of the state are regulated.

I wouldn't take for granted that in the case of the United States thought emanates from below as you say. The great ideologues, to use a bad word or a word that has become bad, of North American independence—at least in the case of Jefferson—also thought from above to below. What happens, of course, is that, like a flash of lightning, or the glass pole that enters the water, they become refracted in accord with reality. One of the greatest texts in the history of humanity is the United States' Declaration of Independence, according to which every man is born free, and so on. But this did not prevent, during an entire century, this same republic, born out of such an important war for independence, from maintaining a system of slavery, which is the most flagrant of contradictions. Of course, and this is stating the obvious, not even the opinion of the slaves was taken into account. The men in favor of North American independence, who kept slaves for over a century, also exterminated the indigenous people who now live in concentration camps that today are called reservations. The concentration camps of Hitler and Stalin are a scandal to me, but why do we overlook the fact that they continue to exist on this continent? And in Europe of course something similar occurred. For this reason I said to you what is the alternative? I would like to know in the course of human history an alternative in which thought is not articulated first on the level of the thinker. This is something that occurs in even the best intentioned of cases, for example in Martí, Bilbao, or Mariátegui,[2] who wanted with the greatest desire to interpret the sense of the collective group. I don't believe for a minute, regarding all of this, that Latin American thinkers differ so much from thinkers from other parts of the world.

But we Latin Americans live in a world that is a dichotomy, a bit schizophrenic regarding the question of idea and reality. . . . Or don't you agree?

Undoubtedly there is a dichotomy between those who impose arrogantly their criteria, at the expense of doing harm to their respective societies, and those who make every effort to interpret such societies.

I have no desire to vent my disdain for Sarmiento, I've already said what I had to say about him and perhaps I went too far. But in some cases it's really terrible, because the implantation of Sarmiento's criteria in the case of Argentina was monstrous: his plan included the physical destruction not only of the indigenous people but also of the gauchos and even of the mixed bloods who were emerging in Argentina. It's terrible to read Sarmiento's instructions to the general in question, telling him: there is nothing more beautiful than to come back with your arm bathed in the blood of the gauchos. It wasn't Hitler who said that, and it wasn't in Germany that it was said. It was said precisely on this continent and it was Sarmiento who said it.

The case of Sarmiento and his theme of civilization versus barbarity is an unfortunate one, no?

I believe that men like him ended up being fatal for this continent and for all of our people. Fortunately, they didn't succeed in exterminating the entire Argentine populace. And in Argentina a very illustrative case occurred: Sarmiento and his disciples sought to whiten their country, a desire that was not unknown in Cuba. This was also one of the goals of José Antonio Seco,[3] one of our own. I'm from a neighborhood called La Víbora, a more or less humble neighborhood where once during its history there were two barber shops, one for whites and another for blacks. When does a Cuban cease to be white or cease to be black? Sarmiento and his cohorts encouraged the arrival of a large immigrant population in the hope that the backward Argentines, mixed bloods, and so on would be transplanted by these new arrivals. But with this immigration not only did future millionaires arrive, but also, in great numbers, future workers who in the end did not embrace Sarmiento's cause and were in reality Argentina's salvation. Because of them Argentina did not become another Rhodesia. In all of this I have entertained the idea that possibly Sarmiento would have been quite happy to be not a Latin American but rather a *latinoamerikaan*.

But do you consider yourself, more white or more black?

That is completely unverifiable. When I was a child my father, who was a professor, would take me to his classes and a colleague of his once said: how handsome your son is, he looks like an English prince. And I more or less introjected, as the psychoanalysts say, that very idea until the moment in which I had to face the reality that no Englishman would ever take me for one of their own while, on the other hand, when the nationalization of the Suez Canal occurred, my Arab friends, with whom I interacted, came and embraced and kissed me, speaking to me in Arabic, because physically I look like a Semite. Since I am of Hispanic origin, it is more than likely my ancestors were Arabs, Jews, whatever.

Does race exist for you?

No, because everything is relative. There is a type of human being who in Havana is called a white from the eastern part of the island, who in that very area where he comes from is considered white but in Havana is seen as a mulatto. I am a white person when contrasted with someone from Tanzania, but compared to those living in Finland it is obvious that I am a mulatto. But there really doesn't exist a boundary, simply because such a boundary doesn't exist in nature either. There are, of course, obvious physical features, including physiological characteristics, but these have no cultural nor historical repercussion.

Do you agree that in all of this thought about our founding fathers, whom you appear to admire, it is in the final analysis nothing more than a kind of syncretism of Romanticism and Iluminism, as Sartre would say, that integrates a ton of Western categories such as the concept of progress and historical stages with the epic, and these are concepts that have nothing to do, for example, with the great majority of the inhabitants of Mexico, with those of the highlands of Bolivia, or with the phenomenon of Cuban Santería? Doesn't it seem that these are people whose approximation to the world has more to do with Rulfo than with Marx, Rousseau, or Beethoven?

Actually, the thought of the Enlightenment, as Alejo Carpentier would say ironically, has been very strong in the founding fathers of independence. Romanticism was also very strong in figures like Bilbao; but when we get to Martí we're no longer talking about a thinker who emanates from the Enlightenment nor are we talking about a Romantic in the historical and concrete sense of the term, nor about a liberal. Martí easily transcends liberalism, even in its most radical aspects, and accedes to another stage of thought. A stage in which we still find ourselves. Some have suggested, I among them, but this is very debatable, that it no longer represents, as in earlier centuries, the point of view of a growing national bourgeoisie, which unfortunately became frustrated in all of our countries because it became little more than a pulley between the metropolis and the village. The ideological base of Martí, together with others like Betances and Hostos in Puerto Rico, is affirmed in the feelings of sectors that are much more popular in their makeup, those who belong to a small, radicalized bourgeoisie, of middle class and poor campesinos, of an incipient proletariat, and so on. My criterion is that Martí did not write the last stanza of the Bolivarian poem, but rather the first of another that is far from being conclusive and that has scarcely been outlined. Martí is not only the last of the great liberators of our continent in the nineteenth century, but also the first of them in our America during the twentieth century.

Why do you give such great importance to Martí? It would seem that he was some kind of oracle....

He's not an oracle, but he's not just any nineteenth century thinker either. In his last letter to the Mexican Manuel Mercado, which is unfinished, he says: "I'm in danger of giving my life out of duty because I understand the situation and I have the drive to accomplish it, that is, to prevent without further delay the United States from extending its domain as far as the Antilles and from allowing its great force to fall upon our America." It is no longer the last liberator of the nineteenth century who is saying this and proposing independence from Spain. Martí is proposing our independence from the new metropolis of our continent, namely, the United States. In this sense Martí is a key figure, he is an axis point in our America, in our action and in our thought. He establishes the basis for a task to come which is precisely what we are living dramatically at this moment in our history.

Why did Bolívar's dream or project fail? The Cuban Revolution was the last great attempt at realizing this dream, this project, and, well, there have been a series of problems that all of us are well aware of. Why has this become an impossible dream?

I believe it's not just a question of a project that has failed as much as that of a project that has been proposed. The reasons for which it could not be realized during Bolívar's time are objective and clear in nature. The thirteen North American colonies shared among them a level of culture they had inherited from England which, of course, our continent could not inherit from Spain because Spain did not have this level of culture and no one can give what you don't have. In the United States, an insertion in history was initiated by the English who led modern capitalism, which was simply taken a step further by the North Americans.

Our world, from Mexico to Tierra del Fuego, was a gigantic one with little or no communication. It was a world of countries or pieces, I don't know what to call them, that were very isolated from one another. Dispersed over an enormous continent, there were no structures or social conditions, either economic or geographic, which would allow Bolívar's great project to be realized. It was materially impossible for Bolívar to create the United States of South America because of the economic poverty and the immense spaces that existed between one country and another, not to mention the lack of political experience that characterized Latin America.

Do you continue to see this dream as a potentially achievable utopia?

I believe that Bolívar's dream is achievable, and as a matter of fact, time and time again this dream or project keeps reappearing under one name or another. It was reborn with Che Guevara. What was it that Che sought to achieve in Bolivia? Simply, to create a Bolivian army. Of course, this Bolivian army would not be oriented by the enlightened thought of Bolívar, but rather by the thought, let's call it socialist, of our days, but it is in any case part of Bolívar's plan.

But that took place almost twenty-five years ago and it was a resounding failure. . . .

We can't embrace Bolívar's project as is, because that would be a big mistake, but yes we can do it within the context of new circumstances that have emerged. . . .

But what happens to this Latin Americanist sentiment, for example, when you realize that today's Mexico, the great precursor of Latin Americanism, seeks a strategic alliance with the United States? Or the case of other countries, such as Chile and Venezuela?

I feel several things regarding this. The Mexican people are a great, very complex people; their country has tremendous problems and shares an immense border with the United States. And throughout Mexico's history it has made certain efforts to draw closer to the United States and one of these is certainly reflected in the Free Trade Agreement. But its action has not prevented Mexico from maintaining a very important attitude of solidarity with Cuba.

There is no doubt in my mind that government leaders have to be realistic. Perhaps the task of dreaming belongs to the poets, and the politicians have to be necessarily more realistic. No leader from this continent or from any other can be asked to stop being realistic and to cease confronting reality. If there were no blockade in Cuba, as there has been for the past thirty years thanks to the United States, which has forced us to link up with other countries at the expense of our sovereignty, I don't see why Cuba could not have trade relations with the United States. With what right would I censure a leader of some Latin American country for maintaining economic relations with the United States when we ourselves would have these same relations were it not for the blockade? Now do you think that those same leaders, because they do this, are going to hand over their respective countries to the United States? Frankly, I doubt it.

Don't you believe, even though it may appear strange, that perhaps the only possibility of attaining Bolívar's dream, with the next century in mind, would be to incorporate the United States within this dream?

It has been said that the convention proposed by Bolívar to foster his grand project that finally came to fruition in 1826 in Panama sought to exclude the United States. But it didn't turn out that way. There was a misrepresentation made by Santander[4] and in the final analysis that congress turned out to be a total disaster as all of us know. But we shouldn't forget that the instructions carried by the North American delegates were to boycott the convention. But the most important thing is that we are no longer in the times of Bolívar; it's no longer 1826 or even 1926; we are at the end of this century. Will an alliance with the United States come about? I want to tell you several things concerning this that may appear contradictory. Up to the present time there has been an imperialistic Pan-Americanism. But this is not the only Pan-Americanism that is possible. I am a firm believer in Pan-Americanism, but not in an imperialistic Pan

Americanism. Obviously, I believe, in spite of all the great differences that exist between us, that from one pole to the other there is something that we call America, and something that we call American, and that something reveals itself, among other things, in the identification that we feel with so many North American intellectuals who in Cuba are esteemed and loved. Some of them even lived in Cuba, like Hemingway, who is perhaps loved as much in Cuba as he is in the United States, and others, like Emerson and Whitman in the nineteenth century, are so important that it is difficult to conceive of our own thought and literature without them. I believe in America. But given the current circumstances, placing the United States and our countries in the same sack would really be to throw fresh meat to the lion. Changes are needed in us and in them for that Pan-Americanism to work harmoniously so that it's not just another name for the destruction to which we have been subjected. Will the external debt be eliminated? Will a new economic order be created? Will our primary resources be paid for at the price that corresponds to their value? Will we receive from the United States manufactured products at a fair price? If all of these conditions are fulfilled, I don't see why the United States could not be integrated into this greater America, especially at this moment when so many communities and so many countries on this earth are disintegrating.

Do you see such a union as better than an Ibero-American community?

I believe that we, so to speak, are tied into more than one community. An Ibero-American community has the advantage and disadvantage that Spain and Portugal are no longer great powers. As a matter of fact, they stopped being so in the seventeenth century and the advantage is that in not being superpowers they cannot exert dominance over our countries. Therefore, such an Ibero-American community is really a meeting of peers. As a matter of fact, if we take Spain's very important literature from 1898 to the present, it does not resist comparison with important Spanish American literature from 1898 to now. Without going any further, Rubén Darío, the father, the initiator of poetry in the Spanish language in this century, was not born in Spain but rather in Nicaragua and was educated in Chile.

I believe therefore that these communities that we have been talking about, the American and the Ibero-American, can come to be more than just a dream, something more than a mere utopia, in the most fleeting sense of the word, because, to a certain extent, they already exist. For example, Cuban music and the music of the Caribbean did not begin in the Caribbean but in the Deep South of the United States. There is an American cultural and musical community that goes from the South of the United States to the Northeast of Brazil, that leaps over hurdles, borders, political regimes, and so on. We are a cultural unity and in this sense we are already united.

And, beyond the cultural, do you see a political or economic alliance . . . ?

Unamuno used to say: you don't have to live in the now but in the context of centuries. I agree with him but, at the same time, you have to carry out certain small and great tasks that at times are dramatic in nature, as we Cubans have had to face and which we too have had to carry out. Not to mention other things, so that within a few centuries this potential design can become a reality. The United States is an extremely complex country, one that I know well and that I love a great deal. I detest the politics of the North American government but I hold no rancor whatsoever toward the people of the United States. I say this so that you see that I am not speaking like one of those enraged anti-Yankees for the simple reason that I'm not one of them. The United States, whose decadence is obvious and which has already begun even though it continues to be the leading military power in the world, is permeated by what earlier was called the "third world." Even some of its most eminent intellectuals are part of minorities. For example, Edward Said, a professor at Columbia University, is a member of the Palestinian National Council as are a host of Latin Americans. Within a very short time the largest Spanish American country will be located in the heart of the United States. . . . That is great, and it's the way in which the Roman Empire was eaten away from within. Immigration acted like a force of termites and this is something that is not going to stop because, as the economic situation in our countries gets progressively worse, migrations to the United States will be even greater. A lot of people have left Cuba because they disagree with the Revolution but very many people have also left for economic reasons, which is something that has always occurred in this country. So if the United Sates changes drastically, why not think that things can be different? This will not come about tomorrow, and it's not going to be with President George Bush, I really don't know under what president it will occur, but change is on the way, because basically change is inevitable. If certain changes are produced, which would mean that the United States would no longer seek to devour us, I don't see how we could deny such a reality.

Until a short time ago the models to be followed by Latin Americans were the United States on the one hand and Cuba on the other. To a certain degree these two paradigms have been seriously questioned in Latin America. Do you believe that a new model has to emerge?

In general, I don't like the term model, and I never apply it in the generic sense to Cuba's case. I have to tell you that I don't believe in models,

I don't believe in the Cuban model or in any other. I don't believe at all that another Latin American country should entertain the idea of carrying out another Cuban Revolution. I do believe, however, that in the margins of models and plans, there is a notorious failure not only of the United States, whose decadence has begun, but also of a capitalism dependent on Latin America, and on this it seems to me that finally we Montagues and Capulets can all agree.

According to you where will this general decadence lead us?

It will lead sooner or later to revolutionary situations in Latin America and this will engender new realities that at this time I cannot foresee. I almost dare to say that happily I cannot foresee them. I don't want to know about the future, I simply want the future to surprise me. As a matter of fact, after the Cuban Revolution there were important processes taking place on this continent, none of which assumed or repeated the Cuban model. I recall the immense happiness we felt, I remember it as if it were yesterday, when the Popular Unity triumphed and then the triumph of Allende in the presidential election. A Soviet friend of mine said to me: but how can you Cubans be so happy when this triumph in Chile is the triumph of another socialist way that is not yours? Let's be brutally frank, it's not the path of a *guerrilla* that has garnered power but rather that of elections. I replied to her: we aren't enamored with the means but rather with the ends. If Allende actually succeeds in unleashing a socialist process through his way, that in itself is a joy that will fill all of us with glory in the final analysis.

If there was on this continent a government leader who had the audacity and the courage to carry forward another distinct process of reform it was Allende.

I remember when I was in the United States in 1982 and saw the movie *Missing* by Costa Gavras. I watched it with tears in my eyes. I cry, I have to admit this, like Tomás Borge, I cry when I see a movie of this type. But what terrified me as I watched this movie was how in it the North American conscience was to a certain degree cleansed and was preparing itself for new misdeeds. Where now? In Cuba? In Nicaragua? In El Salvador? With an honesty that is exemplary the United States, its journalists and its ethical politicians always recognize the country's crimes, albeit a little bit too late.

But that movie is a thing of the past. Now there have to be other premieres....

Yes. Reflecting seriously on this, the United States must change drastically so that this entente that you speak of can become a reality. The United States' model, its plan has lost its attraction for the world but it still has an immensely powerful army. When I lived in modest neighborhoods there was always the neighborhood bully waiting on the corner and you had to go into the street with a rock in your pocket because if the bully appeared you would let him have it. Latin America has a giant bully to the north and you have to be careful where you walk, because when you least expect it he invades your territory. Just as he did in Cuba in 1961, the Dominican Republic in 1965, Grenada in 1983, and Panama in 1989. How will we ever enter into some kind of union with this gangster? How could you imagine my meeting with this bully without carrying forty rocks in my pockets? It's impossible for us to surrender meekly to this union while the bully continues his abuses. This type of union is one of the lion and the lamb. I believe that the lions should join with the lions and what we should propose, what our goal should be, is to become lions and not Rotarians. When we succeed in becoming lions then we'll meet with that other lion, but in the meantime, what we cannot do is go inside the lion's cage so he can eat us up piece-by-piece, which is precisely what he wants. As a matter of fact, it bothers him, it bothers him immensely, everything we do collectively. We are in the presence, to put it in the most academic term possible, of a shameless local gangster whose name is the government and administration of the United States. I have nothing against the North American people, in fact I esteem them so much that I hope that someday they can get rid of that administration and that government and at that moment we will sit down together at the negotiating table whether it be in Iowa, in Cordoba, in Havana, or anywhere else.

What did you feel when the Soviet Bloc came crashing down?

It wasn't good news. On the other hand, one has to make certain distinctions. The situation in Eastern Europe was the situation of countries where the socialist revolution had arrived at the point of the Red Army's bayonets, and for this reason it was a very difficult situation, because although it is true that the problem of basic material needs was solved, it was also true in these countries that no one felt they had a government that they themselves would have created. In the case of what was the Soviet Union, there was indeed a real revolution. But there is no doubt that there were also grave problems in the interior of the Soviet Union that all of us recognize. Those problems were revealed a long time ago by the opposition movement to Stalin. Who hasn't read, for example, Trotsky. Many of Trotsky's texts that I have reread, now seem to be very pro-Soviet, it's quite curious. *The Crimes of Stalin, The Betrayed Revolution* . . . The other day one of the leaders of the Cuban Revolution said to me why talk about a thinker like Deutscher,[5] whose book *The Unfinished Revolution* seemed to him to only help the Soviet Union? Those problems, on the level of politics, were denounced by Khrushchev in 1956, so that actually all of this thinking was already part of the public domain. And all of this occurred three years before the Cuban Revolution. For that reason when they link us to Stalinism, they're really stating an anachronism. And so, what happened, happened, and for me it is not good news. The Soviet Union should have undertaken major reforms, to overcome the difficulties of the system and advance toward a socialist horizon and not retreat toward a past within capitalism. That's my reply.

In any case, if I were an historical entomologist, which I'm not, I would take a good long look at that anthill to examine the world's first case in which a pacific movement, as the Chinese would say when they were at odds with the Soviets, occurred from socialism to capitalism. It really isn't a pacific one, but for the time being we are witnessing that involution. Because for me capitalism is something evil, it doesn't have to be so for the rest of the world, but since I see it as something bad, it's not good news to hear that socialism is undergoing an involution toward capitalism. The true challenge began with Gorbachav's initial postulates of *perestroika, glasnost,* and so on. If only they had overcome the profound problems that existed—bureaucratic, ideological, economic—and attempted to go further. But it was done this way, and the result is they have gone back instead of forward.

Don't you believe that capitalism has some virtues?

I don't believe that capitalism is a good system, I don't fail to recognize its virtues, but I believe that its defects far outweigh its virtues. I believe that it implies a great deal of suffering, an enormous misery. I am not ignorant of how capitalism was formed. It's interesting, sometimes, when you read Marx's *Das Capital* to remember this. One tends to forget that Marx was not an economist, but rather a revolutionary who studied economics, which is quite different. And there are several pages in *Das Capital,* for example, where Marx describes how the English field-workers were stripped of their lands, and finally left on rocky terrain that they could no longer cultivate so that they became proletarians. And thus was invented the proletariat, in a terrible way. I do not forget that page in which Marx did little more than transcribe the famous English blue books of the factory inspectors. . . . It is there that we see how the original accumulation of capital came to be. On the one hand it was done to the detriment of the rest of the world by enslaving it: Africa, Asia, America; and on the other, it emerges through the violence perpetrated on its own people. That's what is known as the accumulation of capital. How are the countries of Eastern Europe going to produce the original accumulation of capital? Are they going to participate again in world distribution? Who are they going to exploit? Because, as far as I know, without such exploitation there would be no England, no France, nor Germany nor the United States. I repeat, I cannot look sympathetically upon such an involution. If they are not going to produce this original accumulation of capital based on the pillaging of a world already divided up and pillaged and based on the exploitation of its workers, how will they carry it out? It's something I ask myself. I am always moved to know that a man in England can place a box that once contained codfish in Hyde Park, stand up and say whatever he wants, with the exception of attacking the monarchy, and this is a precious manifestation of liberty. I regret that it also was done at the same time in which Gandhi was ordering his followers to lie down on the tracks of the British rail system in India as a form of protest to stop the trains, the English did not stop them, and, finally, when the harangue of that admirable dreamer in London came to a halt in Hyde Park there were thirty thousand dead men left on the English railroad tracks. Freedom that is achieved at that price is a great shame; the freedom that the United States enjoys today is also a great shame because it has been achieved at our expense. This freedom presupposes our enslavement, poverty, exploitation, and misery.

Notes

1. Henri Bergson (1859–1941), a French philosopher who opposed the neo-Kantians, Positivismo, and materialism. His principal works dealt with the questions of knowledge, memory, and intuition. He was a member of the French Academy and received the Nobel Prize for Literature in 1927.

2. José Carlos Mariátegui (1895–1930), Peruvian politician and man of letters. He was the editor of the journal *Amauta* from 1926 to 1930, and was a leader in the struggle for the civil rights of indigenous peoples. Included among his principal works are *Siete ensayos de interpretaciión de la realidad peruana* (Seven Interpretive Essays on Peruvian Reality) and *Escena contemporánea* (The Contemporary Scene).

3. José Antonio Saco (1797–1879) was a writer from a leading Cuban reformist group. His principal work is *La historia de la esclavitud* (The History of Slavery).

4. Francisco de Paula Santander (1792–1840) was a Colombian military official and politician. Upon the death of Bolívar, his political enemy, he served as president of New Granada from 1832 until 1836.

5. Isaac Deutscher, historan and biographer. Among his principal works are *The Political Biography of Stalin* (1949), the *Biography of Trotsky* (1954–1963), and *The Unfinished Revolution* (1967).

The Historic Significance of the United States

Armando Roa

Armando Roa (1915–1997), one of Chile's most renowned psychiatrists, was the author of more than two dozen books and founder of the journal *Clinical Psychiatry*. As a member of the University of Chile's Medical Faculty he was the first to offer courses on ethics to his medical students, which eventually led to the creation of the Center for Bioethical and Humanistic Studies in 1988. Through his profound knowledge of philosophy, anthropology, and literature he brought a new approach to the humanistic aspects of medicine. The selection here is from his *Chile y Estados Unidos: Sentido histórico de dos pueblos* (Chile and the United States: The Historic Sense of Two Nations) (Santiago: Dolmen, 1997), 63–69, 72–77, 91–93. By permission of Armando Roa Vial.

1997

Since the beginning of the twentieth century the United States has played a preponderant role in the destiny of the world and, for even longer, in the destiny of this hemisphere. We have become accustomed to seeing the United States as an epilogue of the West, a civilized, concrete example of European culture, and this disturbs our historical judgment; we cannot understand how a country that was purely imitative, oriented above all toward the production of material goods and the epitome of estrangement from the creation of civilization itself, could somehow possess an undeniable dynamic value.

It is true the United States has not participated directly in the birth of philosophy, the arts, or Western science, nor even in the most theoretical formulations: relativity, non-Euclidian mathematics, quantum physics, linguistics, psychoanalysis, phenomenology, existentialism, structuralism. It is, however, imperative not to make a mistake here, because its contribution to the creative development of such fields of knowledge is undeniable with respect to their point of departure in Europe. In medicine, for example, one of the United States' most fertile areas, even though it did not take the initiative in such notable discoveries as bacteria, internal secretions, conditioned reflexes, genetic codes, sulfonamides, penicillin, antipsychotic drugs, and anxiolytics, which emerged in other countries, it has, nonetheless, taken the derivations of these discoveries much further.

If the United States were merely a country in constant imitation of others and with an almost primeval nostalgia for comfort and technology, as it is habitually characterized as, then it would be always waiting for new forms invented by Europe and would take them "passively" and would therefore be unable to free itself from the imperialistic logic of countries that provide it with cultural values.

The transplantation of European civilization to the United States is evident: technical progress, mechanization, computerization, comfort, the speed of public transportation, among others all depend to a critical degree on electricity, optics, chemistry, and biology. But, and this is what is interesting to prove, these technologies have not been imitated "passively"; rather they have been grafted onto a North American cultural structure that is original and profound; only in this sense an assimilation of foreign forms does not pose a danger, quite the contrary, it represents a natural tendency of a vigorous culture. As a matter of fact, it can be asserted that computer science, in spite of its remote origins, was born and developed in North America, opening up a whole new historic era.

On the other hand, cultures that are alive tend to expand "their truth" throughout the world and imperialism represents, in the material sense, this tendency. History causes the two classic stages of every country to coincide with its universal hegemony. Just remember what happened in Chaldea, Persia, Greece, Carthage, Rome, and Spain in the sixteenth and in England in the seventeenth and nineteenth centuries.

In other words, while we viewed North America as a kind of copy of Europe, the history of its present appeared incomprehensible to us. Little by little, we have come to discern the primary cosmic attitude of this country and today we consider it distinct from the cultures of Europe, South America, and other countries around the world.

Being on the Surface

The first North American characteristic that draws our attention for its importance is the presence in its cultural manifestations of a world without mystery. It is almost as if it saw a being's intimate essence turned outward, facing man and converted into a succession of phenomena susceptible to investigation, and in this way these beings appear infinitely knowable and controllable. For the United States the occult is not, to a certain extent, a nature that is different from the known, and what can be taken in by the senses includes the intelligible and even the question of identity.

North American culture is not interested in earlier philosophical hypotheses about ontological cosmic structures; it trusts that with science and technology the question of being will be opened up to it immediately; it goes to this essence, studies it, investigates and uses it. Being, apart from this, possesses worth in this context, to the extent that it serves man. Truth is proven in its practical performance, as William James has stated. There is no room for pure philosophical knowledge in a world the United States perceives as illumined; activity, the intimate utilization of all that exists, comes to play a fundamental role.

The oriental perceives in the sensorial a veil of being itself and Heraclitus, in Greece, still believed that "nature enjoys hiding itself." For the European the sensorial and the intelligible are realities and knowledge and dominion over them, even though they may be attained through the use of Kant's categories, is authentic. The European, however, maintains a kind of self-withdrawal because despite everything, he knows there are densities that he will not be able to penetrate.

The United States is the country that converts metaphysical depth into mere surface, into something visible and, consequently, into mere phenomena capable of being conquered.

As an example of what has already been asserted, we notice that painting in the United States, in general, lacks perspective: the chiaroscuro, the play of shadows and light, allowing the most important aspects to be conjectured behind what is visible to the eye, is practically alien to this art. Its architecture, taken as a whole, is one of precise forms and flat surfaces; interiors that are completely illuminated do not allow for corners of mystery nor capricious reliefs that elude the rational. The skyscraper, one of this country's inventions, in its initial stages was a very useful and novel type of building, but until recently it was alien to the question of space as a beautiful, autonomous, creative reality, alien to that vital space that is so important in gothic and baroque architecture. The space of the skyscraper was conceived in the beginning as an operative place for human work; its worth was reflected in its efficiency. Later it became more beautiful, acquiring a certain nobility. Some architects like Lloyd Wright and others open new horizons full of a powerful imagination in this architecture, which seemed, however, not to contradict the general spirit, the orientation toward sensorial light, which has always been typical of U.S. culture.

This way of looking at reality's face is also reflected in its literature. Poe attempts to make us understand that the mystery of things is really the work of the emotions, of the somber and dark atmosphere, and of a technical defect in our way of penetrating them. With diligence, patience, and effort even the most obscure situations, the most unexpected and intricate occurrences uncover their logical explanation, and finally reveal themselves as something completely natural. Keep in mind his admirable elucidation of crimes, where everything that was an impenetrable enigma suddenly appears as pure clarity.

Whitman is perhaps the most diurnal of Western poets; he has eliminated the night; he knows the miracle of the sun, the dazzling aspects of the human body; he is almost the antithesis of Holderlein and Rimbaud:

Book III: Song of Myself

To behold the day-break!
The little light fades the immense and diaphanous shadows,
The air tastes good to my palate

Dazzling and tremendous how quick the sun-rise would kill me,
If I could not now and always send sun-rise out of me

We also ascend dazzling and tremendous as the sun,
We found our own O my soul in the calm and cool of the daybreak.

There is an abyss between the world of Whitman and the South American world intuited by Neruda in which the enigma is the impenetrability of matter, the life underneath such matter in the midst of its dark interior, of its existence that, at times, is spectral in nature:

Someone who waited for me among the violins
discovered a world like an interred tower
sinking its spiral farther down than all
the hoarse sulfur-colored leaves:

farther down, within geology's gold,
like a sword enveloped in meteors,
I sank my turbulent and sweet hand
into the earth's most profound genitals.

The Value of Corporeality

Since there is a parallel or identification for North Americans between the external and the internal, each and every thing actually reveals its structure through its own physiognomy; the form that the surface takes comes to be primordial. Forms taken in by the senses are no longer fortuitous for the real; they emerge out of necessity, no other ones could have resulted. The more perfect the being the more rigorous this specific physiognomy which reveals precisely this degree of perfection. We owe to the North Americans the highest comprehension of the metaphysical value of "the surface," of that which is observable by the senses, either directly or indirectly, comparable only to that comprehension which, through other means and from other roots, emerged from the heart of the Egyptians. For the European the human body with the form it possesses presents itself as a fact because of biological causes, without one being able to offer any intimate reasons; for the North American, the human body presents itself as a right, since all reality can be reduced to the observable and the scientifically investigative. Such a conviction impregnates the North American's entire culture. In brief, this culture is the only one built on the corporeality of entities, and as long as we do not understand this principle, the North American's power and the type of freedom he retains will remain enigmatic to us.

In North American culture the human body, for example, contains explicitly everything that matter encloses. Dead things are formless, just as their matter is formless and chaotic; in man the same matter has been ordered and vigorously open. Man is the world made word; we can read in him the entire universe. If he speaks sincerely from his very self, he always speaks the truth. The inanimate is that same man as potentiality. Such is, for example, the fundamental thought of Emerson, very different, it is true, from that of Fichte, who, however, seems to influence him profoundly. In Fichte man evolves through thesis and antithesis until he attains the infinite; in his nature light and darkness struggle in search of the Spirit; in Emerson man is a closed and luminous totality who is barely affected by time.

The North American vis-à-vis the Socioeconomic

If the body is an absolute and unrepeatable reality, one can understand why it must not be jeopardized at any price. Love, in the sense of a total sacrifice of the self or asceticism on behalf of a more perfect and free life, but depriving the body of its physical pleasure, are concepts that are far from comprehensible to the North American. A culture such as his always tends to save and exalt the corporal. Comfort and technology are not only simple means as in Europe; they possess the rank of fundamental ends.

The North American family is not something that is very strong from within; it lacks in its depth the reciprocal sentiments of integration and solidarity. Tied by biological, emotional, and economic links, it comes apart easily as soon as one of its members feels that his rights have not been satisfied or respected, and one reaches an age in which dependence among its members is no longer necessary. Ties to the paternal home are not very strong.

Naturally, there is love, but it reaches souls almost exclusively by way of the body. Eugene O'Neill has captured this well in *Strange Interlude*, in which the value of the individual, physically and physiologically, reaches an extreme in the arousal of love.

In novels such as *The Grapes of Wrath* and *Tobacco Road*, for example, the immediate relationship of the family to the economic possession of the land is an interesting one. Every emotion is linked to possessions, to the property of wealth and well-being; it is not a question of loving the land because one was born on it or because of nostalgic ties to it, but to the extent that the possessed is better known and therefore able to obtain a greater yield when it is worked. Without a doubt there is a sensitivity for the beauty of the landscape and one's contact with nature, but this does not signify an affective tie to a specific land.

In the face of any threat of poverty the land is abandoned and in such behavior there is a world of difference between the North American and the South American. The "huaso," the "gaucho," the plainsman, the fisherman, the shepherd in Tierra del Fuego share the same attitude, forming a direct unity with the soil; that is where the soul is to be found, in that specific land there is an "ontological" something that does not exist in any other. Often they can find better economic conditions somewhere else, but they reject them—unless extreme abject poverty threatens them—when confronted with the irresistible attraction of the sea, the plains, or the jungle in which they were born. The South American *caudillos* administer their countries as if they were haciendas and it is this metaphysical sense of the land that makes such *caudillos* consider themselves organically masters and one with the land; they incorporate it into their very being.

The North American novel and theatre often establish themselves within the realm of a socioeconomic problem and also within the principal solitude of the individual who, within his perfect completeness, feels emotionally estranged from the other. The community is almost only about material interests. The economy is the first objective value in a culture of corporeality. Instead of the psychic problems of European characters—or of the economic by way of the psychological—instead of the South American relationship man-land, there emerges as the illuminating destiny of life the antithesis of wealth-poverty. In *Emperor Jones* by O'Neill, there is no fear of a loss of empire (a lack of a sense of honor) but of the loss of riches; and in his flight the emperor has only nightmares about corporal suffering: he sees himself punished, offered for sale as a slave, surrounded by fantastic monsters, and so on. In all these works the supreme tragedy is man threatened corporally and economically, and a famous one, *Uncle Tom's Cabin*, was in fact born out of the horrible punishment and corporal torture to which the slaves were subjected.

Imperialism and Democracy

The conception of each individual as distinct from another gives rise to two important facts: the North American considers the destiny of his corporeal self as superior to any other destiny and according to this perception he is capable of triumphing over all kinds of obstacles including the bellicose invasions of other peoples, to assure his own prosperity. As soon as his well-being is assured, he feels for others the respect of all spirits toward the absolute, an extreme respect for privacy, a living moralism. Thus emerges the exploitation of countries under his dominance, which pays no attention whatsoever to any moral precept when wealth is a consideration, nor to democracy, with its respect for human rights, minorities, and the supreme value of each man for the simple reason of his being one, without relying on questions of social or economic class, or race, or physical appearance.

In no other country outside the United States, at least to the superficial eye, would friendship, the social relationship of equality, for example, between a plumber's wife and that of an entrepreneur, banker, or senator be so presented, even though given a deeper analysis of the situation one notices a certain disdain for the poor, for people of color, for those who profess specific religious faiths. Looking down upon the poor also has its origin in considering poverty a symbol of punishment due to sin, in accord with a certain Protestant mode of thinking, according to Max Weber. God rewards the persistent virtue of work and frugality with economic power, the source of independence, comfort, and corporal freedom. In addition, this is a strongly held belief of some of the branches of Protestant religions.

The North American aspires to wealth in order to save his body from nature's contingencies and also to pamper it to the maximum degree. Once having achieved this he can then devote himself to what remains: power and apparent political dominance. That is why his imperialism is so different from that of other countries; and we should add here that the type of imperialism practiced reflects the type of culture being described. He is not fundamentally interested in political power over the countries he dominates, but he is very interested in economic power, which allows him to use these countries when he needs them. He intervenes militarily when his meddling in other countries runs into danger. In this way, and without the costly risks of European-style colonialism, he exercises his hegemony, at times disguised, over a large part of the world.

The Culture of Corporeality

When speaking of corporeality and the world as a surface, we wish to underscore that these are personal experiences so rich, attractive, and enigmatic that they have always preoccupied and fascinated man. In fact, very significant countries over the course of history have been dazzled by them—take the case of the Egyptians for example—and converted them into a dynamic center of their culture. Culture is, to a certain extent, the image of the world of each country in relation to what it considers a worthy human destiny and, up to the present time, almost no country has centered that destiny to such a degree on the preservation of a body that was always youthful, agile, healthy, efficient, beautiful. If we think for a moment about the corporal organism, the exact functional and specific relations between near and distant cells, the biochemical transformations occurring in infinitesimal time, the importance of the visible form in social success, and all of this on the margins of consciousness, we begin to see how far we are from a simple sketch of corporeality. This word evokes, as far as the spirit is concerned, the most mysterious and enigmatic of worlds. We find ourselves in the presence of a mystery when we realize that the deepest level of organic wisdom, with its vitality, harmony, and rhythm, is achieved outside the intervention of conscious knowledge.

Thus, in our judgment, North America adds another truth to history. Technology is not, as is often commonly believed, the important thing for North Americans, because technology is also European, rather what matters to them is a universe of values created around fundamental experiences of individualized corporeality that have yielded as a result a furor for technology and democracy, to the extent that these favor a kind of happy state which implies a relationship with the utmost corporal pleasure.

The United States and South America

Pan-Americanism proposes the uniting of our destiny with that of North America based on the concept of geographic unity; however, it is absurd to assume as the fundamental cause of one's destiny the question of spatial relationship. Such destiny involves bodies and souls who hardly allowed themselves to be determined exclusively by space.

Between the culture of corporeality and the South American world centered on the essence of matter in itself, seen as something profoundly sacred, fierce, intimate, multiple, and qualitatively diverse in each of its existent forms, there is a great abyss. That essence Neruda compares with wood, Borges with a labyrinth, and in Rulfo and García Márquez it appears as a subtle matter, immutable, in which each individual repeats himself in his individuality across generations, as if everything continued to be the same, except for the constructs created by man, which in his hands tend to become ruined, disintegrate, grow old: it is similar to a constant tendency toward the ruin of nonhuman material and an eternal return of the human individual, a world, in any case, bearing little resemblance to the ebullient European Darwinian world and the North American world in which the individuality of man is unique in each one and ends with death.

For the South American, even the earth becomes fragmented into places with their own soul, while the North American perceives it essentially as something more or less neutral, identical, horizontal.

In certain aspects we are closer to Europe; our attitude regarding being is perhaps more objective—like the European—and for this reason we do not presume it to be totally clear nor more explicit in our personal structure, nor radically cognizable or controllable. We tend more toward transcendence. We love the body, but our terrestrial purpose is to discover, through the corporal sign, the secret of ourselves and of the things around us.

The distance between Emerson and Lacunza—a South American genius from the past—is the same that exists between the world free of original sin of the Man-God and the fallen world redeemed by the God-made-Man, who lives the expectation of salvation through the process of conquering the world.

When two cultures, which is the same as saying two cosmic images and two destinies, are divergent, they cannot be joined artificially except at the expense of the weaker.

Thus the cultural invasion of North America—and not its mere influence, which is desirable and valuable—contains a danger for our own very existence if we do not affirm our mode of intimate being, if we do not try to develop our own institutions in art, philosophy, the sciences, daily existence and at the same time if we do not seek elements from cultures that preceded ours so that we do not become blinded by the excessive light of the most recent culture.

Spanish America should collaborate with North America and with other countries to the extent that it belongs to a universal collectivity, it should assimilate the most it can from all of them, but without forgetting that just as the social common good is precisely that to the extent it serves people, the universal, historic good is truly this to the degree that it vivifies the soul of every country.

Countries have a precise mission and they cannot be estranged from it because of circumstantial interests, without flirting with chaos. Men live only when they establish harmony between their life and their culture. Only the person who works for the growth of his culture works for the good of mankind. In this respect we do not believe in the "cosmopolitanization" of cultures, as it is fashionable to call it today, and which represents one of the many assertions of our so-called postmodernity.

A Wall of Lies

Mario Vargas Llosa

Mario Vargas Llosa (Peru, 1936–) is one of Latin America's most important novelists and essayists. His novels *La ciudad y los perros* (1962, The Time of the Hero) and *La casa verde* (1966, The Green House) made him an instant success and one of the principal writers of the Latin American boom of the 1960s. In addition to these two books some of his most memorable works include *Conversación en la catedral* (1969, Conversation in the Cathedral), *Pantaleón y las visitadoras* (1973, Captain Pantoja and the Special Service), *La tía Julia y el escribidor* (1977, Aunt Julia and the Scriptwriter), *La Guerra del fin del mundo* (1981, The War of the End of the World), *Historia de Mayta* (1984, The Real Life of Alejandro Mayta), *La fiesta del chivo* (2000, The Feast of the Goat), and *Travesuras de la niña mala* (2006, The Bad Girl). In 1990 he ran for the presidency of Peru as a candidate for the Frente Democrático but was defeated by Alberto Fujimori. His experience of running for political office is reflected in a fascinating memoir entitled *El pez en el agua* (1993, A Fish in the Water). He was awarded the Nobel Prize for Literature in 2010. The following essay first appeared in the Spanish newspaper *El País* on October 22, 2006. By permission of Agencia Literaria Carmen Balcells S.A., Barcelona.

2006

The Congress of the United States has approved a bill calling for the construction of a 700-mile (approximately 1,200 kilometers) wall along its border with Mexico that will cost a total of seven billion dollars, to stop illegal immigration. President Bush has promised to enforce the law immediately. For someone like me who is writing this and is fascinated by the contamination of reality by fiction, this news couldn't possibly be more bewitching. Why? Because this wall will never be built and if, by some miracle, it were, it would serve absolutely no purpose. This is something everyone knows, beginning, of course, with the legislators who approved its construction as well as with the U.S. president himself.

Why, then, all the theatrics? Because on November 7th elections will be held to replace all the members of the House of Representatives, as well as a part of the Senate and state governments. The congressmen who seek reelection wish to use their approval of the bill as proof that they have begun to act forcefully against the dangerous Satan embodied by illegal immigrants, who take jobs away from U.S. citizens and exhaust the funds of Social Security (another striking fiction).

The wall of lies will go through four states: Arizona, California, New Mexico, and Texas, and will consist of two barricades and a futuristic system of lights, fences, sensors, and all kinds of radar to ensure that it is absolutely impenetrable. Now, what purpose will it serve to shut off in this way some 1,200 kilometers when another twelve hundred miles of border (about 2,000 kilometers) remain open and across which Mexican, Central American, and South American immigrants can slip into North American territory without serious problems if they should wish to avoid the discomforts of trying to pass through the barricaded and electrified sector?

But these are mere conjectures without any deep roots in reality, in which the construction of this fictional wall, in order to materialize itself, will have to overcome a myriad of obstacles already anticipated by the U.S. media, which, I have to confess, I read, listen to, and watch, with great pleasure, in newspapers, radio, and television. For the time being, a countless number of mayors and governors from the four states to be traversed by the wall have already let it be known that they will demand that the millions to be spent on the construction of the wall should instead be invested in the repair of infrastructure—highways, schools, and public service installations. Several indigenous communities have also raised the roof threatening lawsuits to prevent the construction of the wall from breaking up their cultivated and grazing lands while other electoral districts, left out of the construction plan for the fantasy wall, are threatening judicial action for being discriminated against. But more than anything else, it is the powerful environmental organizations who have come to the fore explaining that they will use all of their political, judicial, and civic resources to prevent this plundering and contaminating monument from being built because it would cause serious devastation to the environment. The marvelous part in all of this is that the legislators, trying to cure themselves before the illness takes hold, have inserted a tricky clause into the law that allows the government to use part of the wall's budget for the construction of roads!

If the wall in question were to survive the great number of judicial obstacles that await it and that, in any case, will paralyze its construction for many years to come, the wall will not serve in the least to cut off the entry of undocumented immigrants into the United States. There are countless ways to demonstrate something that is there right in front of you, and anyone who can see and who is not blinded by prejudice will recognize the malignant fiction that proposes that immigrants do more harm than good to the host country. This morning the press here in Washington indicated that according to an official report, "Hispanic" immigrants just last year sent to their families back home the astronomical sum of 45 billion dollars, 60 percent more than two years ago, when the last research on this topic was carried out. From this figure, the biased deduce that these immigrants are causing a terrible hemorrhage of North America's patrimony. But a true reading of this figure should evoke, on the contrary, a feeling of admiration and enthusiasm since it means that these immigrants from Latin America produced for the United States last year a wealth that is four or five times greater, that is, money that has stayed within its borders and served to increase the nation's revenue. And 200 to 250 billion dollars is an appreciable contribution to an economy that, as all statistics have shown, is enjoying at this time an extraordinary bonanza and has the highest index of employment of all the world's developed countries (barely 4.5 percent unemployed).

But to understand why this imaginary wall will be unusable—an involuntary and rampant sculpture rising and falling among the gorges and mountains of Arizona and scarring the California and Texas deserts—rather than using mere statistics, which hardly ever convince anyone, it would be better to tell the story of Emerita (I'll call her that because I know several Guatemalan women with that pretty name). I met her three years ago, when I spent another semester, as I am now, here in Washington. She was recommended to us by neighbors, who had her clean their house twice a week. We hired her and she did a magnificent job, because in the two hours that she was with us with her polishers and vacuum cleaner and dusters, she would leave the house as spotless as a Swiss butcher shop. At the time she charged us sixty dollars for those two hours.

Now, back in Washington, we were lucky to hire her again. This time she charged ninety dollars per day. Actually, she's giving us a discount, because all of our neighbors pay her one hundred dollars for this service (which is performed, in the majority of cases, by Hispanic immigrants). Emerita is a Central American who has been in the United States ten years now and she makes out quite well with her English. She has a late model Buick station wagon and ultra-modern equipment for sweeping, polishing, cleaning, washing, and dusting. On Saturdays — she works six days a week and rests on Sunday — her husband helps her; the rest of the week he works as a gardener. I don't know how much he earns, but Emerita cleans an average of four houses a day, and sometimes five, which means that she has a monthly income of no less than 8,000 dollars. For this reason she and her husband have already been able to buy themselves a house here in Washington and another in their native country.

Before coming to the United States, this couple could barely survive economically, living at a bare subsistence level. But the worst thing about it, says Emerita, wasn't that "but rather the fact there wasn't any hope of making a better future. That is the big difference in the United States." Yes, in effect, that is the enormous, the overwhelming difference, and that is why so many thousands, tens of thousands, millions of Latin Americans, who know the story of Emerita and her husband, follow in their footsteps, escape their failed countries, where there is no hope, and they come to this one, crossing rivers, climbing mountains, hiding in vans or paying countless and very efficient mafias who obtain false passports, visas, permits, and anything else they might need to enter the United States where — they know this and that's why they come — they are awaited with open arms. The real test is that all of them obtain work almost immediately.

They are the jobs, of course, that U.S. citizens don't want to do. Cleaning houses, taking care of the sick, working as night watchmen, roasting under the hot sun as fruit and vegetable pickers, and in the factories and businesses performing the most elementary and precarious tasks. Nobody but these Latin Americans are willing to do such hard work and considering the standard of living in this country they are badly paid for what they do. But as far as they're concerned, they are not; for them those bad salaries are a fortune. And, therefore, those same U.S. citizens who rant and rave about the dangers of immigration hire them without the least objection, because, thanks to the Emeritas of this world, their houses are left shining, their factories running, and thousands of institutions and services are kept busily engaged.

The only way to halt immigration is for Mexico and Central and South America to begin offering their very impoverished masses better opportunities and the hope of advancing and improving their lives that Hispanics encounter in the United States and that is the great inducement for them to break their backs working day and night, in whatever they undertake. All of this is wonderful for them, of course, but, even more than for them, it is wonderful for this country—a country of immigrants, something we shouldn't forget—that, thanks to the energy and spirit of sacrifice of these 40 million Latin Americans, continues to prosper and grow despite the very difficult political and international problems that it now faces.

The 7 billion dollars it would cost to build the wall of lies would be much better used, as far as illegal immigration is concerned, if, instead of wasting this money on a fiction of cement, which, if it did exist, would soon become a wall with more holes in it than a Swiss cheese, it were invested in factories or credits destined to create jobs on the other side of the border, or if the United States were to completely open up its markets to Latin American products, which, in addition, would benefit enormously local consumers. But all of this belongs strictly to the realm of reality and it's well known that human beings—including *gringos*, who pride themselves on being practical—often prefer the magic of fiction to unadulterated harsh reality.

PART TWO

Travelers from the South

Moral Geography

Domingo Faustino Sarmiento

Domingo Faustino Sarmiento (Argentina 1811–1888), educator, man of letters, politician, diplomat, is one of the outstanding representatives of Argentine romanticism of the nineteenth century. Because of his intense opposition to the dictatorship of Juan Manuel de Rosas and his Federation he was forced to seek exile in Chile, where he lived almost continuously from 1831 to 1851. During these years he was a journalist for *El Mercurio*, wrote countless books and articles, and even served as a representative of Chile in the United States, Europe, and Africa. During his stay in the United States, he became a close friend of Horace Mann, whose educational ideas he later transplanted to Argentina when he served first as its minister of education and then as president from 1868 to 1874. Among his most important books are *Facundo: Civilization and Barbarism* (1845), *Travels in the United States* (1847), *Recollections of a Provincial Past* (1850), and *On the Condition of Foreigners* (1860). The selection included here is from *Travels: A Selection*, translated by Inés Muñoz (Washington, D.C.: Pan American Union, 1963), 175–192.

1847

I have given you a picture of the way of life in the United States. If it is not the foundation of its prosperity, in any case it is a reflection of it, just as man's fingers are the faithful servants of his thought. Moreover, there is a moral geography in this country, the chief function of which I must point out. Taking the foundation for granted, you will appreciate the civilizing currents that carry improvements, enlightenment, and moral progress to all parts of the Union.

You know the history and the position of the thirteen original states of the American Union. For two centuries England implanted here great political and religious ideas. Bancroft has made an inventory of these ideas, showing the locality where each took root: the Pilgrims in New England, the Quakers in Pennsylvania, the Catholics in Maryland. That colonization was not so much one of men who moved from one country to another as it was of political and religious ideas that required air and space in which to expand. Its result was the American republic, prior to the French Revolution. The Declaration of the Rights of Man [sic], made by the United States Congress in 1776, is the first page of the history of the modern world, and all the political revolutions that follow on the earth will be a commentary on those simple principles of common sense.

The Declaration of Independence was like the "Be fruitful and multiply" uttered by the God of the Hebrews. From that time on, ideas and men began a march toward the interior; the republic began to create territories that later became states, like a polyp that throws out new arms from its body. Notice the development of the South American republics and see what a difference there is. Chile has subdivided her ancient provinces but without increasing her populated territory nor the number of her cities. The ancient United Provinces of Rio de la Plata see their territory dismembered and made into feeble, absurd states, while those provinces that still bear the name of Argentina lose population daily, while the groups of ancient cities die out, like lights that are extinguished. In 1790, for example, Maine had 96,000 inhabitants; in 1800, 151,000; 228,705 in 1810; 1,372,812 in 1820; 1,918,608 in 1830; and 2,428,921 in 1840.

Another movement of expansion is added to this movement of concentration. Mississippi appears in 1800 with 8,850 inhabitants, and in 1840 it has 375,651 inhabitants. Arkansas is not heard of until 1820, when she shows a population of 14,273, which by 1840 has grown to nearly a hundred thousand. In 1810 Indiana had 4,762 inhabitants, and 685,866 thirty years later. Recently Ohio, with a population of 40,365 in 1800, showed an increase of more than a million and a half. You may well be amazed at this deluge of men, which the early settlers in a barren desert saw arrive and establish themselves in the surrounding country. I was shown a man who was not yet old, who had seen the birth, development, and growth of one of these states. Whence come these men, since there are no longer Deucalions who produce them by throwing stones behind themselves? Although the immigration from Europe appears to be very large, it ranks second in the successive waves of immigration. The old, or adult, states produce those who keep appearing. The Indian hater goes ahead, scattering the members of this strange instinctive sect, whose only dogma is to persecute savages and whose only wish is to exterminate the indigenous races. No one has commanded it: he goes alone into the forest with his rifle and dogs to hunt savages, pursue them, and make them abandon their fathers' hunting grounds. After these men come the squatters, misanthropes in search of solitary dwelling places, the emotion of danger and deforestation as a pleasure. At a distance come the pioneers, opening up the forests, sowing the earth, and spreading out over a vast area. On their heels come the capitalists with their projects and with immigrant laborers, building cities and villages where the terrain makes it advisable. Another set of immigrants follows immediately, to stake claims, settle, and take root. They are young, industrious, and mechanical minded and come from the older states to make their fortunes.

In this growth of the North American population there are different and very marked degrees of civilization, little noticeable at the extreme points. This is due to the dispersal of the inhabitants in the West, and the rude labor in the fields, and in the South to the presence of slaves and to Spanish and French traditions. A half century would suffice for the incurable barbarism of our Argentine countryside to be revealed at the extreme points of the Union, were it not that the vital, regenerative elements surrounding our country keep the masses in a constant state of movement and prevent the distant sections from complete degeneration and stagnation.

Strange to say, in this country the European immigration is an element of barbarism! The Irish or the Germans, the French or the Spaniards—with a few natural exceptions—come from the needy classes and, as a rule, are ignorant and always unaccustomed to the republican methods of the world. How can one make the immigrant suddenly understand the complicated mechanism of municipal, provincial, and national institutions and, above all, indoctrinate him with the Yankee's passion for these institutions, so that he regards them as part and parcel of his very existence to such a degree that, if he carelessly neglects them and all they represent, he fears that his life and his conscience are both endangered? How to accustom the foreigner to the town meeting in which the townspeople often gather together to express their sentiments? And, once this has been done, and a series of "and be it further resolved" has been voted, how to make him feel that relief and unburdening experienced by the North American, as if he had performed a deed or vanquished the opinion he opposed? And so, in this manner, the foreigners in the United States are a seed of trouble, a leaven introduced yearly into the bloodstream of that nation that was educated long ago in the practices of liberty. The Whig political party—the most reasonable group—has often tended to limit immigration and especially to prolong the period of time required for an immigrant to become a citizen and enjoy full political rights. A native party—today extinct—tried to create a sort of fanatical nationalism, similar to our own Americanism, although due to very different motives. But at the first signs of trouble, interest waned in the new states. The older states did not need the foreigners since they were already densely populated and held little attraction for newcomers. But it was very different in the western states, which from time to time cheapened citizenship, vying with each other in lowering the term of residence and omitting some of the requirements.

The social organization of the nation has very efficient means of combating the relaxation of the elders' discipline caused by the spread of the population throughout the countryside. But these means were ineffectual because of the steady influx of hundreds of thousands of *I bàrbari* from Europe while there were thousands of millions of acres of forests that could be felled. Permit me to enumerate the purifying and cultural forces that are so attractive and so important.

The daily mail is the most obvious force. The mail comes to the doors of every distant village and a newspaper will contain a topic for conversation as well as information about events in the Union. You can realize that it is impossible to remain a barbarian when the mail, day by day, is doing away with the indifference born of isolation. Do not forget that the mail travels over 134,000 miles and in some places has the aid of the telegraph.

I omit the civilizing and stimulating influence of the daily newspapers.

Trial by jury frequently summons men from the country to come together to judge criminal cases. The uncouth judge hears the accusation and the defense weighs the evidence, compares laws, becomes accustomed to the procedure, and decides conscientiously. The jury system has created a horrible civil crime, known as Lynch Law, where the crime is not punished by legal procedure. Jesus said: "Wheresoever three shall be gathered in my name, I will be with you," and Lynch Law says to the Yankee in the forest: "Wheresoever seven of you shall come together in the name of the will of the people, justice will be with you." Beware in the far West or in the slave states of arousing the ire of seven judges, who are more terrible than the invisible judges of the secret tribunal of ancient Germany. The law permits and those grim consciences feel no more remorse than did the Spanish inquisitor who witnessed the burning of the victim that this cunning had led to the stake. Thus religion and democracy become criminals when their principles and objectives are exaggerated.

The election of a president has an equally civilizing influence. The North American votes fifty times a year. The candidate defeated in the election for director of public instruction throws himself with the same ardor into the election for sexton of his chapel; if he loses he hopes with redoubled fury for the post of attorney, representative, or governor of his state. Nor is he any less excited over the necessary elections for changes in the chamber of deputies, and for a whole year he cherishes ill will against one candidate for the presidency and for the other. Then the Union is really shaken to its foundations; the squatters emerge from the forest like shadows summoned up by a conjurer. The fate of each one of the forest dwellers depends upon the outcome; they feel their very existence is threatened if the Whig candidate—regarded as a reactionary—triumphs. If the election is not what they hoped for, they clench their fists and return to their homes, vowing to revenge themselves when they vote for the pastor of their sect.

The presidential election is the only bond uniting all the extremes of the Union; the only national interest that simultaneously moves all the citizens and all the states. The electoral contest is, therefore, a rousing influence, an education and a stimulant arousing the life that has been dormant because of distance and rough labor.

But the greatest influence is that of religious sentiment. A lukewarm Catholic arriving here from our countries would surely be amazed to see how high religion is held in the midst of so much liberty. One finds the Bible everywhere throughout the Union; from the log cabins in the woods to the rooms in the large hotels. It works for good or for evil, according to the effects of the daily reading of it. I say for evil because attachment to the letter of the text produces disastrous consequences in narrow minds. For a long time the law of Moses was the rule in New England, exactly as it stands in every verse and phrase of the Bible, as the ideal of perfection. On board a ship there was talk about the marvels of chloroform. A doctor assured the group that it could be used without danger in childbirth. "And would you use it for your wife?" asked a Puritan who was present. "Why not?" answered the doctor. "I would certainly not use it," answered the questioner seriously. "That would depend upon how much confidence each one has in its efficacy." "No, sir; it says in Genesis: 'The woman shall bear with pain'; you would go against the will of God." As you see, the question of chloroform was viewed from the standpoint of conscience and its usefulness measured by the yardstick of the Bible.

The Yankee's nasal accent, more pronounced in the interior of the country, comes from the daily reading of the Bible. But in spite of this slight inconvenience, it has other great results. Although history is distorted, the moral precepts and evangelical phrases remain in the reader's memory, and the minister's sermons refer to points which the listener knows but whose significance has escaped his untutored mind, with the result that he desires further enlightenment. So the words fall like rain upon thirsty soil, not as often happens with our common preachers whose words are cast to the wind in public squares, spiced with vulgarities that serve as stimulants when they reach the public's ignorant minds. The polemics of the various sects give force to these sermons, and a man's whole life is not long enough to penetrate the many mysteries in his sacred book. Sixty-seven theological schools spread religious science throughout the Union, whereas there are barely ten schools dedicated to law, producing, nevertheless, more than twenty thousand lawyers. The number of original works on that subject in the United States is three times larger than the works devoted to scientific investigation. This national trait will render this nation an entity apart from the rest of the modern world.

Itinerant preachers who travel continuously through the remote countryside keep the sacred fire alive. They are rough, energetic men who spend their lives in this mission, carrying this ferment everywhere, awakening the spirits and arousing the people to a contemplation of eternal truths. These are true spiritual exercises, like those of the Catholics, but more spiritual because they do not threaten the people with the pains of Hell. The pastor or pastors, united in a religious meeting in the open air or in an improvised shed, arouse the sluggish minds of the country people, and present them with an image of God in a grandiose, inconceivable form. When the stimulus has proved effective, they send the women to one part of the woods and the men to another, that they may meditate alone and contemplate their insignificance, their helplessness, and their moral defects.

The results of this moral cure are strange and accountable. The women become delirious; they turn and twist around on the ground, foaming at the mouth. The men weep and clench their fists until finally a religious hymn, sung in chorus, begins slowly to soften this saintly bitterness. Reason is regained, consciences are calmed; and a profound melancholy, mingled with an expression of moral goodness, appears on all faces, as if sentiments of justice had been strengthened by the purification of the spirit. Unbelievers who have witnessed these scenes in the country attribute the strange effects of the word to the excitement produced in the brain by elevated ideas in people who, on account of the monotony of their isolated lives, spend months without feeling any pleasurable or painful emotion. This is a drama between God and his creature, and the action of the drama keeps awake the audience, which is the most lively part of the play. Perhaps the brain moves like other parts of the human body. In any case, the inhabitant of the Far West in no way resembles the uncouth pastor or laborer of our countryside, since he is fully prepared to hear the divine word through the reading of the Bible and the theological commentaries of the divines. But what seems to me important in all this is that, by means of the religious exercises, the theological discussions, and the itinerant preachers, that great human mass lives in a state of ferment and the mind of the most remote inhabitant is awake, alive, and ready to receive all kinds of culture. This resembles a cask that—regardless of the quality of the liquid it contains—continues to be usable; but if it remains empty, the staves become twisted and the hoops loosened, and with the action of time and weather the cask becomes useless for all time.

There is still room for another civilizing element; the most active in carrying on the religious, political, and industrial life in these towns, filled with the ancient spirit of the colonies and imbued with the modern ideas of progress. They are the descendants of the old Pilgrims, the heirs of their traditions of resignation and able to endure the hardships of manual labor. They are also the elaborators of the great social and moral ideas that make up the North American nation—the inhabitants of the New England states: Maine, New Hampshire, Massachusetts, and so on. Here you have the Brahminical race of the United States. Like the Brahmins who came down from the Himalayan Mountains, the inhabitants of these old states have spread to the western part of the Union, educating by their example and practice the new centers of population that have arisen without skill or science on the face of the scarcely deforested land. You will remember that the Pilgrims were one hundred and fifty wise men, thinkers, fanatics, enthusiasts, politicians, and emigrants, tempered by all the hardships that can befall men. You, doubtless, remember that they did not wish any servant to embark with them when they left the shores of Europe, so determined were they to till the soil with their own hands and not recognize any social inequalities in the new country they were going to establish in America. And you will recall that they gathered together beneath an oak where Boston now stands, and, after giving thanks to the God of Israel for their safe arrival, they discussed what laws to set up for the glory of Jehovah and their personal freedom. And finally, you will remember that in that epoch these men established public schools and obliged the parents, tutors, or guardians of children to give them elementary spiritual education and teach them manual work for their bodies' sustenance. Well then, the sons of that select portion of the human race are today still the teachers and directors of new generations. It is believed that more than a million families throughout the Union are descendants of that noble stock. They have impressed upon the Yankee physiognomy that calm goodness one notices in the more educated class. They spread throughout the Union the aptitude for manual skills that makes a North American a peripatetic teacher; they also spread the iron will that combats and overcomes difficulties, as well as moral and intellectual traits that put him at the same level, if not on a higher plane, as the best in the human race. These emigrants form the North exert a disciplining influence upon the new towns and infuse their spirit into the meetings which they promote and preside over. At the same time, they instill the practice of the American institutions into the schools, books, and the elections. The great colonizing enterprises—railways, banks, and associations—are begun and carried on by these men. So it is that the uncouthness resulting from isolation in the woods and the relaxation of republican practices introduced by the immigrants are checked by the descendants of the Puritans and the Pilgrims. Consequently, there is an ebb and flow between these two opposing forces, and no matter how rapid the spread and mingling of people may be in the Union, in the long run there will be a homogeneous people who will conserve the new original type and the traditions and progress that distinguish the inhabitants of this country. Does anything like this occur in such a constant and striking manner anywhere else in the world?

You may believe that these instruments of national culture and refinement, being heirs of the Puritans, retain their ideas unchanged and constitute a separate sect. From the religious point of view, the United States presents the same spectacle as do the customs and the surface of the earth. In no part of the world can it be said with greater truth that God is made in the image and likeness of man. The North Americans have the lofty ideas concerning God that, in their essence, have been transmitted from the Hebrews by way of Christianity. But the religious sects and practices are adapted to the popular intelligence. They either descend to a kind of fetishism, lacking only idols and magic powers, or ascend to pure philosophy—deism—without losing their profoundly religious character or abandoning the great moral teachings of Christianity. As in all eminently religious countries, today there are in the United States saints, prophets, messengers from God, as well as visible ascent and descent of the Holy Ghost and communion between heaven and earth. New religions are being born and promise to embrace all the world; the Mormons are of yesterday and their inspired members and high ecclesiastics perform miracles. In witness to this, while I was living in the United States, an irreverent man discovered that the pale light that shone from the face of a holy man was caused by rubbing phosphorous on it. The venerable prelate was not daunted and claimed that all miracles had been prepared in this manner, and there was no falling off in the faith and fervor of his followers who today are more than a hundred and fifty thousand.

There are dancing religions, and the faithful, after hearing the pastor's prayer, fling themselves into dancing until the spirit of the dance possesses them. Then they start making frantic and indescribable contortions. They finally fall down, crazed and exhausted, believing themselves to be inspired. As I have seen in Paris, the *bal Mabille*, the *Reine Pomaré*, and Rigolette and other celebrities perform fantastic pranks, I am not easily impressed by these manifestations of the Holy Spirit. On a higher plane there are more respectable varieties of Christians in the United States, such as Baptists, Methodists, Presbyterians, Congregationalists, Christians, Episcopalians, Lutherans, Reformed Germans, Roman Catholics, Friends, Universalists, Unitarians, and other sects, among which I include pure deists; for such is the tolerant and religious spirit of the country that the negation of all religion—which we call impiety—forms a separate sect against which no voice is raised. As an example of the comparative numerical strength of these sects, I note that the Baptists have 1,130 churches and 1,907 ministers; the Catholics, 912 churches and 54 priests; the Unitarians 200 churches and 174 ministers; and the smaller sects proportionately few churches and ministers.

I have used the word "tolerant" in the genuine sense the Americans give to this word. The religious sects in the United States form real confraternities and religious nations, in spite of their intermingling with others in the cities and in the country. The doctor, the clerk, the butcher, the family apothecary, and even the shoemaker must belong to the same faith as his employer. There is an undeclared war, and proselytism in a sense. But tolerance is shown by the indifference with which a Methodist will listen to a criticism of his dogmas by a Catholic and vice versa, because the Catholics in the United States, who profess religious intolerance as a dogma, are like those tigers without teeth or claws that are raised in a house. Up to now no one has heard of Catholics having bitten anyone in the United States, where they enjoy religious liberty to the full, although every year they save souls from the tempter's deceitful wiles.

This religious chaos, these hundred contradictory truths, are gradually undergoing a change for the better. While the Mormon barbarism is making progress, the religious philosophy of the descendants of the Pilgrims influences the lower social classes, bringing the opposing viewpoints nearer together and creating bonds between them. Eventually these sects will be absorbed into the Unitarian group, a new sect that is pantheistic in that it admits all differences and respects all baptisms through which grace has been transmitted. It aspires toward loftier regions and, discarding all religious interpretations, unites in a single embrace Jews, Mahometans, and Christians. It dispenses with miracles and rites as mere rhetoric, and as being incompatible with the organic form given by God to the human spirit. The only dogma they admit is Christian morality as the expression and rule of human life, as a point of union available and acceptable to all nations. This is their only dogma, as virtue and humanity constitute the only cult and the only practice recommended to believers.

This religious philosophy has spread rapidly in the six New England states, with its center in Boston, the Athens of North America, and its adherents are the most learned men in the states.

As you can see, the Puritan spirit has been active for two centuries and moves forward toward peaceful and conciliatory aims, always progressing without warring against existing conditions. It influences conditions without violent destruction, as was attempted by the philosophy emanating from Catholicism in the eighteenth century and which has made little headway. If you remember the religious spirit in Franklin's writings, you will note that these ideas have already appeared in the philosophy of common sense started by that great practical man.

I end all this, my good friend, with something that will make the Good Yankees' hair stand on end with horror. It is that they are advancing straight into a unity of beliefs and in a day that is not far distant the Union will show the world the spectacle of a devout Catholic country without an apparent religious form. It will be philosophical, without having abandoned Christianity, exactly as the Chinese have finally come to have a religion without a cult. It was their great apostle Confucius, the great moralist who, aided by reason, came upon this axiom: "Do not do that which you do not want to have done to you," adding this sublime corollary: "Sacrifice yourself for the masses."

If this comes to pass—as indeed it must—what a boon this experiment in this country will be for the dignity of man. This will come about through equal rights, moral elevation through the elimination of religious sects that now divide men and through the increase of physical faculties and the application of eminently civilized methods to the well-being and progress of humanity. The principle of religious tolerance that is written into all constitutions and has become axiomatic is North American; and it is in North America that, for the first time, that word was spoken which was to staunch the blood that has been shed in torrents from the world's earliest day, and has reached us in only slightly diluted form. Catholics, Quakers, Calvinists, all these variations of the same faith, came to the North American colonies to live side by side, without mingling. Their hatreds had fostered wars in Europe and were gaining ground in the colonies. The Pilgrim Fathers were the most zealously exclusive group because, as Bancroft says, they had crossed the world to enjoy the privilege of living for themselves alone. Religious wars and persecution had broken out among the unfortunate survivors of a common shipwreck who did not give each other mutual aid to mitigate their misfortunes. In Europe the Anglicans persecuted the Dissenters; the Catholics persecuted the heretics; and the Inquisition and Calvin vied with each other in burning, as did popes and kings, Mahometans and Christians, to such an extent that one could not know where to turn without running the risk of being converted into a beefsteak. In February of 1631 there arrived in America a young schoolteacher filled with the spirit of God and endowed with precious gifts. His name was Roger Williams. At that time he was little more than thirty years old, but his spirit had already matured a doctrine that assured him immortality, while its application has given religious peace to the American world. He was a Puritan and he came to escape persecution in England, but his personal injuries had not dimmed his clear intelligence. His deeply spiritual character had understood the nature of intolerance, and he—and only he—arrived at the principle that is the only effective remedy for intolerance. He announced this principle as the simple proposition of the sanctity of conscience. The civil magistrate could repress crime, but could never regulate opinions; he could punish offenses but could never violate the freedom of the spirit. This new idea contained a complete reform of ecclesiastical jurisprudence, erasing from the code of laws the crime of felony for nonconformity, extinguishing the bonfire that persecution had kept alive for so long, repealing all laws that made religious observance obligatory, abolishing tithes and all mandatory contributions for the support of the church, giving equal protection to all forms of religious worship without allowing the civil government to align itself against the mosque of the Mahometans, the altar of the fire worshippers, the Jewish synagogue, or the Roman cathedral.

Roger Williams's principles got him into constant trouble with the government of Massachusetts. Williams made no pact with intolerance because he said: The doctrine of persecution for reasons of conscience is actually and lamentably contrary to the doctrine of Jesus Christ.

The magistrates insisted upon requiring the presence of every person at divine service. Williams disapproved of the law, considering it a clear violation of the rights of man to compel him to foregather with those of a different belief. To drag to the temple unbelievers or those of ill will was for him to sanctify hypocrisy. An unbelieving soul, he added, was dead in sin, and to force a man who is indifferent to one belief to join another was like changing the shroud of a corpse. No one should be forced to worship, without his own consent, for the sake of keeping up a belief.

Is the laborer not worthy of his hire the Puritans answered him. Let him who hires him pay him, answered the heresiarch of tolerance. His perspicacity led him to foresee the influence his principles would have upon the government of societies. During the last days of his life he restated his early ideas:

"It will be an act of mercy and justice toward the enslaved nations, to break the yoke that oppresses the soul, and make it possible for every interest and conscience to preserve liberty and the peace of all" (George Bancroft, *History of the United States*).

And there was light! From Williams's time until now some countries have speedily, and others unwillingly and complainingly, been obliged to stop their evil conduct and the burning of human beings for the greater honor and glory of God.

I am unable to stop when I embark upon the field of theology. As you see, I become a Yankee and I even begin to speak with a twang when I read these arguments. But even if it annoys you, I must point out one of the forces of regeneration, instruction, and help to the sluggard whom the intelligent concern to the American mind is forcing to march forward. Its forms and origins are religious, even though its effects are felt in all social matters. I refer to the spirit of religious and philanthropic association that moves thousands of men of good will to carry out laudable enterprises and devote enormous fortunes to achieve these aims. In this respect the North American has created spiritual needs that are as costly and necessary as material needs. The time, effort, and money employed in satisfying these spiritual needs show how active is the moral life of this people. Who could imagine a more indefatigable propagandist than the exclusive Catholic for whom there is no salvation outside the church, and who is in possession of the truth from which so many have strayed? Ask the most intolerant priest how much he has in his purse for reducing the number of infidels and the moral betterment of the masses. Very little, unfortunately, and that little is not due to a religious sentiment that animates him but to the personal qualities and propensities of one who is dedicated to works of philanthropy and propaganda. Would it occur to anyone in Spanish America to start a crusade against drunkenness? In the United States there are already thousands of zealous propagandists of temperance and thousands who have signed a pledge not to drink liquor until the human race has cured itself of this illness that undermines all economy and destroys all morality.

The North American fulfills his duties and satisfies the needs of his heart and his spirit with his money. If he had to render an estimate of his yearly expenses, he would say one hundred for food and clothing, twenty for the propagation of good religious ideas, ten for philanthropic works, fifty for political ends, and thirty for civilizing barbarians. Distributing the fruit of his labor in this manner, he takes the liberty of appearing egotistical, hard and mercenary.

The American Temperance Society dates from 1826, and in 1835 there were in the country eight thousand branches and a million and a half members. Aid to drunkards is not limited to a good example. Four thousand distillers of alcoholic beverages dismantled their distilleries, eight thousand merchants stopped selling liquor, and one thousand two hundred vessels set sail without carrying any spirituous drinks. The Massachusetts legislature forbade the sale of liquor in smaller quantities than fifteen gallons. The Tract Society, with the objective of improving the shifting population—such as sailors and others—published in 1835 fifty-three million pages. The American Sunday School Society, established in 1824, collected 136,855 pesos a year ten years later, had brought out 600 publications, and was in touch with 16,000 schools, 115,000 teachers, and nearly 800,000 pupils.

From the foundation of the American Bible Society until recently, it has received two million and a half pesos, and put into circulation nearly four million copies of the Bible. I omit the missions in the Orient, in which countries one mission alone maintains 308 missionaries, 478 schools, seventeen printing presses, and four presses for printing books in languages with names that are still unknown in Europe. The results of the American missions in Hawaii are too well known for me to even mention them, since my purpose is to point out their civilizing influence and the forces constantly working for the improvement of morals, religion, and politics. It is not unusual to see a banker like Girard who leaves a million and a half dollars to found a college for the education of young men under certain conditions stipulated by himself. Nor is it unusual to find other philanthropists, like Franklin, who leave a fund, which, with interest added to interest, is still being used at the end of two centuries. In all these vast and complicated projects, the great, dominating idea is equality; the sentiment is religious but free from exterior forms; the medium is association, which is the soul and the basis of the national and individual life of this country.

The Race Problem

Ciro Alegría

Ciro Alegría (Peru, 1909–1967) was a famous Peruvian novelist, journalist, and politician. In 1930 he joined the Aprista movement, which was dedicated to social reform and improving the lives of the country's indigenous population. His novel *El mundo es ancho y ajeno* (Broad and Alien Is the World) won the prestigious Latin American Novel Prize in 1941 and brought him immediate international attention. This novel has since been published throughout Europe and North America. The selection included here is from his "El problema negro," which first appeared in his book of memoirs: *Mucha suerte con harto palo: Memorias*, prologue and notes by Dora Varona (Buenos Aires: Losada, 1976), 215–216. By permission of Dora Varona.

1941

Just as the Indian problem interests me, so too does the black problem, and in general the problem of oppressed minorities. I believe that a free America, to which we all aspire, will never be achieved as long as we maintain situations involving the privileges and conflicts of castes and races.

If we take a close look, we will realize that the black problem in North America is essentially a white problem. I am not only referring to the fact that the white man, as is always the case, is suffering the boomerang effect, which is an undeniable strategy of oppression. I allude to those North Americans who have freed themselves rationally from racial prejudice and yet, unconsciously, encourage it. In such a context they prefer not to face the problem and avoid socializing with blacks.

I had a colleague at work who was the daughter of a Colombian father and German mother. Born in the United States, she spoke better English than Spanish, and given the great assimilative capacity of the United States, she had become totally North Americanized. The countries of her father and mother are definitely far from her mind. A blue-eyed blonde, slim, with democratic ideas much like in the New York style, she was one of those by-products of tomato juice, steak, the daily bath, sports, and Jefferson, with a certain supplementary dose of Elsa Maxwell, the society reporter, and *The Nation*, the liberal weekly. We became good friends and not just because she read my books. We often took walks together and engaged in many conversations. I was convinced she had no racial prejudice. And I was right in this respect, but I should qualify my statement.

One day I asked her to go with me to the home of the black poet Langston Hughes, who had invited me to listen to a few songs and speak with some people of color. The young woman, much to my surprise, refused my invitation outright. I thought it was because Hughes was accused of being a Communist. (I should point out that I do not know if he is. He never spoke to me about this and I considered it an indiscretion to ask him.)

I also assumed my friend was afraid to go to Harlem, where Hughes, of course, lived, since this neighborhood is notorious for its frequent robberies and often aggressive behavior. Having discarded these and other assumptions, the young woman burst out:

"I can't explain it. . . . I don't hate blacks nor do I look down upon them. . . . I have read extensively and I know there are no such things as inferior or superior races. Rationally I understand all of this, but when I am in the company of blacks, I don't feel comfortable. . . . I become annoyed. I can't seem to avoid it. . . . Why would I want to ruin your meeting? It's not that I have anything against blacks, please understand me, it's just that I can't be with them."

I could write many more pages about similar reactions. Among my white North American friends, one of the few who welcomes blacks into his home was David Davidson, who at the time wrote short stories, and later, as I was happy to see, published a successful novel. His wife was also a writer. The blacks who were invited to his home were colleagues.

There is in the United States a psychological conditioning that has been created over the centuries, which will make the true eradication of racial prejudice a slow process.

In general, North American blacks maintain an attitude of sly belligerence toward whites. More than the low salaries they earn and the hard and menial work they have to do, the disdain they feel projected by whites toward them bothers them deeply.

We are headed to Harlem. Let's go, for example, to the Small Paradise or to any nightclub whether big or small. The first attitude of blacks, even those who are doormen or work in the coatroom, is of a certain hostility. Many dislike the idea they may be looked upon as something strange. Others, feeling very much at home in their own neighborhood, assume an air of defiance that in downtown New York they do not have. It's worth noting what happens when we say a few words to them in Spanish and add that we are Latin Americans. The gestures of annoyance and defiance disappear. Their press has told them, undoubtedly exaggerating as it generalized, that we Latin Americans lack racial prejudice. I have repeated this experiment many times, because South Americans who have come to New York often asked me to serve as a kind of elder statesman, and this experiment has always ended up producing the same results.

Within the many nuances that the black-white problem has, there is one that attests to how much disdain can intensify the spirit of combat. It is known that blacks, in the United States as well as anywhere else, are becoming whiter after so many years of intercultural mixing. Many of them end up looking white and opt to move out of the city and live like whites. Others, a number that is quite large, refuse to renounce their black identity. They proclaim themselves black. This topic is the object of a great deal of controversy and Doctor Du Bois, the famous black educator and writer, casts his vote in favor of this second option.

At Howard University, a black institution close to Washington, D.C., the professors once gave a luncheon in my honor and I became friends with the professor of Spanish American literature. I visited his class many times, and little by little, the impression of seeing everything in terms of black and white began to erode. There was a young girl in the class with golden hair and green eyes. She could have been taken for a classic Dana girl, in whose features the artist Dana had created the archetypical Yankee female. I asked her, to see what she would say, why she was studying at a black university when she could go to a white one. The reply of this black-white girl impressed me as much as the one of the white girl who had no black blood.

"It would be a disgrace," she said, "to renounce my race would be to renounce my dignity. If they look down on us, then in time they will have to swallow their disdain. Let them yield a little. . . ."

In the United States, the word "black" does not signify so much a racial condition as it does a human situation. I myself have used it in such a sense. According to anthropological data eighty percent of so-called North American blacks have characteristics of the white race or some other.

Having produced a biological mixture, the color barrier is a paradox, a conventional social attitude or an unconscious leftover of racial prejudice. Good Americans will make it fall one day.

English Lessons

Germán Arciniegas

Germán Arciniegas (Colombia, 1900–1999) was one of his country's leading intellectuals as a journalist, historian, diplomat, essayist, and educator. He played a prominent role in introducing North Americans to the history and culture of Spanish America and in addition to his duties in his native country as minister of education, he also taught at numerous universities in the United States, including Columbia University (1947–1957). Some of his most important books include *Biografía del Caribe* (1945, A Biography of the Caribbean), *El continente de siete colores* (1965, The Continent of Seven Colors), and *Nueva imagen del Caribe* (1970, A New Image of the Caribbean). The following selection is from his *En el país del rascacielos y las zanahorias* (In the Country of Skyscrapers and Carrots) (Bogotá: Librería Suramérica, 1945), 27–30.

1945

A somewhat esteemed Englishman introduces himself in this way: "I am Mr. John Nielsen, N-i-e-l-s-e-n." This is due to the fact that in English it is taken for granted a word is pronounced one way—something that really is not exactly so—but in any case can be written a thousand different ways. It turns out that even the spelling may not be completely clear, especially if it is done over the phone. In such a case, the most discreet and common thing to do is say: "Mr. Arciniegas. A as in Argentina, R as in Russia, C as in Colombia, I as in Ireland, N as in Nicaragua, I as in Italy, E as in Estonia, G as in Greece, A as in Afghanistan, S as in Somalia." In this manner, being the language of Shakespeare—the reader will forgive my not spelling out all the letters of the name Shakespeare—and since the language is so concise, a name can go on indefinitely.

To offer the reader a practical example, I am going to mention what happened to me yesterday. I had to phone Professor Nielsen, which is pronounced Nilson, and it's spelled just as I have written it. I looked for his name in the telephone book and found: "Nielsen (if you do not find the name you are looking for, see Nealson, Neilsen, Neilson, Nilson or Nilsson)." These are the six ways they have for saying Nilson.

When spelling a name you can show special deference toward the person you are addressing, taking as a guide for the letters something that attracts you in particular. If it's a farmer you can say to him: "Arciniegas, A as in artichoke, R as in radish, C as in cauliflower," and so on, and compose a kind of victory garden with all of your favorite garden produce. Also some people take advantage of the opportunity to speak about their country—I always say C as in Colombia—or to publicize the country's products. I remember that a Mr. Mejía from Antioquia, who was the sales representative in the United States for the country's coffee plantations, always started to spell his name like this: Medellín, Excelso . . . (this is the premium brand of Antioquian coffee).

The confusion produced by this question of language is not limited to the minuscule accident of people's names. As a principal thesis you can say that every English word is a hieroglyphic. I published a book, which in the Spanish edition is called *El caballero del Dorado*. Here it is *The Knight of El Dorado*. But because in English "night" and "knight" are pronounced in the same way, when I speak of my book no one knows if I have written a nocturne or a book about knightly adventures. In theater programs, to get around this confusion, instead of writing "night" as it is spelled in the dictionary, they write "nite," which is exactly the way it sounds. This can mean night as well as knight, but the indication of 8 p.m. allows you to understand that it refers to night. The "gh" that has been suppressed in these brochures is a combination of two letters that are used in English to mislead.

When the earlier-mentioned version of my book was published, the editors added to the cover a clarification: "Germán Arciniegas (is pronounced Hair máhn Ar-seen-yáygus)." This clarification was indispensable. But if the reader wishes to know more about the fate of my name in this country, I can inform him that one day in the newspaper one of my lectures was announced in the following manner: "Today Dr. Arthur Nagus will give a lecture on Latin America."

The difficulty with English is, on the one hand, to be found in the utterance of sounds, which we cannot produce like the misters can. When the uninitiated realizes that each of the vowels is pronounced in four or five different ways, he begins to swoon. The effort realized to produce "r's" or "s's" not only causes a great fatigue for those who are used to Spanish but also leaves on their faces a pitiful look, a look of great ineptitude. I usually offer this explanation to my academic colleagues: "I'm not an idiot: it's just that I don't know English." Thus I say in confidence, which they in turn reproduce confidentially: "No, the gentleman is not stupid; it's just that he doesn't know."

My experience is that more than anything else the English language resembles an infirmity. It is what grammatically we would call the disease of the tongue. Its manifestations are the faces of ill people that we project every time we try to speak it, and the fatigue such attempts produce in us. When, after two or three years, two friends who have traveled to the United States get together again, their first conversation seems to be of a clinical nature: "Look, I continue to speak bad English, but I've gotten better as far as pronunciation is concerned but I feel worse and worse in "espelin." (The word is "spelling" in English; it means orthography. We Spanish speakers say *espelin*.)

The only consolation in all of this is to see the misters experience the same trouble in our countries. All of us remember that wonderful anecdote told about Charles the Fifth, who arrived in Spain without knowing a word of the language, and who would spend hours listening without saying a word. One day a peasant came to talk to him, after noticing him with his mouth open in the central plaza of the town. "Your Majesty, please close your mouth and realize that the flies in this town are pretty insolent." After all, Charles the Fifth was no dummy. And if at times he had the look of an idiot and at other times that of a constipated person, it was all simply a question of language.

The First Surprise (Selection)

Luis Alberto Sánchez

Luis Alberto Sánchez (Lima, 1900–1994) was a Peruvian politician and man of letters whose more than seventy books include biography, literary criticism, philosophy, history, poetry, and fiction. He was a leading member of the Popular Revolutionary Alliance (APRA), which was founded by Víctor Haya de la Torre to combat imperialism in Latin America. Sánchez served as president of Peru's Senate in 1966 and headed the commission to edit the constitution of 1979. He was also a candidate for the first vice presidency under the candidacy of Luis Alva Castro in 1990. The following selection is from his *Un sudamericano en Norteamérica: Ellos y nosotros* (A South American in North America: We and They) (Santiago de Chile: Edicones de Ercilla, 1942), 75–83. By permission of Instituto Luis Alberto Sánchez, Lima, Peru.

1942

The first surprise was that they were also people like the rest of us. A North American who does not know South America in depth will probably think I am joking. Nothing of the sort. Just as they bring their air of superiority to our lands and are amazed when they discover that in Panama, El Callao, and Valparaiso instead of hordes of plumed savages waiting to receive them, groups of attractive young men and women, impeccably dressed, climb on board the ship. So too it is with us South Americans. Even though the culture may tell us something else, secretly we expect to see, as we arrive in New York, a bunch of gangsters, vamps, and boxers.

Praised be the movies! There is no North American who doesn't confuse a Latin with a Mexican and a Mexican with an outlaw. Praised be the movies! Our prejudice notwithstanding, New York disappointed us with its undeniable normalcy.

In the first place, the skyscrapers. The movies, the Hudson River, and Immigration employees attempt to detract from their importance. The big screen has us so accustomed to what they look like and the bureaucrats of Immigration keep us at such a great distance from being able to see them up close, that, nonetheless, they turn out to be familiar to us before we even get to know them.

Second . . . a pleasant and humanitarian conquest of New York occurred, which began on Pier 52, the day we disembarked.

The customs inspector, in charge of our baggage, is an elderly gentleman with teeth missing, just like any South American employee. He is smiling and cunning and, in addition—what is most typical—has the look of someone who enjoys his drink. At least that morning he had had his drink of whiskey, because his breath, his patience, and his loquacity all gave him away. Formally he asked us if we were carrying contraband of any kind: we answered no. In accord with common practice, his authoritative pencil indicated a reply at the bottom of our customs form. Then, another question: "Any liquor?"—"Yes, one bottle."—"Nothing else?"—"No, nothing else."—A bottle of what?"—"Of *pisco*." The old man opened his eyes widely, pondering what he had just heard:—"Peruvian brandy," we explained. Shaken by an intimate laugh of ethylic fraternity, the inspector added only: "That's good!"—and he proceeded to stamp our form.

Arriving in New York had been like arriving in Valparaiso, in Buenaventura, or in Havana—where there are no political police who look upon everyone as a potential suspect.

Blessed be *pisco*!

The following surprise had nothing to do with the landscape nor with public functionaries but rather with people themselves.

According to the canons of routine information, a North American is always a Yankee, always a kind of pachyderm with blue eyes and blonde hair who chews gum, smokes big cigars or a thick pipe. The *gringas* are all either platinum blondes, with stunning eyes, suggestive and ravishing looking women—or their counterpart, elderly women tourists treating the country they visit as if they were in a museum.

Well, both on and off the dock we saw only brunettes—just as in South America. With dark or brown hair—just like in South America. There was a bit more color in their dresses; less formality in the way men dressed, although breaking with a delightful North American tradition as important as the discovery of the light bulb, we noticed they sported many semistiff collars and not so many soft ones, that sublime conquest of the democracy and comfort afforded by North America.

Buenos Aires, you say? Perhaps. Yes, that's exactly what many of these men reminded us of, so formal in their stiff white shirts and their jackets made of pure wool—and the smoky cigarette instead of the pipe or cigar. European finery, which in exchange for our vitality they offer us the old age of their civil armor made from much cotton and wool.

I must confess that this was not a pleasant surprise, quite the contrary. But the United States, as it evolves, has begun to adopt several European formalisms, instead of sticking to its guns as a champion of invigorating informality, a kind of sporty *sans-facon*. Years ago, Lincoln governed this country from the heights of his awkward stature and he did so without the least bit of affectedness, a man who was the essence of virility and integrity. They refer to him as "Abe" with total confidence, and he liked to talk to all kinds of people, to sit in the sun and meditate on his destiny, to page through books, to quote the law, pick his nose, and give a skeletal texture to the country that was still colonial in nature, and for this reason, fragmented. His coat was famous for its long tails and his trousers for how tight they were and not always fitting exactly. But he was even more renowned for his judgment, which was always impeccable, for his unequaled impartiality, his daring and tenderness. General Ulysses S. Grant, on the other hand, was a coarse man. He had been shaped by the war and made decisions with the speed of cannon fire. He chomped on an enormous cigar, like any cowboy from the West, but he also knew how to chew on his thoughts and he continued the exemplary work of "Honest Abe." Theodore Roosevelt had been a Rough Rider in Cuba and he preserved during his administration the fearlessness and thundering indiscretion typical of the warrior of the Cuban *manigua* and the great white hunter of Africa. Out of pure naiveté he never vacillated for even a moment in uttering, "I took Panama," labeling himself forever with the title of abusive and imperialistic. (Nowadays such things are not said: they're simply carried out—and then covered up.)

These are not the times of the Apostle or of the Hunter. Nevertheless, because of the fact that a man of patriarchal appearance, wounded physically by pain, directs from the White House the lives of 133 million citizens and a number of other subjects, one can say that things have acquired a less frugal tone: more seasoned, although not always savory. The stiff collar that is now demanded in some offices, the manners, a bit sophisticated of high dignitaries, all of these indicate a change of mentality that is more profound than what at first sight seems to be the case. And the change has occurred to such a degree that just as it was a luxury before to be, as Walt Whitman used to say, "the man in shirt sleeves," today it is to be, as Sumner Welles, for example, would want, a man in a stiff collar, with a cold demeanor and words—and thoughts for that matter—measured in centimeters and kept, at times, in the refrigerator.

Let's not deceive ourselves, however. We're in New York, a cosmopolitan city; we are also referring to Washington, which is a vast governmental office, but the two are not, thank goodness, the United States. Whoever confuses New York and Washington with the entire Republic is well on his way to making a big mistake. The bad thing is that all South Americans who come here are forever seduced by the lure of New York, and often, which is even worse, by just one of its neighborhoods, Greenwich Village, when they possess a certain imagination and a little arrogance, or by Radio City when they lack the former and possess the latter in great quantities.

Naturally, these are the thoughts that come to mind at the end of several months of walking around and keeping my eyes open. That first day, finally getting off the boat—we hadn't disembarked for weeks—I had other impressions about which I must inform the unsuspecting reader so that he will be educated in the art of avoiding the risks of the newly arrived in a great cosmopolitan and mechanical metropolis.

This was the era of rationed food! During one such opportunity I learned several things: one of them was that speed is a concept more relative even than Einsteinian space. Let's see how.

Alberto Rembao, the great heart of Mexico, who is always in tune with Manhattan, took us to placate our hunger to one of the thousands of Childs restaurants in the city. From the "menu," which was attractively decorated with colors and names, the powerful voice of a steak drew our attention. We responded to its beckoning. But the minutes went by, cutting through time, and prolonging our hunger. At the end of thirty eternities and another thirty agonies, the waitress showed up declaring, with the all too well known "sorry," that serves as the prologue to everything, neither the steak nor that other whim we had entertained could be served to us because of the first of one hundred reasons sounded by the bell ringer: there weren't any more steaks left. Philosophizing in silence and afflicted by our hunger, we began to yearn for our South America, where such a reply would have been met with a deluge of comforting insults.

And this wasn't all, because forced to eat a dish we really didn't want, we had to put up with the obligatory accompaniment of certain gravies and vegetables and the inevitable pie, all of which we would have exchanged gladly for a simple steak, something solid and with fewer frills. Our intestinal democracy felt the strong urge to intone a culinary Marseillaise against the dietary totalitarianism of Childs's debatable democracy.

If we had adopted the procedures of the Count of Keyserling, we would have to infer there are grave consequences concerning the proper functioning of the cosmos. We will resign ourselves to continue jotting down our discrepancies, a reflection of any "Latin" who has just arrived in this country.

We protest *in pectore* against the ritual serving of ice water as an obligatory aperitif. We protest the unavoidable succession of *appetizer, soup, vegetables*, and *dessert*. And, also, the serving of coffee in the middle of the meal. And that morning, having verbalized our protest, we dedicated ourselves to observing around us the goings and comings of this great human swarm, seasoned with lots of dogs, decked out in luxurious trappings, who would be the envy of the street urchins of our America, who were more abandoned, the poor things, than the dogs in North America.

A Trip to New York

Ernesto Cardenal

Ernesto Cardenal (1925–) is Nicaragua's former minister of culture (1979–1987), an ordained Catholic priest, political activist, and one of Latin America's most highly esteemed poets. Author of dozens of books of poetry, Cardenal is known for a poetic world that fuses art and politics in which the social criticism is never strident and overbearing but indirect and suggestive of the need for social reform. Some of his most representative works include *Salmos* (1967, Psalms), *Homenaje a los indios americanos* (1969, Homage to the American Indians), *La hora cero y otros poemas* (1971, Zero Hour and Other Documentary Poems), *En Cuba* (1972, In Cuba), *El Evangelio en Solentiname* (1975, The Gospel in Solentiname), *Canto a un país que nace* (1978, Song to a Nascent Country), *El estrecho dudoso* (1985, The Dubious Strait), *Cántico cósmico* (1989, The Cosmic Canticle), *Vida perdida* (1999, Lost Life), and *Seis cántigas del cántico cósmico* (2003, Six Songs from the Cosmic Canticle). This selection first appeared in Spanish in *Casa de las Américas*, v. 14, no. 82 (January–February 1974), 70–82. By permission of the author.

1973

I had the impression that afternoon that I was still on my island of
    Solentiname
and not looking out a window at the bay of New York.
Ships below scarcely moving, our plane also proceeding slowly
    Kennedy heavy with traffic at that time of the day

we had to circle New York for an hour
What miracle had deposited me upon Manhattan that late afternoon
circling around skyscrapers colored by the setting sun?
From the seat next to mine (empty) I picked up a copy of the *New Yorker*
"This week Washington awoke from a stupor called Watergate."
Senator Fulbright fears that the country will become a totalitarian system.
Ladies and Gentlemen: Kennedy Airport is still backed up with traffic

leaning against the window, the water of New York's harbor
the plane as if anchored to a cloud doesn't move
An ad from an island resort—swimming pool tennis cottages water sports
      The Island Company, Ltd., 375 Park Avenue
A cartoon of a fat man holding a newspaper as he says to his wife
"I've worked so hard and the *New York Times* refers to me as only 'a suspected head of the Mafia'"

Ladies and Gentlemen . . . now we've been picked up by radar and
we are headed directly to Kennedy on automatic pilot
factories, trains, little suburban homes, all identical, cars the size of toys
and now we're on the Tarmac. Along with a hundred other planes, like sharks.

Gerard was waiting for me, a young bearded man, the one who brought me
miraculously to New York, he prefers I call him Tony
we head to Manhattan in his old car, rivers of cars
he called me to participate in the charity drive for the earthquake victims of Managua
without having anyone to pay for my trip, he says
      he already got someone, God takes care of everything.
      He works
with orphans, drug addicts, poor Puerto Ricans
he was walking through the ghetto when he got the idea for a fund drive for Managua
he didn't have a headquarters, he flunked out of Columbia, looking toward heaven
he saw the Episcopal cathedral of St. John the Divine, went in
      And the bishop said "Why not?"

        New York convicts donated paintings done by them
        Native Americans also contributed fabrics and ceramics
more rivers of cars trains trucks, the super highways crisscross
        he's a Catholic he tells me and also a Buddhist
he worked before in St. Patrick's Cathedral, he couldn't continue
    there
        the current cardinal is worse than Spellman
on the highway there rises up before our eyes ads for gas stations drive-
    in motels
        A melancholy cemetery of automobiles in the twilight
several hippies have camped in the monastery of Gethsemani, he says
boys and girls, the abbot allowed them
the monasteries in the United States are becoming empty
young people prefer small communes. I tell him
that Merton once said to me that those orders would disappear
and that the only thing left would be small communes
        the sky the smog and the ads
            rectangular forms among the smog
and the contemplative orders almost all of them Tony says have a
    bourgeois mentality   middle class
Indifferent to the question of war. And to Revolution.
            LIQUORS—DRUG-STORE
"Does New York seem very changed to you?"
I was here twenty-three years ago. I tell him: "It's the same."
        the rows of traffic lights red and green
        and the lights from the taxis and buses.
            "Madison Avenue" Tony says. And laughing:
"It's funny: Ernesto Cardenal on Madison Avenue": And I look
the deep canyon, the deep gorge of buildings
where the hidden persuaders hide behind their glass windows
      they sell automobiles of Happiness, Consolation in a can
        (30 cents)
           The Coca Cola Company
we cross the canyon of glass windows and billions of dollars.
"For centuries they didn't eat meat; now that many of us are
    vegetarians
they eat meat," he says. From a narrow side street the Empire State
    Building
        (I barely see its lower part). In the depths of Imperialism.

"Famous monks come here to give lectures on asceticism and
                they stay at luxury hotels." And now at the West Side
                    Cafeteria—Delicatessen—Dry Cleaning
We arrive at Napoleon's apartment, 50th and Tenth Avenue.
On the sidewalk, teenagers, blue jeans and blue eyes,
standing with their bicycles or sitting on the stoops....
The bell doesn't work but Napoleon and Jacquie were waiting for us.
Napoleon Chow of Chinese and Nicaraguan ancestry
and Jacquie who is an anthropologist specializing in Turkish culture.
The small, monastic apartment; but with Persian tapestries.
I call Laughlin, at his home in Connecticut.
He's surprised: "What the devil am I doing in New York?"
He laughs from Connecticut. He'll come Monday so that we can get
   together;
in his house in the Village.
Napoleon and Jacquie are doing yoga. They fast completely
for many days, other days they cook and very well, Chinese
                Turkish, Nicaraguan food
("food as happiness; a sacrament")
There's an Angora cat who defecates like people on the toilet.
Thursday night, the Cathedral of St. John the Divine
110th Street, it opened its bronze doors to the exhibition
      I read my Oracle about Managua (the part that has to do with
         the earthquake)
among paintings done by convicts, the ceramic works of native
   Americans.
A rabbi with a long beard prays: "Our culpability
in these tragedies" And the Dean of the cathedral: "Our System
Oh Lord, which aggravates these catastrophes" (And I think: the
   Somozas
      an earthquake that has lasted for forty years). Brother David
a Benedictine: "And it's in New York, Lord, who would have
   guessed it
where you bring us all together from diverse countries and religions
to pray for Managua and to meditate
      on how much here should be destroyed"
Dorothy Day, ill, could not attend.
María José and Clemencia, two beautiful Nicaraguan women (I knew
   their father)

ask me in what condition were certain streets left (I met him once
on that night in April
        when we were going to attack the presidential residence—
Chema, he was tortured and killed)
I just say to them: "I knew your father"
In the choir, slides (radiant colors) of the Rubble.
Corita (formerly Sister Corita) donated six paintings for Managua.
        Daniel Berrigan is expecting me tomorrow.

Central Park (uptown): And I say to myself: that's where the swans
   are.
I remember my Liana, and the swans.
She got married. The swans are probably still there.
Luis, once, wanting to catch a swan, a day of hunger.
I saw the people once again in the streets speaking by themselves.
   "The Lonely Crowd."
With Napoleon and Jacquie in Times Square, nothing to see
and along 48th Street among the titillating porno movie houses.
        An empty store, two policemen taking notes
The store windows shattered, and no one takes notice (on Broadway)

With Daniel Berrigan at the Thomas Merton Center
Daniel (Dan) in blue jeans and sandals just like me, his hair
   Like that of a street tough after a fight
and the smile that was evident in the photos when he was captured
by the FBI (jubilant among the sullen FBI agents)
   he had read my Psalms in prison.
and also there is Jim Forest (pacifist) with a big mustache,
younger than I thought. He wrote me once
He said that Merton had given him a crucifix that I had made in the
   Trappist monastery
        He has just come from Washington, from a protest march
from the Watergate Building to the Department of Justice.
And Berrigan sitting on his desk, his chiseled face
against his knee, his thin hair in his face. He has scarcely recovered
from his time in jail, I'm told. And a young girl:
"People take for granted that torture doesn't exist in the United
   States"
This is a group of contemplatives and resisters, Berrigan says.
   Meeting one night in a convent in Harlem
   they got the idea to found this Merton Center.

they study the mysticism of a variety of religions and also of Native
    Americans
"Merton endured horrors in the monastery" Dan says
          and all of us know this. And Jim remembers
when they prohibited him from writing against nuclear war
because it wasn't a monastic subject.
Dan: "He told me he would never again consider becoming a monk
but since he already was, he would continue to be one."
"He was going to go to Solentiname after Asia, right?" Jim says.
          And Dan: "Are you sure he's not there?"
And also Dan:
"It's a terrible drug that we have here: the 'Contemplative Life'.
You meditate. Without thinking at all about the war. Without
    thinking
At all about the war. You can't be with God and be neutral at the
    same time.
The true contemplative life is resistance. And poetry,
looking at the clouds is resistance, I discovered that in jail."
I tell him to go to Cuba, and he: I'm still out under certain conditions.
          I also tell him: "In Latin America
We are integrating Christianity with Marxism."
And he: "I know. But not here.
Here it's Christianity with Buddhism.
Jim, all of us are already Buddhists, don't you think?
Isn't there Buddhism in Latin America?"
                              "No."
Tomorrow there will be a celebration at the Merton Center
The marriage of his brother Philip, the other priest,
And the former nun Elizabeth McAlister — and we're invited.
Philip poured blood in Maryland over the draft records
Later Philip and Daniel burned records in Catonsville
with homemade napalm (powdered soap and gasoline)
and Jim also burned, using napalm, the records in Milwaukee
          (and they have only been released from jail recently)
It is said that Merton once planned a similar action.
There's a young girl fasting because of the bombing of Cambodia.
          On the wall is a poem by Berrigan about Vietnam
          in large sheets joined together like a mural.
As I leave Dan gives me a big loaf of bread.
A big round loaf, baked there in the oven, of pure wheat.

With Napoleon and Jacquie on the way to the movies to see a
   Cuban film
Memories of Underdevelopment
                    in it they don't idealize the Revolution
a documentary piece—a meeting of writers—
      and I believe I see Roque Dalton in the documentary
Fidel giving a speech (and a part of the audience in the theater
   applauds Fidel).
      A ton of people on the sidewalk dressed formally: the Opera
      Tony's aristocratic Italian grandfather
      left him an estate on the outskirts of Rome.
He'll probably give it away to someone. He doesn't want to be a prop-
   erty owner.
And Tony said: "Holy Communion" (his eyes burning in his head)
"Communion is my greatest link with men every day
Communion for me is the greatest revolutionary act in the world."

Philip Berrigan and Elizabeth McAlister
accused by the FBI of trying to kidnap Henry Kissinger
         The marriage celebration in the Merton Center
Contemplatives and radicals, pacifists, ex-prisoners many of them
         anarchistic Christians and Buddhist Christians
and in this celebration a Eucharist with songs of protest
         everyone sitting on the floor
after the gospel Jim speaks, then Dan, a young woman
who has just poured blood on Richard Nixon's dining room table
and the walls of the dining room she covered in blood, while as a
   tourist
she toured the White House (the Press did not report the incident).
   She awaits
trial, perhaps years in jail, pregnant.
Dan Berrigan blesses a bread similar to the one he gave me
and wine glasses. The bread broken and passed from one to the other,
   and the wine.
Afterwards, a collection . . . for the poor accused of Watergate
         "Our adversarial brothers."
Back to the party. Dan says: "No more religion,"
Gallons of California "rosé" and "white" wine on one table
rice pudding with raisins, apple pie, cheeses on the other table.
A young man with lots of blonde hair says hi to me, Michael Cullen.

He read my Psalms in prison he says,
and I've read about him.
He gives me a brochure he distributes: If Mike Cullen is deported
He was born on a farm in the south of Ireland, he came at the age of
    ten, not
to make money. He studies in the seminary. Got married. Sold
    insurance
But felt the suffering of those living in rat infested apartments
and the blood being spilled everywhere in Indo China
he burned his draft card. He burned
with Jim the draft records in Milwaukee
        the 1-A draft cards destined to burn bodies in Asia
now they want to deport him, he believes they will deport him he
    says sadly
someone who passes by put money in his pocket and says to him
        "keep going" and he smiles (a sad smile)
he says to me: "The American dream has become a nightmare."
All the television cameras are on Philip and his wife.
"I believe in the Revolution," he says. "My contribution is not
    violent."
Phil with his blue eyes. Built like a rugby player
        the Gary Cooper of the Church.
Elizabeth, gentle: they got married she says to help each other in the
    struggle
and they will build a commune to help others continue the struggle
            Dan with his radiant smile
                    and his inner Zen peace.

Upon leaving the Doubleday Bookstore on 5th Avenue
several men and women with white tunics dancing on the sidewalk
and these young people with shaven heads (dressed in white) look like
    Trappist novices.
            In a store window:
            Mink. Persian lambskin jacket. Diamond brooch
            with rubies . . .
A young man with a circular badge pinned to his chest: IMPEACH
    NIXON
                Plastic looking women.
I cross the street fearfully: WALK—DON'T WALK (in red)
The sales clerks from the stores almost all of them Cuban

and it seems to me I'm listening to
                              revolutionaries speak.
A dirty sky. Police sirens.
Old women speaking among themselves
The colonel spoke about that French Dominican here who said to
    him:
"Ever since I came three months ago I haven't been able to pray."
The Museum of Modern Art. Without time to go in. And for what
    purpose?
Frank O'Hara used to work here. His poetry he would write
                      during lunch hour—sandwiches and Coca Cola
Once we corresponded with each other.
Now I've bought his LUNCH POEMS ($1.50) in Brentano's
and the automobiles remind me of his death
          run over in New York (during his lunch hour?)
                    WALK—DON'T WALK
Dorothy Day is expecting me at the Catholic Worker Tony says.
She remembered on the phone that she had once written to me.

A paperback bookstore on 5th Avenue
Lots of books about Indians, Pawnees. Sioux. Hopis. The
Hopis, anarchists and pacifists for 2,000 years, gandhians
they never declared a war nor signed a treaty (not
              Even with the United States)
and now I'm going to meet with Kenneth Arnold at twelve o'clock
my editor in English of my *Homage to the American Indians*
also here is the autobiography of Black Elk
          he once came to New York with Buffalo Bill
houses as far as the sky, lights taken from the power of thunder claps
he says that here he was like one who never had a vision.
Red Fox also with Buffalo Bill. He loved the Indians, he says
he defended them in Washington. Time to meet with Kenneth.
He came from Baltimore. We agreed to meet in the Gotham Book
    Mart.
I Have Spoken, I already have it. Contains Seattle's speech
            Seattle wrapped in his blanket as if in a toga
    with his famous voice understandable a half mile away, in the
            middle
of an uncultivated terrain: "My words are like the stars
that never change. What Seattle says, the Great Chief of Washington

believe it just like the movement of the sun or the seasons"
    It's raining outside, a rain without smell
and it's almost time for lunch
      NO SMOKING
"And when the last of my people has died
and they speak of my tribe as a story from the past"
the rustling of tires on the wet streets
   neon reflections upon the wet asphalt mirror
"and the children of his children believe themselves to be alone
in their fields, in their storehouses, in their tents they will not be
  alone.
When the streets of their cities are quiet and you
Believe them to be empty, they will be filled with the spirits of the
  dead.
Did I say the dead? There is no death. Only a change of world."
I leave with books of new homage paid to the American Indians
and I go to the Gotham Book Mart—three blocks—and there is
  Kenneth.
He is young, with a beard. Miss Steloff also present, her silver colored
  hair
this bookstore's famous lady. And I was here once before
for a party for Miss Edith Sitwell. Miss Steloff
invited the Colonel and me and we brought Mimi Hammer
and Auden, Tennessee Williams, Marianne Moore, Spender were
  there . . . Kenneth brought the jacket of *Homage to the American*
  Indians
and we go to a Chinese restaurant a half block away and
   a chow mein lunch but first a couple of cold beers.
This abundance of books about Indians, he says
started about a year or two ago. The theme of the Indian has become
  fashionable.
He also has a poem about Indians, rather
about Buffalo Bill, his great grand-uncle. Yes, Colonel William
  Frederic Cody (Buffalo Bill)
   was the brother of his great-grandfather

Tony comes to get me and apologizes for the car.
His own broke down. This one, a luxury model, is his father's.
  (Ashamed)
Invited to lunch by Brother David's mother

(with Napoleon and Jacquie). The apartment in an elegant
   neighborhood
      along 5th Avenue. She's the Baroness of Austria
but she works as an employee. She gave away her wealth.
A young woman has brought me a gift: a poster of Watergate
—Nixon in the photo as a gangster with the caption WANTED
          Brother David asks me
"What should I tell the abbots of the monasteries in the United
   States?"
I laugh. "Seriously, as if the abbots as a group asked for my advice?"
"They wouldn't follow it." "But what would you say to them?"
"That they should be communists."
A young woman: "Why society first
and not the heart of man? First, the inner being!"
I say to her: "We are social beings. Social change is not external."
             The lunch: yoghourt with strawberries
                a black bread and another very dark one, milk
                bluish looking grapes, red apples, yellow bananas
                honey, the most delicious I have tasted in my entire life
No liquor at this lunch. I'm the only one who smokes
    ("The air is impure enough without having to breathe in more
       smoke")
Brother David speaks with several small beads in his hand.
I ask him: "Can Buddhism and Marxism be integrated?
"Through Christianity. You have brought
Christianity and Marxism together, and we, here, Christianity and
   Buddhism."
He also says to me: "Pentecostals . . . maybe it would be better for you
   not to see them.
They seem possessed by the spirit, but they continue with the
   Exploitation."
          Tony leaves us to be with his orphans.

12th Street. Near here is where Joaquín had his apartment. In that
   building,
      I'm almost sure.
A seller of old books in the Village fascinated by my shirt
      my Nicaraguan *campesino* shirt of coarse cotton
asks me who invented it.
      A sign in gold: MONEY (Pawnshop)

I ask for Charles Street: A neat man on a bench: He
doesn't know, he says. Can I give him a dollar? He hasn't eaten in two
  days.
    Parra was in Chile.
On all the television screens Dean testifying against Nixon.

    Washington Square: Rock in the park
a microphone with electronic crazy music frenetic listeners
thousands of long-haired figures howling with the band black blond
  black women
with the band, barefoot women bearded men bejeweled or in rags
howling with the band, kicking the grass or
lying down smoking kissing one another drinking cans of beer.
A group of lesbians shouting. Further over *Gay Liberation* with a flag
passive in the face of the Methodists giving them a sermon Bible in
  hand
with a choir of stern looking women wrapped in clothing down to
  their ankles.
    Crossing the street
two gays each licking
the same cone.

the neighborhood of beggars and the Catholic Worker.
Armando Morales' studio, La Mecha; in the Bowery
It's a warehouse. No bathroom (he sponge bathes in the sink
standing on an edition of the New York Times so he doesn't wet the
  floor)
With California wine we reminisce about Managua before the quake
in front of canvases of La Mecha that the gallery sells for 10,000 dollars.
The ashtrays sardine cans the kind you open with a key,
their tops only rolled halfway back and piles of these ashtrays.
    He explains: the Gallery prices each item, and these are
the stocks of a painter. One of Morales' buyers
invests in him just as he would in General Motors. If the price goes up
(the stock) they will invest more in him. And if sales come to a halt
    the Gallery could no longer drop the price
even if La Mecha was dying of hunger—the drop in price would create a panic
among the "stock holders" of Morales' intricate colors and mysterious
  nudes.

He paints his colors and then he covers the whole body in black.
He shaves it with a Gillette, scraping the black, and
over the shaven parts he paints all of the colors once again.
"By now I know how to paint" he says "I can paint whatever I want.
      The difficult part is—what to paint"
We recall that cantina in Managua called The Five Sisters.
We recall several super Muses that we loved, more or less.
And when we found out that we were on the police list of
    homosexuals
        —he for being a painter and I for being a poet.
And he recalls that bordello called the Hydrangea and I tell him that
it wasn't located where he said, but rather in another area, and that it
    no longer exists
afterwards they built on that spot the Church of the Redeemer
    (La Mecha laughs)
and that I at the time already a priest, said Mass there, until the
    Superior forbade it
because of my anti-Somoza preaching (La Mecha laughs even more)
    and besides
There's no longer the Church of the Redeemer, it collapsed in the
    earthquake—
        He can't donate paintings for the earthquake relief collection
            his paintings belong to the Gallery.
On all of the TV stations Dean continued testifying against Nixon.

Laughlin is a man as tall as the door and
(as I already knew through Merton) brimming with love.
When we went in he asks about Nicanor's wine.
Where's the wine that Nicanor left? He takes from the refrigerator
The white Portuguese wine Saint Something that he left there the
    last time
That Nicanor visited. Here we are with a glass in our hand, still with-
    out tasting a drop
And Laughlin raises his glass to heaven as if celebrating an Offertory:
"For Tom. I'm sure he'll enjoy the get-together
wherever he may be!" And I: "He's here." Nicanor Parra's wine is
delicious. "It's strange," Laughlin says, "after his death
it was obvious that each of his friends believed himself to be Merton's
    closest friend."
After a pause and a sip of wine: "—And actually he was."

He speaks with Napoleon Chow about China and with Jacquie about
     Turkey.
He gives us some of New Directions' latest books.
We quickly signed the contract for my new book *In Cuba*.
More wine. Margaret Randall seems happy in Cuba—how wonderful
He sympathizes a lot with her, even though he doesn't know her
               He tells us (it still hasn't been made public)
About Merton's falling in love two years before his death.
In 1966. In the spring. He and Parra were in the monastery.
A very beautiful girl. Love like a flash of lightning. "Madly in love"
     he says
          "But he didn't want to stop being a monk."
Then I say that he is a good poet, I've translated him, and he says no
     he isn't
Pound told him he isn't. He would edit his poems
with that famous pencil of his. He told him: "Do something useful"
     and he
became an editor. No one had an editor in those days, only
     Hemingway
He attended the University of Ezra in Rapallo. He'd have lunch with
     Pound
and his wife in the Albergo Rapales. After swimming or tennis
and readings of Villon, Catullus. . . . Pound was his spiritual father.
          He tells the story: Once Somoza robbed one of his uncle's mines
—James Laughlin is the grandson of Laughlin, the king of steel—
          "Of course he knew," says Laughlin (he being Nixon)
We finish off Nicanor's wine and go to a French restaurant
three blocks away.
"He liked his solitude a lot and he also liked people.
He loved silence—but also conversation.
Merton was gregarious, you know, and a perfect monk."

Midnight. In a tobacco shop the morning edition of the New York
     Times
          NIXON KNEW SAYS DEAN (we bought it)
On the subway an ad for the Army: young men graduating—
          . . . after graduation think about a career in the Army. . .
And the dark subways are now painted all over on the outside:
names of boys and girls in a variety of colors
          Alice 95   Bob 106   Charles 195

and the express trains go by as if they were covered by flowers
(their names and streets where they live) "They write them down
so that someone will know who they are, to be real," Napoleon says
    painted with spray cans of all types of colors
and there are names that are up to a meter tall
    Manuel . . . Julia . . . José . . . (many of them Puerto Ricans)

Slums "with no more beauty than that of the clouds"
36 East First Street (Bowery)
with a surge of emotion I saw the small sign on the front of the building: Catholic Worker
a fat man lying on the sidewalk asks me softly for a cigarette
    moved I enter this sacred place
she wasn't in, but soon she comes walking along the sidewalk with other women
    thin, hunched over, white hair
she's still beautiful at 78
I kiss the saint's hand and she kisses me on the cheek.
Just like my grandmother Agustina during the fifties (when she
could still read and was a reader of this woman)
This is the famous House of Hospitality founded by
Peter Maurin and Dorothy Day during the Great Depression
where they offer food and lodging free to all who come
    drunks crazies drug addicts bums who are dying
and it is also the headquarters of a pacifist and anarchistic movement:
its objective: a society in which it is easy to be good.
    Soon the poor would arrive for dinner.
I was studying at Columbia and even there we learned
that a saint had died in the neighborhood of the poor.
Peter Maurin, an activist and saint,
preached in the parks:
    "Fire all the bosses." Or
    "Giving to and not taking from
    is what makes a person a human being."
With just one dress, faded and not the right size. Without her own bed
in this place that he founded, not even a corner for her books.
    She walked without looking at the traffic lights.
And she devoted herself from that point on to
"works of mercy and rebellion." A life of daily communion and
    participation

in every strike, demonstration march, protest or boycott.
Volunteers come here to work: students, seminarians
professors, sailors, also beggars, and sometimes they
stay their whole life. Many have gone to jail or are still there.
Hennacy fasted in front of the government buildings
with a protest sign, handing out flyers and selling the newspaper
and he refused to pay taxes because 85% of them go for the war
he worked as a field laborer in order to pay no taxes.
Hugh, a thin man, in short pants sandals and a poncho
also did penance in the streets.
Jack English, a brilliant journalist from Cleveland
was a cook at the Catholic Worker and later he became a monk.
Roger La Porte was a handsome blonde 22 year old; he sacrificed
   his life
by setting himself on fire with gasoline in front of the United Nations.
And a former marine, Smoky Joe, who fought against Sandino
in Nicaragua, died here as a convert to antiviolence.
      Here is where Merton worked before becoming a Trappist.
The newspaper is still sold for a penny
as when Dorothy Day first stepped onto
    Union Square to sell it on May 1st (1933)
It was the third year of the Depression
      Twelve million out of work
and Peter wanted with this newspaper something more than just a
   publication of opinions
he wanted a revolution.
       The pots are now steaming
the poor are already beginning to arrive, the homeless, those in the
   Bowery
are starting to line up. "The other United States" Dorothy says
    men displaced by machines
    and abandoned by Holy Mother the State.
Shouts. Someone has entered kicking and punching
    —Two from the Catholic Worker take him outside gently.
"We never call the police because we believe in nonviolence."
And she also tells me: "When I visited Cuba
I saw that Sandino was one of their heroes
and I enjoyed this. Because when I was young I collected money
   for him,
when I was a Communist, before converting to Catholicism.

And I saw Sandino's principal generals (not him)
in Mexico: with their big hats, eating hot dogs
        Why hot dogs I have no idea"
And lifting her white head energetically: "Castro's Cuba
I am acquainted with it, as I already wrote to you. I liked it."
Shouts. Now it's a dwarfish woman. And someone leads her away
    gently
        Lifted up in the air like a doll.
She tells us that now she is helping Chavez's workers
boycotting the A & P chain. And she prays, she says
that the United States will suffer a purifying defeat. She speaks of
Joan Báez who sang beneath the bombardments in Hanoi. She says
that Hennacy said: "Contrary to what people think
we anarchists are not doing the bombing but rather the government."
        And there is no peace because the streets would be left without
            traffic
the factories would be shut down, with birds singing on the machinery
just like she witnessed during the Great Depression. She speaks of the
    horrors
that she has seen in the Women's House of Detention
the times she has been jailed. And looking at the poor who enter
she repeats what Peter would say: "The future will be different,
    If we make the present different"
A reverent good-bye to this saintly anarchist
and to this sacred place where everyone is welcomed, all free
        each one according to his own needs
        each one according to his abilities.

DOWNTOWN. UPTOWN. Bang, bang. The trains go thundering
underground UPTOWN and DOWNTOWN
with the names of poor boys and girls painted like flowers on them
    Tom   Jim   John   Caroline
the name and sad address of where they live. They
are real. So that we know they are real. Bang bang
the express cars on the high tension wires with
their luminous ads for Calvert, Pall Mall, and the Army
            think about a career in the Army

It's night, near Wall Street, in an apartment without furniture
priests and lay people and Marxist Protestant ministers

"Change the system in which profit is the goal of mankind"
"Christian ethics do not belong within the confines of a private
    morality"
"The vision of the Kingdom of God is subversive"
One person works with computers, another with the poor.
Sunday night, and floors of buildings still lit on Wall Street.
They're screwing us.
    "Hello Bogotá"
            "Hello ITT"
two twin skyscrapers taller than the Empire State
the upper half of both still lit up
manifest in the sky behind the crystal windows Imperialism
Hello we wanted more drought
    Who is that other monster that rises up in the night?
The Chase Manhattan Bank screwing half of humanity.
Behind Wall Street, the Brooklyn Bridge, like a lyre of lights.
In the shadows two young men breaking into a car or so it seems.
    Our pale satellite above the Brooklyn sky
    flat like a rugby ball.

Early next day. Tony takes me again to Kennedy
in his Franciscan car. Six days in New York.
    The collection will be for consciousness raising,
"Not for any institution!" Tony said. For no institution.
I did not get a window seat. Upon takeoff, way below
    (scarcely a glance)
the silhouette of skyscrapers in a sky of smog from autos
    acids and carbon monoxide.

"We Didn't Go North to Pick Flowers"

Víctor M. Espinosa

This interview was conducted by Víctor M. Espinosa in San Diego de Alejandría, Mexico, in May 1992. The original may be found in Jorge Durand's *El Norte es como el mar: Entrevistas a trabajadores migrantes en Estados Unidos* (The North Is Like a Sea: Interviews with Migrant Workers in the United States) (Guadalajara: University of Guadalajara Press, 1996), 234–249. Jorge Durand is a research professor of anthropology at the University of Guadalajara. In addition to the aforementioned text his books include *Crossing the Border, Beyond Smoke and Mirrors: Mexican Immigration in an Era of Economic Integration, Miracles on the Border: Retablos of Mexican Migrants to the United States,* and *Return to Aztlan: The Social Process of International Migration from Western Mexico.* By permission of the University of Guadalajara Press, Mexico.

1992

Don Miguel Gutiérrez is a native of the altiplano community of San Diego de Alejandría. It was there that he learned from his father and fellow countrymen all he needed to know about migration. But his father, a laborer and migratory worker for many years, didn't want his son to follow the same path he did. If he had wasted his life in the North it was precisely so that his children would not have to do the same thing. But there was little he could do in this sense—his three sons were already in the North; the only thing he succeeded in doing was instilling in them the need to return to their homeland.

The story of Don Miguel is undoubtedly unique. His goal in life was to work his own lands, and to realize this dream he let other opportunities pass him by. First he was a "maestro" and migratory worker, until he became a union leader and legalized his situation in the United States. Later he was a university student and a teacher and completed his formal studies in agronomy. But the same day he graduated he opted to go north to work in order to save money, buy some land and a tractor.

At first he was the butt of his countrymen's jokes, but little by little they began to understand what he had accomplished. He had several different jobs and by the time he managed to get a good one, the period he had given himself to work in the United States was up.

Now he works in Mexico, in his native village, farming his own lands, subject to the unpredictability and vicissitudes of the weather, which is what anyone who grows corn has to endure.

My father was born in 1922. From the time he was a child he worked as an irrigator at the San Isidro hacienda, owned by Don Fernando Valdivia, and he helped my grandfather work his land. When he was twelve years old he was sent to school and after completing the third grade he left his village for the Lagos seminary where he was to continue his primary school education. He only studied there for a few months because my grandfather found himself unemployed when the San Isidro hacienda was divided up among the agrarian reformers of 1937 and therefore he had to return to his village and help my grandfather support the family.

In those years things got so bad for the village that many migrated to Mexico City. My father had received news there was work to be found there and so he decided to try his luck. He left in 1940 at the age of eighteen and lived with several of his friends. He worked for a while as an employee in a store, then later in a furniture factory, until he found a job in the Mundet soft drinks factory.

In August 1942 he heard on the radio that all those wanting to go to the United States to work legally should go to the hiring center that had been set up in a football stadium. My father told me that despite the intense propaganda the government engaged in, the rumor had circulated that it was all a trick to send Mexicans off to war. He recalled how the rumor spread because in May of that same year the Germans sunk the ship the *Potrero del llano* and Mexico was suddenly compelled to enter the war officially. In addition, in August that same year the Law of Obligatory Military Service went into effect. The fear felt by the people only increased as blackouts occurred and emergency drills were carried out in some neighborhoods.

One day, I think it was in October, my father was in his truck on the way to work when he passed by the stadium and saw the lines of people who were waiting their turn to work as day laborers. He decided to take a look at what was going on. While he waited in line he remembered that my grandfather had once told him that if he happened to go north, he shouldn't do it illegally because he had gone to the United States in 1910 and nearly drowned attempting to cross the Rio Grande.

When it was his turn the first thing they did was examine his hands, and since he had been a *campesino* they were full of calluses; they also gave him a medical exam. On the third day he was on a train, heading for the United States, with his trip, food, and lodging all paid for. He told me it was a fifteen-car train, full of human arms that the gringos needed for their work and that the last car bore a white flag. They arrived in Juarez and there they were divided up; he ended up in a group of young men who didn't know the North at all. When they told him he was going to the Imperial Valley he imagined a really beautiful place.

When they arrived, my father said, everyone was taken by surprise, there were nothing but ranches surrounded by desert, far from any kind of a village, with ranchers who worked with draft horses and an occasional tractor. They were even more disillusioned when they showed them where they would live and sleep, as if they were out camping.

They began to work right away in planting watermelon seeds; these were twelve-hour work days, from six in the morning until six in the evening. The watermelon harvest was to begin within six months, but his contract was up and he returned to the village in May 1943, I believe. He tells me that all those who went north with him came back wearing nice jackets and pants and carrying a lot of dollars on them.

That same year he was hired again; this time they sent him to San José, California, to work on the railroad tracks, as part of a roving crew that laid and replaced tracks. He worked ten hours a day and was paid fifty-seven cents, ten cents more than in the Imperial Valley. The work was real hard; they had to move the tracks, between just the twelve of them, with pincers called *troncas*. He had been there for more than a year when news reached him that the war had ended, and they refused to renew the contracts of these workers, so he returned to San Diego the last day of December 1945.

When he arrived he found my grandfather in very bad health. He died in March 1946 and my father stayed to tend to what he had left him: a chickpea harvest and a few animals. He could no longer go north.

That year, as soon as he had harvested the crop, he left again for the United States; this time he was hired in Irapuato. He had to go to Montana and work in agriculture, because there was no longer any work for Mexicans in this sector of the economy. He worked in the fields, in the weeding of the beet crop, using a little hoe known as the *cortito*, infamous because it required them to be bent over the whole day.

This time they paid him per contract, that is, according to the number of sacks he picked. They kept only six workers, five from San Diego and one from Arandas, and they were to do all the work in two months, because afterward they would be taken to Wisconsin for the potato harvest. The final days they worked until ten o'clock at night in order to complete the work.

They went by train to Wisconsin, but they arrived before the actual potato harvest, so in the meantime they were put to work picking cherries, in small buckets that were narrow at the bottom and wide at the top, for which they were paid twenty-five cents a bucket. My father scarcely made enough money to eat, and besides, they didn't pay them until they finished their work for fear they might desert. Since these were states that were quite remote, it wasn't easy to find people to work on the ranches. They were there for several weeks and still it wasn't time for the potato harvest. As a result, my father got in touch with a good friend who was working nearby and whose sister in Chicago worked in a meatpacking plant. He proposed they take off and try their luck in Chicago, taking advantage of the fact they were not too far from the city. He felt hopeful because the job meant more money; he had spent very little and during that whole period he was still not married.

They left by train and journeyed for fifteen hours, feeling a bit afraid because this was the first time they were traveling as illegals. He told me that whenever he saw a *gringo* in uniform he always confused him with immigration agents.

In Chicago he went to the home of his friend's sister. He obtained work immediately in the packing plant, where they paid him ninety-five cents a day and he worked eight to ten hours. His job was simple: put sausages into small baskets with wheels so that the women could pack them. He had barely worked three months when December arrived and he and his friend began to reminisce about the holidays in the village: the strolls around the plaza and the serenades. Since they were both bachelors they decided, out of pure nostalgia, to return to San Diego. But when they reached the border, the *Migra* caught them as they were getting out of a truck in Laredo and locked them up in a basement for a few days. Later they were taken to the other side of the bridge and set free on the Mexican side. They reached San Diego on January 6th, two days before the fiestas came to an end. Shortly after he arrived, my father was offered a job in the municipal president's office as treasurer. He knew nothing about politics but since many people were going north, and those who knew how to read and write were in a minority, without realizing it, he ended up working in the president's office for ten years, not leaving San Diego again until 1962. That year Samuel Correa became president and they couldn't reach an understanding with one another and he was removed from his job. He decided it was time to return again to the United States.

But this time he didn't go as a laborer because that year, a cousin of his offered to help him with his papers and since he was on good terms with the head of the ranch where he worked, he obtained for my father "a promise to work" document, whereby the rancher formally asked him to work, and the whole question of papers took six months to resolve.

He left in August 1962 for Santa Maria, California, with his cousin, to pick raspberries, but they paid very little, and the raspberries didn't even taste that good. After two months the season came to an end and he decided to return to his village.

The following year he went to Soledad, California, with a sister whose husband had taken her there to live, and an uncle who had been the first person from San Diego to go to that state. The uncle had already begun to find a place for relatives from the village. My father's first job was washing dishes in a field where they fed the laborers, but he didn't like it because he was paid barely fifty dollars a week. He lasted only one week and then went to talk to his uncle who told him that in the ranch where he worked they were looking for an irrigator, but he warned him it was very hard work:

"You get really wet and the ones who work the job always complain of rheumatism; the good thing is there's always work and they give you a lot of hours per day."

My father replied that he hadn't gone north to pick flowers, and so they gave him the job of irrigator. He worked fourteen hours a day, beginning at 6:00 a.m. before daybreak and finishing up when it was dark. He didn't have to pay rent because he lived on the ranch. He liked the work, learned it well, and continued to do this for some twenty years. He'd come and go: he'd work from six to eight months in different ranches and then he'd return to San Diego, where he spent the rest of the year working his own land, some sixty hectares that he bought in 1964 thanks to his work in the North, and he even had fifty pigs and ten cows. In 1970 he returned to Chicago, because in the village friends told him they earned more and worked less, but to make a long story short, reality was very different from what he was told. In Chicago he worked for a company where he earned $2.50 an hour but they only gave him eight hours of work per day, the normal forty-hour work week that paid him at the most ninety dollars a week, because they didn't give overtime to new arrivals, while in California, even though he earned less per hour, he could work—twelve to fourteen hours a week and earn more than a hundred dollars a week. In Chicago he ended up working for the city, for Parks and Gardens, where he earned three dollars an hour, but the problem was the climate, which he never liked.

In 1974 when he returned from the United States, I told him I wanted to go north, but my father was opposed to the idea. He told me that so many years of sacrifice and sleeplessness were precisely so that his children could get an education and not have to struggle to survive in another country, because in the end they were exploited there like slaves.

He returned to the United States, just like every other year, and told me he'd take me with him so I could get to know what it was like, but not until my papers were in order so that I wouldn't have to go as an illegal. But I had already reached an agreement with my friends and, with his authorization or without it, I wanted to experience in the flesh what the so-called North was all about. I didn't really need to go north because my father always provided for us and I had worked as a teacher for the previous two years in San Diego's secondary school. For this reason I waited until summer vacation and left in August, along with three other friends from the village, heading straight for the border. But luck wasn't on our side; the Migra caught us several times and we had to go back without experiencing life in the United States. All the same, this trip was my initiation and I recall it vividly.

I remember how Chuy Echeverría, Miguel Ramírez, and a son of Cirilo Rocha and I journeyed north; supposedly Chuy Echeverría had already gone once and he was the one who knew the famous San Marcos–Carlos Bad route. He told us we would arrive in Tijuana, the Libertad neighborhood of the city, and from there you could see a pair of antennas and you had to continue to follow the light from between the hills, without the need of a *coyote*, because knowing the way made everything else easy.

Chuy told us that in order to avoid the problem with the famous *cholos* who gathered in the Libertad neighborhood, we were going to leave in the late evening, after sunset so we could still see where we were going. We walked and hid, then started walking again, and in one of these moments the Border Patrol spotted us and as they approached we looked for a place to hide, but the Migra found two of us. We were close by, hiding about fifteen feet away, in the underbrush, and since they only saw two people, they were satisfied, arrested the two and left. The bad part was they took with them the one person who knew the way; we stayed there not knowing what to do; we ate and then started walking, and what else could we do? We walked almost the entire night; within a short time all of this turned into a kind of fiesta; we found ourselves in the company of a lot of other people, whole groups doing the same thing we were. We joined one of these groups and followed them for a long time until finally we got tired of this and decided to go our own way, ending up in a tomato garden. By that time it was after midnight.

We waited for daybreak so as not to lose our way and as soon as it dawned we naively decided to walk along the highway. It wasn't long before the Border Patrol spotted us and asked what we were doing there.

"Nothing," we answered.

"Okay, then, let's go to Mexico."

What else could we say? They got us out of the United States right away and by morning we were eating *menudo* in Tijuana.

We attempted two more times to enter the country. We didn't run into the ones who were caught during our first trip. We had some money on us because this time we wanted to be prepared, but the ones they caught before, they put on a plane and flew them as far as León, Guanajuato. So for them the adventure had come to an end.

The other friend with me began to lose interest in the whole thing. His money was now running out.

"I'm going back," he said.

"Okay, let's go."

So we returned.

When my father found out he said that if I really wanted to go north, I should go when the season for work began, in March, and not in August when all the work is coming to an end.

I asked for a leave of absence from the school and the following year in 1975 I invited another friend and we left together in March, accompanied by my father. He went as far as Soledad and left the two of us in Tijuana with Jesús Aldana, a *coyote* from San Diego, who would get us across the border. This time we entered without difficulty; they drove us in a pickup as far as Los Angeles; we paid three hundred dollars apiece. When we arrived my father had already obtained my Social Security card. They told my friend that in order to get insurance he needed to prove he was a legal resident; if not, the Migra would be after him, and since we had given the address where we were living, we could no longer stay there, so we left for a month to work in the cleaning and harvesting of beets at a small ranch thirty miles from Soledad. We worked from six in the morning until noon. That was the time the Migra always passed by the ranch, in the daily run it made from Salinas. Those who didn't have papers stopped working and hid in a shed. They didn't show themselves until three o'clock and then worked for another three hours.

When we realized that the Migra didn't show up at the house we returned. I worked for a time with my father on a ranch until I got a better job, in a company that produced dehydrated garlic and onion. During this period my father had initiated the paperwork to make me legal. After several applications they informed us to come in person as soon as possible, before I turned twenty-one, because the procedure was much easier in that case.

Now legal, it was much easier to obtain work, but I still hadn't given up the idea of continuing my studies. When I went back to Mexico in 1975 it turned out they had just opened a college preparatory school in San Julián and I signed up right away. I continued to teach high school and during vacation I would go with my father to the United States for three or four months.

This was how I spent my time when I finished my college prep work in 1977, and with the money I saved from my work as a teacher in San Diego and as a worker in the United States, I went to the University of Guadalajara to study agronomy. At the same time I tried to change my assignment as a teacher in San Diego to Guadalajara but I couldn't, and therefore I asked for a leave of absence, but this time without going off to work.

But it turned out that my savings, consisting of twenty thousand pesos, soon disappeared, I no longer had enough money to continue my studies and, besides, I wanted to get married. With all of this in mind, I left my studies for a year and in 1978 I headed back to the United States.

In a short time, thanks to the political connections I had as a teacher and my friendship with the president of Don Diego's municipal council, they called in a favor from the representative of the district who had good contacts in the Department of Public Education. As a result I was able to get a teaching position closer to Guadalajara: in Cajatitlán.

In 1983 I finally received my diploma in agronomy, and to the surprise of my parents, I decided to return again to the United States. I recall now that they were very much against my decision, but I had my reasons for wanting to go. I had never stopped thinking about the United States, and this time with a specific goal in mind: save enough money in order to get married and be able to continue my studies. When I had about three or four thousand dollars saved, I returned to Mexico and within two months

I was married. I went back to the high school in San Diego to work, without giving up on my plans to continue my university degree in agronomy. Later I asked for an exchange to Ocotlán, and at the same time I planned my return to my second year of university studies. To do this I first had to change my teaching schedule for one in the evening in Jamay, from where I traveled every day to Guadalajara to attend classes at the university, in a small car I bought with the money I brought from the United States because there I learned it was possible to save money. The principal problem with people who go north is that the idea of saving money is the farthest thing from their mind; they don't have the necessary willpower or the necessary ability to save what they earn, because for the most part they make a lot of money; I was well aware of this, and my intention was to buy a tractor, because I was always very good in agriculture. In fact, I wanted to make a living at it, in my own village and on my own land.

My friends thought it was crazy for me to go back to the United States, because in fact I was in the best possible moment of my professional career working as a teacher. I had become involved in politics; at the time I was the general-secretary of the teachers union; mine was an excellent position, because in the district there were only twenty-two of us who were in charge of political affairs under Section 47. All of this represented a great deal of responsibility because political affairs are carried out in Guadalajara, not here, but outside the villages. In the villages at that time the general-secretary could speak his mind, along with the inspector, on issues that involved temporary work and work proposals, and that gave you a certain power that many people used to make money, but I had another trip north in mind, and as far as everyone was concerned, it didn't make sense to be going to the United States again.

I knew that the work I would be doing there would be physical work, that it demanded a tremendous effort; nonetheless, I also knew that if I didn't go then, I would never go, so with all the pain and grief, I left for the United States when I finished my university degree in September 1983.

I arrived in Soledad, California, with Abel, my youngest brother. At the time, David was still there, my other brother whom I had taken north for the first time in 1976. In the beginning I picked lettuce, until it occurred to me that the best way to make money was with the *corridas* in the Salinas Valley. This consisted of following the harvesting of different crops from one ranch to another. During my movements from one to another I lived in my car, a Volkswagen that had only one seat, the driver's, and I put a well-cushioned platform in it to serve as a bed and I even had an electric stove in the car.

At first I had to put up with the jokes of my friends from San Diego. They made fun of me because I had spent my life studying only to end up picking lettuce like the rest of them. I remember that I didn't let them get to me because I had an argument that was quite simple and it shut them up: I was making good money at a time when it was difficult to get work in Mexico, because the economic recession was in its critical stage.

The only thing I didn't like about the *corridas* was having to travel from one place to another. It prevented me from being in school, so that when I could, the first thing I did was study English, because I knew it was the basis for getting the best jobs. What I learned in school in Mexico undoubtedly helped me thanks to my accent, because if you arrive speaking haltingly, with a strong Mexican accent, they view you as someone who doesn't know how to speak English, and therefore incapable of doing anything, at least that's the kind of complex they create in you.

I had been working in the *corridas* for a year when my father, now tired after twenty years as an irrigator, retired in the United States. I took advantage of this opportunity and remained in his job for three years. With this work I was able to save more; soon I bought a house in San Diego, besides the one I already had in Guadalajara in the Residencial Poniente.

My job, as irrigator, enabled me to better establish myself. I started to study everything I always wanted to: mechanics, welding, lamination and painting, writing and editing, philosophy, and I even took a course in education for teachers. The moment arrived when I felt I could understand and write English perfectly, but I still had some problems in speaking. Despite this, and in spite of the fact I had a good job, and instilled by the desire to get ahead, I started working as a mechanic for eight months, without ceasing to read the newspapers in search of a better position.

On one of those occasions an ad appeared that said the Department of Agriculture of Monterrey County, California, was looking for agricultural technicians to help researchers carry out a number of different tasks. I filled out an application, and, to my surprise, within a few days, after they evaluated my qualifications, I was offered the job. I recall that the exam they gave me was easy. I had to identify plants, calculate the proper dosage of insecticide, very elementary things, compared with everything I had studied in Mexico. In addition, the job required experience in agriculture, plants, crops, and the use of farm equipment. My university transcript, which indicated all the courses I had taken plus my experience as an irrigator, all of this served me well.

I worked for several researchers from the University of California. The Department of Agriculture of Monterrey County paid me, and it was an interesting job. There were seven of us, several of whom were internationally recognized scholars in entomology, herbicides, herbiculture, irrigation, and fertilizers. Initially, in economic terms, it was the best job I ever had; I earned between ten and twelve dollars an hour. The problem was I couldn't work more than eight hours a day, and a lot was deducted from my pay for taxes. As time went by I gained their confidence and they began to call me on weekends to do work for the ranchers in the county, and in this way I was able to improve my earnings. I had been working for a year for them when I completed the five-year maximum I had given myself in the United States, regardless of how much money I saved up until then. But at that moment I found myself in the best job I had ever had, so I decided to stay another six months.

In December 1989 I informed people that I would be leaving the job because I wanted to try to make it in Mexico. It probably wouldn't work, I remember thinking, but I had to try just the same. One of the members of the research team promised me a better job, another told me that if I came back to the United States, even for only one or two weeks, I would definitely have work with them.

Fortunately or unfortunately, I decided to return to Mexico because my self-imposed deadline had expired and, besides, I wanted to be in Mexico for a while. I don't know now whether I will return to the United States. In December 1992 it will be two years since I've come back to Mexico. I returned to work in agriculture. The first year was a bad one for me; I invested a lot of money and despite the fact I had a good harvest, I definitely spent more money than I made. But I am going to plant again this year and I hope to have better luck.

The lands I currently own are the same ones my father bought back in 1964, thanks to his work in the North, and which he sold in 1970, because he never derived any benefit from them

In 1988 two of my brothers and I bought those same lands because here you are worth more especially if you have property; to own land is to have prestige. One of my brothers wanted to buy land for a house but I convinced him to buy land to plant. When we lived together in the United States things went well for the three of us. David is currently in charge of a potato packing plant. Abel, the youngest, I put to work as an irrigator on the ranch, and now he works as a welder.

I remember that we spoke every day about our land, always with the illusion of getting ahead. My brothers are still in the North; they come back to Mexico for a while; their intention is to return definitively because they know that here you're somebody and there you're nobody. It doesn't matter what your work is, no matter how good it is. The two of them, for example, have good jobs, but even so they really aren't anybody.

We looked for some land for sale and found out that a good friend of our father wanted to sell his land and since we knew the property, it had belonged to my father, we knew it was beautiful land and so we bought it. We paid ten thousand dollars in cash and five thousand dollars every six months, for a total of forty thousand dollars.

Before I came back we had bought a tractor, several vehicles, equipment, and farm implements and that's why I dedicated my time completely to agriculture. I planted close to forty hectares, all with corn, because there was a great demand for cattle feed in the local market, but it was a difficult year. As a farmer I believe I treated the soil well, that I invested a great deal of money in the land, but I didn't get the results I was counting on. In the first place, the rains were late; it began to rain in July, and once they started they didn't let up until September. But still I had a decent crop. When I had everything ready to be ground, on July 6, the rains came and soaked the entire harvest and I found myself on the verge of losing everything. I owed forty-five million pesos; the following year I planted again but I was more careful with my expenses.

I was invited to participate in one of the PRI groups in the municipality because they knew I liked politics and I had a good reputation due to the fact I was a migrant who had built my home with money I earned in the North and I was also one of the few who could return from the North and have at my disposal anywhere from thirty to forty million pesos. The elections were bitterly contested because one of the PRI groups joined PAN, but in the end PRI won despite losing three seats in the village. Actually we won thanks to the votes of the ranchers. Don Jesús Hernández, also a migrant, was elected president of the town council and I became secretary to the president of San Diego de Alejandría.

Mea Culpa

Eduardo Galeano

Eduardo Galeano (Uruguay, 1940–) is one of Latin America's leading journalists and political commentators. His columns appear in newspapers throughout Latin America as well as in *The Progressive, The New Internationalist, The Monthly Review,* and *The Nation.* His books include *Las venas abiertas de América Latina* (1971, The Open Veins of Latin America), *Días y noches de amor y de guerra* (1978, Days and Nights of Love and War), *Memoria del fuego* (1982–1986, Memory of Fire), *Ventana sobre Sandino* (1985, A Window on Sandino), *El libro de los abrazos* (1989, The Book of Embraces), *Nosotros decimos no* (1989, We Say No), *América Latina para entenderte mejor* (1990, To Understand You Better Latin America), *Ser como ellos y otros artículos* (1992, To Be Like Them and Other Essays), and *Patas arriba:La escuela del mundo al revés* (1998, Upside Down: A Primer for the Looking Glass World). The following selection was a speech given to the annual meeting of book dealers in the United States, American Booksellers Association, in Los Angeles, California, May 26, 1992. It appears in *Ser como ellos y otros artículos* (Madrid: Siglo Veintiuno Editores, 1992), 41–45. By permission of the author.

1992

Twenty-five years ago I tried to take my first trip to the United States. I went to the consulate and requested a visa. The form I had to fill out asked for, among other things, the following: *Are you planning to assassinate the president of the United States of America?* I was so modest at the time that I wasn't even planning to assassinate the president of Uruguay; but I responded: *Yes.* I was sure the question was a joke, inspired by my mentors Ambrose Bierce and Mark Twain.

The consulate denied my request. My response was a bad one. I didn't get it. Years have gone by and, if truth be told, I still don't get it. Please excuse me. I'm confusing this convention of North American booksellers with the confessional of my Catholic childhood. But to whom could a writer better confess himself than to a bookseller? And with a lot of sins to confess don't you perhaps need a large number of booksellers?

Every morning, to start off the day, I have news for breakfast. I read, for example, in the newspapers about the constant scandals that stalk presidential candidates. I must admit I don't understand why North American politicians are bad if they have affairs with beautiful, inoffensive women, and, on the other hand, are considered good if they have affairs with powerful companies that sell arms or poison.

Or I read about the sending of North American soldiers to fight against the drug plantations in Latin America. There's no way to understand this; I just don't get why countries that produce drugs and the people who consume them are evil while, on the other hand, the lifestyle that generates the need to consume them is good.

In the financial pages I read that the United States imported 35,292 Mexican brassieres during 1991. Not one brassiere more, because the quota for brassieres authorized by the government is 35,292. And so, what can I say: I don't understand why protectionist trade barriers and subsidies are good inside the United States but bad in Latin America.

Ah, the fog between Good and Evil. In the American press I see ads exhorting people to buy domestic products, *Buy American!* But then I fail to understand why Japanese products that invade the U.S. market are bad, while U.S. products that invade Latin America are good.

And it's not only the question of products: let's imagine for a moment that Mexican marines invade Los Angeles, in order to protect Mexicans living there who are threatened by recent disturbances. Is this good or bad?

I even ask myself: And I? Am I good? Or am I bad? I am tormented by doubts about my identity: doubts that are typical of us, writers, I know this only too well. It's no mystery to anyone that we writers have a soul that is condemned to the fires of eternal anxiety: at the center of this inferno new doubts respond to each certainty and new questions respond to each question. But my anxiety is multiplying at this end of the century, this end of the millennium, because I too know that the United States is looking for new evils to combat.

Nostalgia for the Empire of Evil: there in the East the bad guys have become good, and the rest of the world has become dramatically incapable of producing the bad guys the military market so desperately demands. I still don't understand why Iraqi soldiers were bad when they took control of Kuwait while U.S. marines were good when they took control of Grenada or Panama; but you have to take into account that Saddam Hussein, who was good until the end of 1990, was becoming bad from 1991 on. Obviously, one bad guy just isn't enough. You can always lay hands on the long-term bad guys like Muammar Khaddafi or Fidel Castro; but you have to recognize that the offer is a poor one.

I confess confidentially, and with all the letters of the alphabet, no matter how difficult it may be for me that yes, it's true, yes: I don't know how to drive an automobile, I don't have a computer, I never went to a psychoanalyst, I write by hand, I don't like TV, and I've never seen Ninja turtles.

And even more: my head is bald and leftist. All of my efforts to grow hair on my naked cranium and to correct my tendency to think toward the left have been in vain. Up until just a few years ago they used to tie the left hand of southpaw children in the schools in order to make them write with the right hand; and it seems that produced good results. To oblige adults to think rightly military dictatorships use blood-and-guts therapies and democracies use television. They've made me try both medicines but they didn't work.

I admit I have a certain biological inability to perceive the virtues of the freedom of money. At the end of last year, let's take as an example, I was with my wife in the middle of a long trip when Pan American went bankrupt. She and I were left literally in the air and planeless. We had to borrow money from a few friends and then I proceeded to interpret the whole episode, following my limited vision of things: I believed that the invisible hand of the market had robbed two tickets from me.

I recognize that I was wrong. I no longer have any hope of recovering even a cent; but now I realize that God did me a great favor. The Almighty astutely used that subtle procedure to convince me you can't go through this world without a credit card.

I didn't have one. I confess this. Until very recently my natural inclination toward evil prohibited this happiness. I used to believe the credit card was just one more trap perpetrated by a consuming society. I believed that the inhabitants of the world's great modern cities suffered the slavery of debt, just as the Indians of Guatemala did on the cotton and coffee plantations. Now the veil covering my eyes has been lifted, and I can see clearly: no one is, if he is not worthy of credit. But now, I am. I owe, therefore I am.

But doubt, that persistent shadow, renews its attack. I get it in my head that my country also owes debt, and that the more it pays the more it owes. And the more it owes, the less the government governs and the more its creditors govern. And still the United States, who owes more than all of Latin America put together, accepts no conditions, it only imposes them. Can it be that it is bad to owe a little and, on the other hand, good to owe very much?

Doubts, doubts. And so many doubts regarding my own work! I wonder if literature still has a future in this world where five-year-olds are already electrical engineers. And I'd like to be able to respond to my question: maybe the lifestyle of our age is not very good for people, nor the environment; but undoubtedly it's very good for the pharmaceutical industry. Why couldn't it also be good for the literary industry? It all depends on the product being offered, which has to be a kind of tranquilizer like valium and glitzy and light like a TV show; something that helps you not to think dangerously nor to feel profoundly, something that eludes dangerous dreams and above all avoids the temptation to live them.

But it so happens that is exactly the literature I'm incapable of writing and reading. Condemned to impotence, I can neither write nor read words that are neutral. And even though I do everything possible, I can't stop believing that these times of resignation, of the discredit of human passion and regret for human commitment, constitute our challenge but certainly not our destiny.

Thank you very much. I have unburdened my conscience, availing myself of the sanctity of the confessional, and I beg you not to forget it. Now I must obtain a visa in order to enter the New World Order. I hope they don't ask me if I'm planning to kill the president.

New York, New York

Mario Vargas Llosa

This essay first appeared in *El País*, June 15, 2008. By permission of Agencia Literaria Carmen Balcells S.A., Barcelona.

2008

Even though under its current mayor, Michael Bloomberg, it's a lot less clean than it was during the Giuliani administration, New York continues to be a fascinating city, the Babylon of the twenty-first century, a modern Tower of Babel, the capital of today's world. I've been to Manhattan many times before, but almost always for just a few days, and usually it was to attend symposia and give conferences, but this is the first time, after nearly thirty years, that I've been able to stay in the city a couple of months, just enough time to take its pulse, to live here and get an idea of what it's like.

This city is small, in numerical and statistical terms, and still, as in Borges's "El Aleph," everything fits inside it, or passes through it, whether it be countries, races, religions, or languages, and everything becomes quickly absorbed by the city, losing its foreign identity while adopting a new one, New York's. It is, at the same time, everybody's city and no one's, a city without its own identity because it contains all possible identities. The Hispanic world, or Latino as they also call it here, is multipresent, and in its bars, department stores, and restaurants, after English, Spanish is the language you hear wherever you go, with all of its Latin American variants, as well as the local Spanish idiom, Spanglish, which is already beginning to generate its own literature. All of this is due undoubtedly to the fact that institutions like Teatro Español and the Instituto Cervantes have such a vital presence in the cultural life of New York. In the former I saw a superb theatrical adaptation of Jorge Amado's *Doña Flor and Her Two husbands* by Jorge Alí Triana, and the Cervantes collaborated closely with the International PEN Center on a symposium that in April brought to New York hundreds of writers from all over the world.

One of the most well-known stereotypes concerning New York is that it is a city of business and little culture, but this notion is quickly undermined paging through *Time Out* or the weekly cultural pages of the *New York Times*. The truth is that, as far as cultural offerings are concerned, there is no other city on this planet that offers as many possibilities, from all artistic domains, as the Big Apple does. Painting, sculpture, classical and modern music, dance, theater, opera, movies, ideas, literature, classes, workshops, conferences, museums, schools of art, academies, all of these constitute a vertiginous dimension of New York life that no one can capture in its totality. The most one can accomplish, devoting a great deal of time to the task, renders a very small part of the total, merely the tip of the iceberg.

For those who are accustomed to working in libraries, like me, the Public Library of the City of New York is a small paradise. Located on Fifth Avenue, between 41st and 42nd Streets, this immense nineteenth-century edifice with thick columns, marble staircases, and immense high-ceilinged reading rooms that are magnificently illuminated lies atop a real subterranean city of several floors where its millions of books are housed, computerized and preserved in air-conditioned rooms that protect them from heat, insects, and humidity. After the Library of Congress and the library of Harvard University it is one of the best-equipped libraries in the United States and one of the most functional and efficient that I have ever used. One of its treasures is the Berg Collection, which was donated by two brothers who were physicians, Jews of Hungarian origin. Thanks to them the library counts, among its prized possessions, a first edition of the *Quixote*, manuscripts by Dickens, Henry James, Whitman, practically all of the diaries and novels of Virginia Woolf, as well as a typed copy of Eliot's *The Waste Land* with corrections and commentaries written in Ezra Pound's hand.

It is also the noisiest and busiest library in the world, because tourists invade its reading rooms taking photos and speaking out loud in the most brazen manner. But you finally get used to all the bustle, as if it were background music. Although the Public Library has the necessary specialized personnel, it, like all cultural institutions in the United States, functions thanks to the help of volunteers, usually retirees, and for the most part women, who offer information and guidance, and help library users to find their way through the labyrinth of this building. I am very moved by these women, some of whom are quite elderly, who are always there on time with a smile on their face, lending the public their services. Civic volunteerism is an Anglo-Saxon institution and without it neither England nor the United States would be what they are.

The very rich cultural life of New York would not exist without the contribution of the society at large, which is what, to a great extent, finances and promotes it. Undoubtedly, the state does too but in a relatively limited proportion, and, at times, its contribution represents only a very small part. It is true that both businesses as well as individuals derive important tax incentives for their donations and for sponsoring cultural activities, but beyond that, a more profound explanation for the astronomical sums of money that foundations, commercial entities, both industrial and financial, as well as private individuals invest annually in museums, spectacles, exhibitions, libraries, conferences, universities, and so on, has more to do with a culture, with a civic awareness that if a society wants to have an intellectual and artistic life that is rich, creative, and free, it is the obligation of all citizens, without exception, to assume this responsibility and to sustain it. This explains why, unlike countries in other parts of the world where philanthropic governments make culture an official product of self-promotion and bureaucratic manipulation, in England and the United States culture possesses a certain independent and inclusive character that guarantees its freedom, its renewal, and its continuous state of experimentation.

In the two months I have spent here I have seen, for example, how the Museo del Barrio, located in Spanish Harlem, has obtained resources for the complete renovation it has undertaken and its plan to exhibit art from all parts of Latin America. It has already rebuilt its beautiful auditorium, a *belle époque* jewel that was previously in ruins. At the formal dinner held to raise money, they collected, in just a few hours, more than four million dollars.

It is true that a cultural life that is barely funded by the state and that depends on the society at large to sustain it can be very costly. New York's definitely is and certain performing arts like the opera and concerts often charge prices that are extremely prohibitive. And yet, everything that is worth seeing is always filled with people in New York, and the great museums, the Metropolitan and the MOMA (Museum of Modern Art), each year receive more visitors than Yankee Stadium and Madison Square Garden.

In many ways, New York has become in this epoch what Paris was for many earlier generations: a place where young and creative artists want to be because they sense that New York is where they will find a stimulating atmosphere for their work and because they know that if they can triumph here then they can triumph throughout the entire world. This occurs not only with musicians, painters, dancers, actors, and filmmakers, but also with writers. I was surprised by the incredible number of young poets, storytellers, and playwrights from different Latin American countries who now reside in New York where they write, trying to make their way in the city of skyscrapers. Some are connected with universities and foundations while others survive the best they can, working in bookstores, at publishing houses, or playing the guitar or the bongos in Latino bars and even on street corners. In spite of all this, they publish literary reviews, give recitals, and in almost all of New York's bookstores there are sections devoted to books in Spanish.

I have spent two intense and exciting months in this bustling city. I lived in the area around Union Square, a charming and animated neighborhood, where I even found European-style cafés where I could go to read a newspaper or scribble a few lines while I had my coffee. And it is also where the Strand is located, the largest retailer of used books in the world. I attended magnificent exhibitions and some theatrical presentations—above all, one of Beckett's with John Turturro, which was splendidly produced. And films, lots of films, taking advantage of the Tribeca Film Festival, which, during a ten-day period, brings to New York movies from all over the planet. And yet, I always had the sensation that there was something missing in this marvelous city for me to feel completely at home. What was it? Age, history, tradition, antiquity. That which is essentially the secret soul of any European city and even of the most forsaken and insignificant town, that invisible presence that establishes a link between yesterday and today, those centuries of adventures, wars, artistic feats, and historical, religious, and cultural upheavals, that have produced the civilization in which we live today. In New York everything is so recent that you have the feeling the past never existed, that life is only a future in the process of creating itself. It must be because I am no longer young, but the feeling that there is almost no life behind us, that everything is only ahead, produces in me a certain anxiety and a feeling of solitude.

PART THREE

The United States as Literary Theme

To Roosevelt

Rubén Darío

Rubén Darío (real name Félix Rubén García Sarmiento, 1867–1916) was a Nicaraguan journalist, diplomat, and poet. He first became recognized as one of the region's most important poetic voices with the publication of *Azul* (Blue) in 1888. This book set the tone for the advent of what has come to be known in Latin American letters as "Modernism." Thanks to this book as well as *Prosas profanas* (1896, Profane Prose) and *Cantos de vida y esperanza* (1905, Songs of Life and Hope), Darío is today considered one of the most important poets in the Spanish language. The title of the poem presented here refers to Theodore Roosevelt (1858–1919), president of the United States from 1901 to 1909. This selection is from *Poesías completas* (Complete Poetry) (Madrid: Aguilar, 1968,) 639–641.

1905

It is through the voice of the Bible or the verses of Walt Whitman,
that one should attempt to reach you, oh great Hunter,
primitive and modern, simple and complicated,
with a certain something of Washington and four of Nimrod.

    You are the United States,
you are the future invader
of a naïve America that has Indian blood,
that still prays to Jesus Christ and still speaks in Spanish.

You are a proud and strong example of your race;
you are cultured, you are talented: you oppose Tolstoy.
And in breaking horses or killing tigers,
you are an Alexander Nabucodonosor.
(You are a professor of Energy
as the crazy people of today would say.)

You believe that life is fire,
that progress is eruption,
that wherever you shoot your bullet,
you lay the future.

No.

The United States is powerful and great.
When it shakes there is a profound tremor
that crosses the enormous vertebrae of the Andes.
When you complain, the voice one hears is the roar of the lion,
It was Hugo who once said to Grant: The stars belong to you.
(The Argentine sun barely shines as it rises in the sky,
and the Chilean star ascends . . .) You are rich.
To the worship of Hercules you join the worship of Mammon,
and as you light the way for an easy conquest,
Freedom raises its torch in New York.

But the America that is ours, that has had poets
since the early times of Netzahualcoyotl,
that has preserved the footprints of the great Baco,
that once learned the alphabet of Pan;
that consulted the stars, that was acquainted with Atlantis
whose name resonates for us in Plato,
that from the earliest moments of its life
lives infused with light, fire, perfume, love,
the America of the great Montezuma, of the great Inca,
the fragrant America of Christopher Columbus,
Catholic America, Spanish America,
the America in which the noble Cuatémoc said:
"I am not in a bed of roses"; that America
that trembles with hurricanes and nourishes itself with love,
men of Anglo-Saxon eyes and savage souls,
beware, that other America lives.

And dreams. And loves and vibrates, and is the daughter of the Sun.
Be careful. Spanish America lives.
There are a thousand cubs of the Spanish lion running around loose.
My God, Roosevelt, one would need to be
the most deadly Marksman and the strongest Hunter,
In order to keep all of us within your iron-like claws.

Well, while you may be able to count on everything, there is one
 thing missing: God!

Selected Poems

Nicolás Guillén

Nicolás Guillén (1902–1989) was born in Camaguey, Cuba, and is recognized as the foremost exponent of Afro-Cuban poetry. In 1953 he was expelled from his native land because of his opposition to the Batista government but was welcomed back by Fidel Castro after the triumph of the Revolution. Shortly after his return he was named president of the National Cuban Writers' Union. Among his most memorable books of poetry are *Sóngoro Cosongo* (1931), *West Indies Ltd.* (1934), *El son entero* (1947, The Entire Melody), *La paloma de vuelo popular* (1958, The Dove with a Popular Flight), *Tengo* (1964, I Have), *La rueda dentada* (1972, The Serrated Wheel), and *El diario que a diario* (1972, The Daily Daily). The selection included here is from *Tengo*, 2nd edition (Montevideo: Editorial El Siglo Ilustrado, 1967), 6–9. By permission of Agencia Literaria Latinoamericana, Havana, Cuba.

1967

I Have

When I look at me and pinch myself,
I, who just yesterday, was a penniless Juan,
and today a Juan who has everything,
I turn my head, and look,
I see myself and pinch myself
and wonder how can this be.

I have, let's see,
I have the pleasure of traveling throughout my country,
master of all that is contained within it,
taking a closer look at what previously
I neither possessed nor could ever hope to possess.
I can now say sugar cane,
I can say mountain,
I can say city,
I can say army,
I exercise my right to say army
now they are mine forever and yours too, and ours,
as well as a great splendor
as if emanating from lightning, a star, a flower.

I have, let's see.
I have the pleasure of going,
me, a *campesino*, a worker, a simple man,
I have the pleasure of going
(it's just an example),
of going to a bank and speaking with the manager,
not in English,
not in the language of *señor*,
but rather to say to him *compañero*, as we say in Spanish.

I have, let's see,
given the fact I'm black
no one can stop me
at the door of a dance club or bar,
or at the front desk of a hotel
and scream at me that there are no rooms,
not even a simple room, I'm not talking about a colossal suite,
just a small room where I can rest.

I have, let's see,
the reality that there's no rural police
to grab me and lock me up in their barracks,
or uproot me and cast me from my land
into the midst of the highways and byways.

Just as I have the land, I also have the sea.
no *country*

no *nightlife*
no *tennis* and *no yacht*,
just one beach after another, and one wave after another,
immense blue open and democratic:
in short, the sea.

I have, let's see,
I have already learned to read,
to tell stories,
I have learned to write
and to think
and to laugh.

I now have the reality of
a place to work
and earn
What I have to eat.

I have, let's see,
I have now what I should have had always.

The Flowers Grow Tall

The following selection is from *Tengo*, 2nd edition (Montevideo: Editorial El Siglo Ilustrado, 1967) 10–15. By permission of Agencia Literaria Latinoamericana, Havana, Cuba.

If I were not a man sure of himself, if I were not
a man who is aware of everything that awaits him

With Lynch at the helm, and Jim Crow in control
and navigating through bloody nocturnal waters;

if I were not an old alligator whose
hide has become thicker with each passing day;

if I were not a black man of universal memory
and a white man who is well aware of his sin and glory;

if I were not a Chinese man free of the mandarin
looking through the eyes of Shanghai and Peking;

if I were not an Indian of stolen copper
who has died poor for four hundred years now;

if I were not a Soviet man whose hands
are well-known for their generosity:

if I were not everything that I already am, I would say that
maybe my enemy would be able to deceive me.

* * *

McCarthy has died, they say. (I myself say: It's true,
McCarthy has died . . .) But the truth is he hasn't died.

He is alive and the barbarian makes no attempt to hide his iron claws
nor the executioner his chair, nor the G-man his jail.

A two-headed monster, that's the real North American,
one half Democrat, the other half Republican;

A two-headed monster, neither one with a brain,
it doesn't matter whether it speaks to us of alliance or progress.

And maybe it's because it speaks to us, no one in our America
(pallid Indian virgin, but not hysterical),

freed finally from the harsh noose of the Spanish
is going to believe the ridiculous manipulations of the Yankee.

An Alliance of Rockefeller with Mr. Ford: that's what I believe,
and the progress coming out of the two, I do not believe, I can see it
    all clearly.

An Alliance between Standard Oil and United Fruit. . . . Of course,
in this way progress between the two is nothing strange.

An Alliance between Chase Bank and the World Bank. My friend
the alliance between two "banks" means progress and money.

But don't anybody start with their road stories
because I do not only think, I have an opinion

that I express in a loud voice and above all I'm a man
who likes to tell things the way they really are.

And I ask questions and I reply and speak up and make demands
and I know when there's much more than meets the eye.

For the Yankee we're nothing more than cheap scum,
tribes that can be easily bought with glass beads and tin trinkets,

imbecilic generals without knowledge and education,
who stand before the slaughtered pig and drool

Argentine good old boys, Peruvian satraps,
betancourts, peraltas, muñozes . . . Quadrumanes

leaping in the jungle; small and lazy people
who dip their bitter darts in the fatal curare.

But because we have forests and coffee groves,
iron, coal, oil, copper, sugar cane plantations,

(what in dollars, means millions)
it doesn't matter that we're Quechuas or Montilones.

They come supposedly to help us progress
and in payment for their help we give them our blood.

If in Paraguay there are uproars against Washington,
then let Stroessner go and help Paraguay.

Let him who placed his government and nation in a bottle
cede power not to the people but to the primitive star

of the foolish general whose stupidity leads him
to sell his home to a stranger, and imprison and offend.

Let a macaque rest his buttocks on the seat,
Bolívar's seat, and through terror and torture

help the supreme guerrilla whose voice bellows in Venezuela
to not break the yoke of oppressive power nor shake the bonds of
   guardianship.

Each day in Colombia soldiers aim their weapons
at the campesinos and workers who assemble.

Help for Chile's copper is of primary importance.
(The copper of the mining companies not the copper of the miners.)

In the unspoiled mountains the Indian's flute sounds sad.
It produces harsh syllables of tin when its voice speaks.

In Brazil, toward the northeastern side of its anguish,
a complicated mixture of blood and sweat irrigates the dejected soil

where Gringos wearing kepis help one another each day . . .
Tell me what you think, Recife. Isn't it true, Bahía?

Central America is a huge plantation that continues to improve,
the banana crop gets bigger, coffee grows without letup.

(At times you hear the hissing sound of the whip or a slap to the face,
a peon falls to the ground . . . in short, it's not that important.)

The helper swallows his English and walks around
self-satisfied, the subdued servant in his vile livery,

who in Puerto Rico gives the orders, that is to say, obeys them,
while Albizu's[1] vast brow glistens.

Alongside the muddy River Plate Buenos Aires sparkles,
but the shadow of the gorilla clouds its brilliance

with its poisonous tongue and its stare filled with bile,
at whose voice beckon the jail cell and the barracks

* * *

Go ahead, Jim Crow, don't stop now; let go
with your victory yell. A great hurrah for the Alliance.

Lynch, go ahead, run, get your whips.
That's the way, that's what's important . . . Hurrah for Progress!

Just like that, from one day to the next (allied on the road to progress
under Washington's directives, which is the voice of authority)

go ahead, make of our lands a Nazi paradise:
with not an Indian, an evil white man, a black or mestizo;

and let us reach that superb summit of culture
where the mechanical genius of a great pure race

shows us the profound technique that it proclaims
in Jacksonville, Arkansas, Mississippi, Alabama,

the expeditious South whose obscene problems
it resolves with whiplashes, dogs and burnings.

But in our America the flowers grow tall.
It brings its people together and polishes its precious stones.
Out of the guerrillas emerge bazookas and poems.
With a vengeful fury our nightingales trill their song . . .

Notes

1. Reference to Pedro Albizu Campos (1891–1965), leader of Puerto Rico's Nationalist Party and an ardent advocate for Puerto Rican independence. He was jailed on several occasions by U.S. authorities for his activist role in the struggle for his country's independence. (Trans. note).

One Hundred Years of Solitude *(Selection)*

Gabriel García Márquez

Gabriel García Márquez (1927–), Colombian novelist, short story writer, and journalist, is considered one of the most important writers of the twentieth century. He has long been Latin America's most translated and published author and in 1982 he was awarded the Nobel Prize for Literature. Over the years he has written some of the region's most significant texts, including *La hojarasca* (1955, Leaf Storm), *El coronel no tiene quien le escriba* (1961, No One Writes to the Colonel), *Cien años de soledad* (1967, One Hundred Years of Solitude), *El otoño del patriarca* (1974, The Autumn of the Patriarch), *Crónica de una muerte anunciada* (1981, Chronicle of a Death Foretold), *El amor en los tiempos del cólera* (1985, Love in the Time of Cholera), *El general en su laberinto* (1990, The General in His Labyrinth), *Doce cuentos peregrines* (1992, Strange Pilgrims), *Del amor y otros demonios* (1994, Love and Other Demons), and *Memoria de mis putas tristes* (2005, Memories of My Melancholy Whores). The following selection is from *One Hundred Years of Solitude*, translated by Gregory Rabassa (New York: Harper and Row, 1970), 223–228. Reprinted by permission of HarperCollins Publishers.

1967

DAZZLED BY SO MANY and such marvelous inventions, the people of Macondo did not know when their amazement began. They stayed up all night looking at the pale electric bulbs fed by the plant that Aureliano Triste had brought back when the train made its second trip, and it took time and effort for them to grow accustomed to its obsessive *toom-toom*. They became indignant over the living images that the prosperous merchant Bruno Crespi projected in the theater with the lion-head ticket windows, for a character who had died and was buried in one film and for whose misfortune tears of affliction had been shed would reappear alive and transformed into an Arab in the next one. The audience, who paid two cents apiece to share the difficulties of the actors, would not tolerate that outlandish fraud and they broke up the seats. The mayor, at the urging of Bruno Crespi, explained in a proclamation that the cinema was a machine of illusions that did not merit the emotional outbursts of the audience. With that discouraging explanation many felt that they had been the victims of some new and showy gypsy business and they decided not to return to the movies, considering that they already had too many troubles of their own to weep over the acted-out misfortunes of imaginary beings. Something similar happened with the cylinder phonographs that the merry matrons from France brought with them as a substitute for the antiquated hand organs and that for a time had serious effects on the livelihood of the band of musicians. At first curiosity increased the clientele on the forbidden street and there was even word of respectable ladies who disguised themselves as workers in order to observe the novelty of the phonograph from first hand, but from so much and such close observation they soon reached the conclusion that it was not an enchanted mill as everyone had thought and as the matrons had said, but a mechanical trick that could not be compared with something so moving, so human, and so full of everyday truth as a band of musicians. It was such a serious disappointment that when phonographs became so popular that there was one in every house they were not considered objects for amusement for adults but as something good for children to take apart. On the other hand, when someone from the town had the opportunity to test the crude reality of the telephone installed in the railroad station, which was thought to be a rudimentary version of the phonograph because of its crank, even the most incredulous were upset. It was as if God had decided to put to the test every capacity for surprise and was keeping the inhabitants of Macondo in a permanent alternation between excitement and disappointment, doubt and revelation, to such an extreme that no one knew for certain where the limits of reality lay. It was an intricate stew of truths and mirages that convulsed the ghost of José Arcadio Buendia under the chestnut tree with impatience and made him wander all through the house even in broad daylight. Ever since the railroad had been officially inaugurated and had begun to arrive with regularity on Wednesdays at eleven o'clock and the primitive wooden station with a desk, a telephone, and a ticket window had been built, on the streets of Macondo men and women were seen who had adopted everyday normal customs and manners but who really looked like people out of a circus. In a town that had chafed under the tricks of the gypsies there was no future for those ambulatory acrobats of commerce who with equal effrontery offered a whistling kettle and a daily regime that would assure the salvation of the soul on the seventh day; but from those who let themselves be convinced out of fatigue and the ones who were always unwary, they reaped stupendous benefits. Among those theatrical creatures, wearing riding breeches and leggings, a pith helmet and steel-rimmed glasses, with topaz eyes and the skin of a thin rooster, there arrived in Macondo on one of so many Wednesdays the chubby and smiling Mr. Herbert, who ate at the house.

No one had noticed him at the table until the first bunch of bananas had been eaten. Aureliano Segundo had come across him by chance as he protested in broken Spanish because there were no rooms at the Hotel Jacob, and as he frequently did with strangers, he took him home. He was in the captive-balloon business, which had taken him halfway around the world with excellent profits, but he had not succeeded in taking anyone up in Macondo because they considered that invention backward after having seen and tried the gypsies' flying carpets. He was leaving, therefore, on the next train. When they brought to the table the tiger-striped bunch of bananas that they were accustomed to hang in the dining room during lunch, he picked the first piece of fruit without great enthusiasm. But he kept on eating as he spoke, tasting, chewing, more with the distraction of a wise man than with the delight of a good eater, and when he finished the first bunch he asked them to bring him another. Then he took a small case with optical instruments out of the toolbox that he always carried with him. With the suspicious attention of a diamond merchant he examined the banana meticulously, dissecting it with a special scalpel, weighing the pieces on a pharmacist's scale, and calculating its breadth with a gunsmith's calipers. Then he took a series of instruments out of the chest with which he measured the temperature, the level of humidity in the atmosphere, and the intensity of the light. It was such an intriguing ceremony that no one could eat in peace as everybody waited for Mr. Herbert to pass a final and revealing judgment, but he did not say anything that allowed anyone to guess his intentions.

On the days that followed he was seen with a net and a small basket, hunting butterflies on the outskirts of town. On Wednesday a group of engineers, agronomists, hydrologists, topographers, and surveyors arrived who for several weeks explored the places where Mr. Herbert had hunted his butterflies. Later on Mr. Jack Brown arrived in an extra coach that had been coupled onto the yellow train and that was silver-plated all over, with seats of episcopal velvet, and a roof of blue glass. Also arriving on the special car, fluttering around Mr. Brown, were the solemn lawyers dressed in black who in different times had followed Colonel Aureliano Buendia everywhere, and that led the people to think that the agronomists, hydrologists, topographers, and surveyors, like Mr. Herbert with his captive balloons and his colored butterflies and Mr. Brown with his mausoleum on wheels and his ferocious German shepherd dogs, had something to do with the war. There was not much time to think about it, however, because the suspicious inhabitants of Macondo barely began to wonder what the devil was going on when the town had already become transformed into an encampment of wooden houses with zinc roofs inhabited by foreigners who arrived on the train from halfway around the world, riding not only on the seats and platforms but even on the roof of the coaches. The gringos, who later on brought their languid wives in muslin dresses and large veiled hats, built a separate town across the railroad tracks with streets lined with palm trees, houses with screened windows, small white tables on the terraces, and fans mounted on the ceilings, and extensive blue lawns with peacocks and quails. The section was surrounded by a metal fence topped with a band of electrified chicken wire, which during the cool summer mornings would be black with roasted swallows. No one knew yet what they were after, or whether they were actually nothing but philanthropists, and they had already caused a colossal disturbance, much more than that of the old gypsies, but less transitory and understandable. Endowed with means that had been reserved for Divine Providence in former times, they changed the pattern of the rains, accelerated the cycle of harvests, and moved the river from where it had always been and put it with its white stones and icy currents on the other side of the town, behind the cemetery. It was at that time that they built a fortress of reinforced concrete over the faded tomb of José Arcadio, so that the corpse's smell of powder would not contaminate the waters. For the foreigners who arrived without love they converted the street of the loving matrons from France into a more extensive village than it had been, and on one glorious Wednesday they brought in a trainload of strange whores, Babylonish women skilled in age-old methods and in possession of all manner of unguents and devices to stimulate the unaroused, to give courage to the timid, to satiate the voracious, to exalt the modest man, to teach a lesson to repeaters, and to correct solitary people. The Street of the Turks, enriched by well-lit stores with products from abroad, displacing the old bazaars with their bright colors, overflowed on Saturday nights with the crowds of adventurers who bumped into each other among gambling tables, shooting galleries, the alley where the future was guessed and dreams interpreted, and tables of fried food and drinks, and on Sunday mornings there were scattered on the ground bodies that were sometimes those of happy drunkards and more often those of onlookers felled by shots, fists, knives, and bottles during the brawls. It was such a tumultuous and intemperate invasion that during the first days it was impossible to walk through the streets because of the furniture and trunks, and the noise of the carpentry of those who were building their houses in any vacant lot without asking anyone's permission, and the scandalous behavior of couples who hung their hammocks between the almond trees and made love under the netting in broad daylight and in view of everyone. The only serene corner had been established by peaceful West Indian Negroes, who built a marginal street with wooden houses on piles where they would sit in the doors at dusk singing melancholy hymns in their disordered gabble. So many changes took place in such a short time that eight months after Mr. Herbert's visit the old inhabitants had a hard time recognizing their own town.

"Look at the mess we've got ourselves into," Colonel Aureliano Buendia said at that time, "just because we invited a gringo to eat some bananas."

Selected Poems

Pablo Neruda

Pablo Neruda (Chile 1904–1973) was the pen name of Ricardo Eliecer Neftali Reyes. He was awarded the Nobel Prize for Literature in 1971 and is widely considered one of the most important poets of the twentieth century. During his lifetime Neruda served in a variety of diplomatic posts as well as senator in Chile's government. He was a close friend of and collaborator with Socialist president Salvador Allende and his funeral in 1973 became the first public manifestation of opposition to the Pinochet dictatorship. Among his most important books of poetry are *Veinte poemas de amor y una canción desesperada* (1924, Twenty Love Poems and a Song of Despair), *Tentativa del hombre infinito* (1926, The Attempt of Infinite Man), *Residencia en la tierra* (1925–1931, Residence on Earth), *Tercera residencia* (1935–1945, Third Residence), *Canto general* (1950), *Odas elementales* (1954, Odes to Common Things), *Alturas de Macchu Picchu* (1954, The Heights of Macchu Picchu), *Cien sonetos de amor* (1959, One Hundred Love Sonnets), *La Barcarola* (1967, The Barcarole), *Canción de gesta* (1970, Song of Protest), and *Incitación al Nixonicidio y alabanza de la revolución chilena* (1973, Call for the Destruction of Nixon and Praise for the Chilean Revolution). This selection is from *Canción de gesta* (Montevideo: Editorial El Siglo Ilustrado, 1970), 23–24. By permission of Agencia Literaria Carmen Balcells S. A., Barcelona.

1970

A Central Land
The waist of the Americas
is formed between two nuptial oceans,
from the Atlantic side is produced sea foam
from the Pacific torrential stars,
the ships from the white polar caps arrive
loaded with petroleum and citrus fruits;
their holds absorbed
our secret mineral blood
that builds the planet's towers
in cruel and dangerous capitals.
This is why the empire
of the dollar was established there along with its sad
    relations:
the bloodthirsty Caribbean cannibals
disguised as heroic generals:
a kingdom of merciless mice,
a heritage of military spittle,
a stinking cavern of bosses,
a trench of tropical mud,
a dark chain of torments,
a string of fundamental sorrows,
and the dollar overseeing this shamelessness
with a white fleet sailing the seas,
extracting the aroma of bananas,
the intense smell of coffee groves,
eternalizing in our innocent world
the Trujillos stained with blood.
This poor America immersed in blood
up to its waist in countless quagmires,
nailed to a cross and covered with thorns,
bound and bitten by dogs,
torn to pieces by the invaders,
wounded by torture and excess,
razed by extraordinary winds,
sacrilegious deals, colossal thievery.
Oh delicate chain of sorrows,
oh reunion of the weeping seas.

To Our North American Friend
This selection is from *Canción de gesta* (Montevideo: Editorial El Siglo Ilustrado, 1970), pp. 91–93. By permission of Agencia Literaria Carmen Balcells S. A., Barcelona.

Man from the North, North American,
industrial harvester of apples
simple as a pine tree in a pine grove,
geographic fir of Alaska,
Yankee of the villages and factories
with a wife, responsibilities, and children,
prolific engineers who work
in the immutable jungle of numbers
or in the production phase of the factories,
broad shouldered and tall workers bent over
between the wheels and above the flames,
heartrending poets you have lost
the faith of Whitman in the human race,
I want what I love and what I hate
to be clear in the words I use:
against you I express only one reproach
for a silence that says nothing:
we do not really know what North Americans
are thinking in the confines of their homes,
we understand the sweetness of the family,
but we also love the sudden flare up
when something happens in the world
we want to share the teachings
but we find that two or three individuals
shut North American doors
and the only voice heard is "Voice of America"
which is like listening to a strange hen.
But apart from this I also want to celebrate
your exploits of both today and tomorrow
and I think that we can all be proud of the delayed Satellite
that you positioned one dawn:
why is it necessary to be in the first room?
In this championship called life
arrogance has been abandoned forever:
in this sense we can go together to the sun

and drink wine from the same pitcher.
You are Americans just as we are
and we do not wish to exclude you from anything,
but we do want to preserve what is ours,
there is a great deal of room for our souls
and we can live without abuse
with an undeveloped liking
until we can say frankly to one another
how far we will go, face to face.
The world is changing and we don't believe
that one has to conquer by means of the bomb and the sword.
On this basis we will come to understand each other
without your having to suffer at all:
we are not going to exploit your oil,
we will not meddle at your borders,
we will not sell electrical energy
to North American towns:
We are a peaceful people who can be
content with what we earn
and we do not seek to subject anyone
to the greed of circumstance.
We respect the space of Lincoln
and the clear conscience of Paul Robeson.
We learned to love you through Charlie Chaplin
(even though his authority was badly rewarded),
and so many other things, the geography
that unites us in this desired land,
all of this indicates the need to say once again
that we both travel on the same small boat:
with arrogance it could capsize:
let's load it up with bread and apples,
let's load it up with blacks and whites,
with understanding and hope.

I Will Begin By Invoking Walt Whitman
This selection is from: *Incitación al nixonicidio y alabanza de la revolucion chilena*. Santiago, Chile: Editorial Quimantú, 1973, pp. 17–21. By permission of Agencia Literaria Carmen Balcells S. A., Barcelona.

1973

It is out of love for my country
that I protest, my indispensable brother,
old friend Walt Whitman with the gray hand,

so that with your extraordinary support,
verse by verse, we will completely
kill Nixon, the bloodthirsty President.

On this earth there is no man who is happy,
no one who lives well on this planet
if in Washington he catches cold.

In beseeching the old Bard to bestow upon me the authority,
I will assume my duties as poet
armed with a terrorist sonnet,

because I must carry out without any sorrow
the sentence, up until now never seen,
of shooting a dedicated criminal,

who in spite of his trips to the moon
has killed so many people on this earth,
that when I try to write down the name of this evildoer,
this perpetrator of genocide from the White House,
the paper flees from me and the pen escapes my grasp.

The Weeping of Jimmy Swaggart

Mario Benedetti

Mario Benedetti (1920–2009) was a Uruguayan poet, novelist, essayist, and short story writer. His works took a noticeable political turn after the military coup of 1973 in Uruguay. After that time he became one of the leading commentators on Latin America and its place within the world. Some of his most memorable works include *Montevideanos* (1960, Montevideans), *La tregua* (1960, The Truce), *Gracias por el fuego* (1965, Thanks for the Fire), *El cumpleaños de Juan Angel* (1971, The Birthday of Juan Angel), *Perplejidades de fin de siglo* (1992, Perplexities at the End of the Century), *La borra del café* (1993, Coffee Sediment), *Andamios* (1996, Scaffolding), and *El porvenir de mi pasado* (2003, The Future of My Past). The following selection is from *Perplejidades de fin de siglo* (Montevideo: Cal y Canto, 1993), 31–33. By permission of Fundación Mario Benedetti, c/o Guillermo Schavelzon & Asociados, Agencia Literaria, Barcelona, www.schavelzon.com.

1988

Saturday the nineteenth, 11:00 p.m., Channel 4 finally broadcasts the long-awaited special of the grand repentance of TV preacher Jimmy Swaggart. Since it is now part of the *vox populi* and therefore *vox dei*, the *peccata minuta* of the reverend was committed in a New Orleans hotel thanks to the efficient collaboration of a local *hetaera*. Proof of the infamous act was carried in a suitcase by another former preacher, Marvin Gorman, whom

Jimmy had placed in the pillory in 1987 for being an adulterer, so that today the two are colleagues in more than one sense of the word.

With the help of a private detective, Gorman was able to record in photos the public figure and the aforementioned woman at the moment they left the motel. One can assume that Marvin's pious readings had been somewhat forgotten, since in the Bible (see Deuteronomy 32:35, Romans 12:19, Hebrews 10:30) it is specified that "vengeance is a prerogative of God that hinders those who try illicitly to seek vengeance on their own." Whatever the situation, what is certain is that Jimmy confirmed, more stupefied than contrite, how Marvin was making a nightmare out of his reasonable dream of a typical Magdalena.

In any case, the great show of Baton Rouge became unintentionally an apotheosis of New Orleans's critical concubinage. Never before had a self-confessed adulterer been applauded, cheered, kissed, and embraced with such enthusiasm by thousands of people. At times their tear-filled and supportive eyes seemed to transmit to the sinner the following: "How good of you, brother, that you made this confession."

It is well known that during antiquity, tears (for example, those of grievers) were kept in small urns or lachrymatories made of glass or porcelain. If that tradition were maintained up to the present day and an accurate record kept on the number of tears shed in this expiation (no longer an appropriate term since in this case it is a question of an *ex-pío*, a formerly devout believer), we'd have to keep them in enormous bottles or barrels. This twentieth-century Jeremias wept, at times like a willow and at other times like a crocodile, but always in a copious, torrential manner. But also the thousands in attendance contributed a weeping that was almost choral in nature and the camera focused with delight on the soaked faces of the son and wife, and there were more than a few who conjectured that the former cried because he was stupid and the latter because she was furious. The sinner asked for a punctual and humid forgiveness from both of them and also from his "adorable and lovely daughter-in-law" (careful, brunette lady, penitent satyrs are the worst kind), and from his "associates" (gathered together and sorrowful, perhaps they cried for their loss of profits), from the members of the choir and the hundreds of millions of television viewers. And of course, from the Lord, Who, if God is truly God, at this point He would be experiencing a completely celestial nausea.

Since it is already public and notorious knowledge, Swaggart and Gorman are not the first reverends of explicit sex. Two years ago the famous Jim Bakker (also accused by Jimmy) succumbed to the delights of his secretary, Jessica Hahn. And even earlier, Billy James Hargis saw his successful career as a TV preacher come to a halt because of his erotic episodes. Truly these reverends have turned out to be the false kind.

The surprising contradiction in all of this is that such mystical-financial Savonarolas, who everywhere they went, denounced the diabolical infiltration of Marxism, ended up themselves becoming "libidinous Satans," who infiltrated their own flock of chaste souls.

After all is said and done, what importance should a mini adultery in a motel have? Only a community of a puritanical, punitive, and hypocritical stripe can attain such exaggeration. Nonetheless, the implacable, truculent, and reactionary preaching of Swaggart and his peers has finally experienced a boomerang effect. His peccadilloes have become great sins, only because they themselves had previously treated sex as a monstrous presence in one's life.

Two years ago Swaggart, when he denounced the extramarital relations of his colleague Jim Bakker, categorized Baker with this delicate metaphor as "a cancer that must be extirpated from the body of Christ." Now he himself has become an extirpative tumor. After his multitudinous repentance in Baton Rouge, this preacher without a pulpit and with his eyes once again rancorously dry perhaps will make his forced vacation more pleasant by reading chronicles about the witches of Salem, who definitely were treated much worse. For Jimmy it will always be a consolation knowing he can recover from this period of transgression, in the relief brought about by forbearance and the prosperity of his stunning mansion and—last but not least—by the terrestrial certainty of an annual income of one hundred thirty million dollars.

The only thing missing now is for someone to give us reliable news regarding the unjustly forgotten harlot of New Orleans. Frankly, I like the young woman. At some point we'll have to pay tribute to her, since it is thanks to her unmentionable profession that today we owe, even though indirectly, the fall of masks (and maybe the beginning of a dismantling) of one of the most talked-about pseudoreligious extortions of this century. And it is not hard to believe that within a short time we may have to enlarge the pillory to make room for other neoreverends whose preaching is all knowing, and whose practice is all lustful.

The American Invasion of Macún (Selection)

Esmeralda Santiago

Esmeralda Santiago (Puerto Rico, 1948–) came to the United States with her family as an adolescent and settled in New York. Among her works are included the critically acclaimed book of memoirs *When I Was Puerto Rican* (1994), the novel *America's Dream* (1997), a second book of memoirs entitled *Almost a Woman* (1999), and her autobiography, *The Turkish Lover* (2004). *When I Was Puerto Rican* was originally published by Addison-Wesley (Reading, Massachusetts) in 1994. The following selection is from the Da Capo Press/Perseus Books Group edition published in 2006 and corresponds to pages 70–74 in the original edition. By permission of the Copyright Clearance Center.

1993

Miss Jiménez sent us out to see the nurse two at a time, in alphabetical order. By the time she got to the S's, I was shaky, because every one of the children who had gone before me had come back crying, pressing a wad of cotton against their arm. Ignacio Sepúlveda walked next to me, and even though he was as scared as I was, he pretended he wasn't.

"What crybabies!" he said. "I've had shots before and they don't hurt that much."

"When?"

"Last year. They gave us shots for tuberculosis." We were nearing the lunchroom, and Ignacio slowed down, tugged on my arm, and whispered, "It's all because of politics."

"What are you talking about? Politics isn't a disease like polio. It's something men talk about at the bus stop." I'd heard Papi tell Mami when he was late that he's missed the bus because he'd been discussing politics.

Ignacio kept his voice to a whisper, as if he were telling me something no one else knew. "My Papá says the government's doing all this stuff for us because it's an election year."

"What does that have to do with it?"

"They give kids shots and free breakfast, stuff like that, so that our dads will vote for them."

"So?"

"Don't you know anything?"

"I know a lot of things."

"You don't know anything about politics."

"Do so."

"Do not."

"Do so."

"Who's the governor of Puerto Rico, then?"

"Oh, you could have asked something really hard! . . . Everyone knows it's Don Luis Muñoz Marín."

"Yeah, well, who's *el presidente* of the Jun-ited Estates?"

"Ay-sen-hou-err."

"I bet you don't know his first name."

I knew then I had him. I scanned Papi's newspaper daily, and I had seen pictures of *el presidente* on the golf course, and of his wife's funny hairdo.

"His first name is Eekeh," I said, puffed with knowledge. "And his wife's name is Mami."

"Well, he's an imperialist, just like all the other *gringos*!" Ignacio said, and I was speechless because Mami and Papi never let us say things like that about grown-ups, even if they were true.

When we came into the lunchroom, Ignacio presented his arm to the nurse as if instead of a shot he were getting a medal. He winced as the nurse stuck the needle into him and blinked a few times to push back the tears. But he didn't cry, and I didn't either, though I wanted to. There was no way I'd have Ignacio Sepúlveda calling me a crybaby.

"Papi, what's an imperialist?"

He stopped his hammer in midstrike and looked at me. "Where did you hear that word?"

"Ignacio Sepúlveda said Eekeh Aysenhouerr is an imperialist. He said all *gringos* are."

Papi looked around as if someone were hiding behind a bush and listening in. "I don't want you repeating those words to anybody..."

"I know that Papi... I just wanted to know what it means. Are *gringos* the same as *Americanos*?"

"You should never call an *Americano* a *gringo*. It's a very bad insult."

"But why?"

"It just is." It wasn't like Papi not to give a real answer to my questions. "Besides, *el presidente*'s name is pronounced Ayk, not Eekeh." He went back to his hammering.

I handed him a nail from the can at his feet. "How come it's a bad insult?"

He stopped banging the wall and looked at me. I stared back, and he put his hammer down, took off his hat, brushed his hand across his forehead, wiped it on his pants, sat on the stoop, and leaned his elbows back, stretching his legs out in front of him. This was the response I expected. Now I would hear all about *gringos* and imperialists.

"Puerto Rico was a colony of Spain after Columbus landed here," he began, like a schoolteacher.

"I know that."

"Don't interrupt."

"Sorry."

"In 1898, *los Estados Unidos* invaded Puerto Rico, and we became their colony. A lot of Puerto Ricans don't think that's right. They call *Americanos* imperialists, which means they want to change our country and our culture to be like theirs."

"Is that why they teach us English in school, so we can speak like them?"

"Yes."

"Well, I'm not going to learn English so I don't become American."

He chuckled. "Being American is not just a language, *Negrita*, it's a lot of other things."

"Like what?"

He scratched his head. "Like the food you eat... the music you listen to... the things you believe in."

"Do they believe in God?"

"Some of them do."

"Do they believe in phantasms and witches?"

"Yes, some Americans believe in that."

"Mami doesn't believe any of that stuff."

"I know. I don't either."

"Why not?"

"I just . . . believe in things I can see."

"Why do people call *Americanos gringos*?"

"We call them *gringos*, they call us spiks."

"What does that mean?"

"Well," he sat up, leaned his elbows on his knees and looked at the ground, as if he were embarrassed. "There are many Puerto Ricans in New York, and when someone asks them a question they say, 'I don't spik inglish' instead of 'I don't speak English.' They make fun of our accent."

"*Americanos* talk funny when they speak Spanish."

"'Yes, they do. The ones who don't take the trouble to learn it well." He pushed his hat back, and the sun burned into his already brown face, making him squint. "That's part of being an imperialist. They expect us to do things their way, even in our country."

"That's not fair."

"No, it isn't." He stood up and picked up his hammer. "Well, I'd better get back to work, *Negrita*. Do you want to help?"

"Okay." I followed him, holding the can of nails up so he wouldn't have to bend over to pick them up. "Papi?"

"Yes."

"If we eat all that American food they give us at the *centro communal*, will we become *Americanos*?"

He banged a nail hard into the wall then turned to me, and, with a broad smile on his face, said, "Only if you like it better than our Puerto Rican food."

Inner View

Christine Granados

Christine Granados (1969–) was born and raised in El Paso, Texas. She is the author of the collection of short stories entitled *Brides and Sinners in El Chuco*, published by the University of Arizona Press in 2006. The story "Inner View" first appeared in this collection and may also be found in *Camino del sol: Fifteen Years of Latina and Latino Writing*, edited by Rigoberto González (Tucson: University of Arizona Press, 2010), 193–200. Reprinted by permission of the University of Arizona Press.

2006

Moist under my arms from my sprint to the building, I walk through the double doors, and a blast of cold air hits my face. Rather than refreshed, I am nauseated. After I sign in with the security guard, I jog down the cavernous hallway, find the glass door I am looking for, and step inside. I swallow and head toward the secretary, whose angular face and slender arms remind me of a TV news anchor. Her face, with its hard, porcelain-like veneer, shines under the fluorescent lighting. I squeeze the St. Christopher medallion in my hand, and her bored expression makes me more uncomfortable. I smile. The secretary's blue eyes give no warmth—all points and hard edges like a cube. She speaks before I do.

"You must be No-ella Boost-a-mont," she says, mispronouncing my name. "Mr. Richardson is expecting you. Please take a seat. He'll be with you in a minute," she says with her eyes already focusing on the computer screen in front of her.

I do as I'm told and sit on the leather sofa. The couch I rest on costs more than the car my father drives. I place my Naugahyde briefcase on my knees. The dark, rich textures of the room are gloomy and intimidating. I feel out of place, like I did in P.E. class in grade school, even a little ashamed of myself. I imagine the walls painted the banana yellow of our living room and think it would brighten up this dreary office, maybe give the secretary something to smile about. I remembered my mother's words as I got out of the car, "Pórtate bien, Noelia, you're wearing a dress. Sit like a lady." I put the briefcase on the floor and cross my legs. The minute I do, the pointy secretary tells me Mr. Richardson can see me now. I stand as if to race.

The smell of coffee hits my nostrils before I see Mr. Richardson. My mouth waters, and I'm feeling comfortable despite the gloominess of the beige walls. Mr. Richardson is all roundness and folds. He reminds me of tía Ofelia's spoiled cat, Gertrudis. He walks around from behind an elaborate chiseled mahogany desk and shakes my hand. As he holds my hand in a stiff, tight clutch, he glances at me—from the diamante rhinestone barrettes in my hair, down to the discount-shoe-store loafers I'm wearing. Even though he doesn't say it, I feel it—cheap. He wants to get right down to business. Doesn't offer me a cup of espresso from the espresso machine behind his desk. He doesn't ask me about my trip. If I'm comfortable, hot, or tired. He wants me to tell him a little bit about myself. Why would I be a good addition to Richardson, Richardson, and Stoddard? Annoyed, I answer, "I've been the office manager of the credit union for five years." I can see Dad's car through Mr. Richardson's window. It's just behind the high-backed chair Mr. Richardson is sitting in. Dad has parked across the street, illegally. ". . . and before that I was a checker at Big Eight, and I'm bilingual." I stare out the window because I see my sister, Teresa, get out of the car.

She's probably had enough, I think. Everyone in the family is inside Dad's blue Chevy in this 100-degree heat, and Dad turned off the air conditioner when he parked. As I got out, he was telling Teresa, "Eres escandalosa. No hace tanto calor." Titi just lifted her thick black ponytail and fanned the nape of her neck, which was drenched in sweat. "You're lucky you even have a car to ride in. I had to walk." I slammed the car door and ran across the street to the plaza, grateful that I didn't have to hear the end of the story again.

"Ms. Bustamante? Is there something outside?" Mr. Richardson asks.

"No, no sir," I say. I try to focus my attention on his face, but I'm distracted by Titi, who is waving her arms wildly, and now my father is out of the car.

I had tried to convince Dad to let me take the bus to the interview.

He'd said, "I'll take you, no problem. When is it?"

"It's Monday," I said. "You'll probably want to rest on your day off."

"Rest? I can rest when I'm dead."

I cringed.

"Lunes, I'll take you to your job interview. We can all go."

"No, Dad, really, I can take the bus," I said, desperately.

"N'ombre, you shouldn't take the bus for such an important day. We'll take you."

I poured him a cup of coffee, and as I handed it to him, I said, "I already planned to take the bus. It's no big deal."

"What do you mean, no big deal." He slurped. "You crazy? How much will it pay?"

"I think $28,000."

Dad whistled, "With that kind of money we can get a new roof for the house. I'm driving you, so you can have some support." He sliced the air with an open hand.

I turned to my mother, who was folding laundry on the kitchen table, and shrugged, as if to say, "Help!"

"It'll be all right," she said, folding my T-shirt into thirds the way I like, "You're going to want someone to talk to after the interview. This way will be better. We won't worry, and don't you worry."

I rolled my eyes in defeat.

Mr. Richardson swivels in his chair, "Oh, I see — a family argument. Amusing, eh. I love the Mexican culture. That's why my wife and I moved here. Actually, my wife isn't too fond of this hot weather." He looks out the window. "They are such an emotional people."

"Yes, I know," I say.

I was pretty emotional when Dad announced we were going to pick up Abuela on the way to the interview.

"We only have twenty-five minutes to get downtown," I pointed to my watch. "There's no time for this."

"It don't matter if you're a little late," Dad said. "It's just an interview, not like you're going to actually be working."

When we got to grandma's house, Dad made us all get out of the car to greet her. I sighed loudly.

Dad yelled, "There's always time for manners."

I didn't want to leave the air-conditioned car but stepped out into the heat, and as I walked towards abuela's gated yard, I noticed the padlock shackle was closed tight. I turned to look at Mom.

"So what's the problem?" Dad called out. "Jump it."

I pointed to my business suit and shoes.

"Oh, forgot. Titi jump it and go get Abuela and tell her we need the key so we can come inside."

"No, Titi," I yelled, "Just tell her to come out because we're running late." I didn't dare look behind me.

Abuela shuffled outside with the key to the padlock in one hand and Titi holding her arm.

"Titi, get Abuela's bag and shut and lock her door!" I yelled and got slapped on the back of the head.

"What are we late for?" Abuela asked, shaking as she tried to put the key in the lock.

One good tug would break the rusted chain that was cinched together by the padlock. I stopped myself from pulling and said, "Let Titi do it, Abuela. I've got an important job interview."

Abuela said, "Titi, get my bolsa."

I loved my sister at that moment because she ran down Grandma's brick pathway and was back a few seconds later carrying the large tote.

Dad said "¡Mira ésta! She has one job interview, and she thinks she can boss us around now."

"No te preocupes, mijo, she's just nervosa," Abuela said. I looked at my watch and saw that we had fifteen minutes to get downtown.

Once we got Abuela settled in the front seat, Mom sat in back with Titi, Joe, and me. I sat in the middle on top of Joe's lap. It was coolest there. The air-conditioner was hitting me straight on, and my makeup stayed in place.

"Would you move your fat head so I can get some air?" Joe moaned.

"Shuttup, I can't go to a job interview all sweaty."

"Why not?" Dad said.

Titi rested her hand on my thigh, but I ignored her. "Because it's unprofessional."

"Unprofessional? If you're sweating that means you're working hard. Any idiot can see that."

Titi rolled her eyes.

"I saw that," Dad said, giving her the evil eye through the rearview mirror. "You keep doing that, and I'll slap you so hard your eyes will roll back permanently. Malcriada."

"Dad," I said, and Titi started to place her hand on me, but stopped and sighed. "This is an office job. No one wants to walk in and see a sweaty woman inside an air-conditioned office. It doesn't look good for the company."

"At least they'll know you're working and not just sitting on your ass, drinking coffee."

"That's the trick, to make people think you sit on your ass—"

Dad said, "Watch your language."

"And drink coffee all day but in reality you're working, working very hard," I said.

"What's the point in that?" he said.

"It gives you more prestige."

"Prestige? ¿Qué es eso, prestige?" He waves one hand in the air. "Sounds like bullshit to me."

"Being late is not good either," I added.

Dad looked at his watch. "Ah, you're not going to be late, mija. We'll be there en punto!"

Grandma said, "I like my coffee with a lot of cream and sugar."

Titi and Joe laughed.

"The best coffee I ever had I drank with a gringa," Dad looked over at Mom, who smiled at him to go on. "My boss's wife. She had a shiny machine. Looked like it was made from rims. The good ones like at the car show Joe took us to. Remember mijo, the trokitas were my favorites and the bombs."

"I liked the girls the best," Joe said.

Titi punched his arm.

"It's true," Joe added. "And Dad didn't mind the view, either."

Mom hit his other arm, and everyone laughed.

"Ay, Dad, it's an espresso machine," Titi rolled her eyes.

"Yeah, yeah, one of those expression machines. The coffee was bien duro, but she gave it to me in one of those coffee cups you girls used to make me drink out of when you were little."

"Demitasse," Titi said, then whispered, "Idiot."

Mom reached over me and slapped my sister's thigh.

"Sorry," Titi said.

Oblivious, Dad said, "You were little, and you both wanted to make my coffee. You shouldn't be sorry. I loved playing with you girls. That's what the gabacha reminded me of, a little girl in a big house all by herself. She kept talking about this machine and how it was from France and what it did, when all I wanted was another cup of coffee, in a real cup."

We all laughed.

"Gabachos," Abuela said, absently. "They love their things and they're always in a hurry."

I tried not to look at my watch.

Mr. Richardson's watch was a gold Rolex. He tapped it every few seconds, while he spoke. "Tell me something . . . Are you of Mexican descent?"

"Descent?" He catches me off guard. "My grandmother's family is from Chihuahua, so, yes, yes, I am."

"I thought so," he says. "I'm sorry, please go on; you were saying you are bilingual."

My head is spinning. I wonder if what he asked is proper. If he just violated my rights. I look at this balding, pale man, really look at him. His eyes are the color of Abuela's brass padlock. There's a spot of hair on his neck just above where his collar chokes him that he missed shaving. His shirt collar, starched stiff, is tinged gray with grime. He taps his Rolex, as if to remind himself he owns it. He seems sad. I wonder if Mr. Richardson's wife is alone right now—alone in her big house.

"Yes, I'm bilingual. I can type a hundred words a minute and write in English and Spanish. Do translations."

I wonder why I tried to get here on time. I feel bad about my irritation at my father, who had grabbed my arm as I opened the car door.

"Remember, mija, men don't like show-offs." He looked serious.

Mom added, "And don't bite your nails while you're talking to him."

My little brother Joe said, "Try not to fart like you do in your bedroom."

This got Titi laughing hysterically, and Dad slapped Joe on the top of his head, "Serio."

I was almost out of the car before my abuela said, "Wait, mija. I forgot to give you this."

I glanced at my watch: 2 p.m., and I thought, I'm going to be officially late for my interview, but still I waited. It took her a few seconds to unclasp the necklace that holds her St. Christopher medallion. I wanted to rip the thin chain off her neck, but I waited.

"This is for good luck," she said, and winked. "¡Que Dios te bendiga! He'll help you charm your new boss."

"Thank you, Abuela." I took it, slammed the car door, and ran.

"You can translate?" Mr. Richardson asks.

"Yes."

"And you're Mexican American?"

"Yes."

"You don't look it."

"Thank you," I say, ashamed.

He smiles and clears his throat. "Most Mexicans I know have an accent."

"How many do you know?"

"Well, the cleaning lady here, and my gardener."

"They're probably recent immigrants or illegals. I've been here for two generations on my father's side and three on my mother's," I say.

"Fascinating," he says, dismissively.

A buzzer goes off, and his secretary says, "Mrs. Richardson on line one."

He presses a red button on his phone and almost touches his lips to the speaker, "Tell her I'm busy."

"She says it's important."

"I'll call her back in ten minutes," he says, agitated.

I try not to roll my eyes or pass judgment, but I do. My interview warrants ten minutes of his time. I prepared all weekend for this meeting, dipped into savings and bought a new outfit, even shoes, and got my hair done. My mind races, and I imagine this man sitting alone with his wife in a large house. He probably doesn't even tell her that he's interviewing someone for a paralegal position. I bet they eat their roast-beef supper in silence, speaking only when they're in bed and turn off the lights. "Night, I love you," they lie to one another. It's what I assume Anglo couples do.

"Sorry about that. My wife calls at least three times a day. Probably wants me to pick up some milk on the way home."

"Bored?"

"Yes, I think you're right," he says.

"Where were we?" he says, and a buzzer goes off again. "What?!" He presses his lips to the speaker as he pushes the button.

"Mrs. Richardson."

"I'll take it," he hisses, then lifts one finger toward me as he picks up the phone. "Hello. Yes. How should I know? I only took two semesters of Spanish." He looks at me and pauses, "Wait a minute. Hold on."

With the phone still to his ear he says, "Excuse me."

I picture a graying, slender woman on the other end of the line, wearing faded denim and turquoise jewelry. I can see her explaining to her friends that she wears rocks embedded in silver because she loves the culture. It's why she and her husband moved to the Southwest.

He snaps his fingers, "Can you tell me how to say, 'Please don't trim the rose bushes' in Spanish? My wife likes to trim them herself," he says, sheepishly, "because the roses are Golden Wings from her Auntie Lem's yard." He covers the receiver of the phone with his hand and whispers. "She wanted to bring a little bit of home with her here."

I pause for a moment, smell the espresso, think about the secretary, the walls, the couch, how much translating I'd have to do for this man, my family sitting out in the car, and I say, "Sure. Here's what you can tell him: 'No riegue los rosales.'"

About the Editors

John J. Hassett is the Susan W. Lippincott Professor Emeritus of Modern Languages and Literatures of Swarthmore College, in Pennsylvania. He is one of the cofounders of *Chasqui, a Latin American Literary Journal*, and served as its editor-in-chief for many years. He received his Ph.D. in Latin American literature and Ibero-American Studies from the University of Wisconsin–Madison. Among his books are *Chile: Dictatorship and the Struggle for Democracy* (with Grínor Rojo) and *Toward a Society That Serves Its People: The Intellectual Contribution of El Salvador's Murdered Jesuits* (with Hugh Lacey). His articles and translations of Spanish American narratives, essays, and poetry have appeared in numerous books and journals throughout the United States. He has just completed a translation of Chilean novelist Elizabeth Subercaseaux's *Las confidentes*.

Braulio Muñoz was born in Chimbote, Peru. While there he was a labor and student leader as well as a radio and print journalist. Upon leaving Peru he served as a foreign correspondent for newspapers and magazines. He holds a Ph.D. in sociology from the University of Pennsylvania. Professor Muñoz has taught in universities in Europe, Latin America, and the United States. He has published several academic books and numerous essays and articles. His latest academic work is *A Storyteller: Mario Vargas Llosa between Civilization and Barbarism* (Rowman and Littlefield). He writes works of fiction in Spanish and in English. His first novel in Spanish was translated into English as *Alejandro and the Fishermen of Tancay* (University of Arizona Press) and won the 2010 International Latino Book Award for best historical novel. His first novel in English, *The Peruvian Notebooks* (University of Arizona Press), was published in 2006. Professor Muñoz has been named honorary professor at the Universidad Ricardo Palma, in Lima, Peru. He holds a Centennial Professor Chair at Swarthmore College.